A Student Grammar of German

A Student Grammar of German is an invaluable reference guide for undergraduates and all intermediate and advanced students. It sets out the grammar of the language in a clear and jargon-free way. Every point is illustrated with numerous examples, accompanied by translations, drawn from a wide variety of printed and electronic media to reflect contemporary usage across a range of registers.

Key features:
+ An overview at the start of each chapter to provide a survey of the chapter's contents and the terms used
+ Layout designed to facilitate ease of reference
+ 'Tip' boxes containing aids to understanding and learning difficult points
+ Authentic examples drawn from a wide range of printed and electronic sources
+ A glossary of grammatical terms with clear explanations and cross-references
+ A full index

Paul Stocker is currently Head of German at Uppingham School, UK, where he was also Head of Modern Languages for twenty years; many of the school's alumni continue with their study of German at university level. He is a Fellow of the Chartered Institute of Linguists and has written numerous books for A-level students and others, including *Wort für Wort* (5th edition 2010), *German for Edexcel* (with others, 2008), *Einsicht* (1988 and 1995), and various titles for the "Teach Yourself" series.

A Student Grammar of
German

PAUL STOCKER

CAMBRIDGE
UNIVERSITY PRESS

CAMBRIDGE
UNIVERSITY PRESS

University Printing House, Cambridge CB2 8BS, United Kingdom

Cambridge University Press is part of the University of Cambridge.

It furthers the University's mission by disseminating knowledge in the pursuit of
education, learning and research at the highest international levels of excellence.

www.cambridge.org
Information on this title: www.cambridge.org/9780521012584

© Paul Stocker 2012

First published 2012

A catalogue record for this publication is available from the British Library

Library of Congress Cataloguing in Publication data
Stocker, Paul, 1950–
A student grammar of German / Paul Stocker.
   p.   cm.
Includes index.
ISBN 978-0-521-81313-6
1. German language – Textbooks for foreign speakers – English.   2. German language – Grammar.
I. Title.
PF3112.S76   2012
438.2′421–dc23

2011053321

ISBN 978-0-521-81313-6 Hardback
ISBN 978-0-521-01258-4 Paperback

Contents

List of 'Tip' boxes   *page* ix
Acknowledgements   xi

Introduction   1

1 Cases   3
1.1   The cases   4
1.2   Apposition   9

2 Nouns   11
2.1   The gender of nouns   11
2.2   The plural of nouns   19
2.3   The declension of nouns   26

3 Determiners   30
3.1   The definite and indefinite articles   31
3.2   The use of the article   32
3.3   Demonstrative determiners   35
3.4   Possessive determiners   37
3.5   Interrogative determiners   38
3.6   Indefinite determiners   38
3.7   Determiners and pronouns: a summary   43

4 Pronouns   45
4.1   Personal pronouns   46
4.2   Reflexive pronouns   49
4.3   Demonstrative pronouns   50
4.4   Possessive pronouns   52
4.5   Indefinite pronouns   52
4.6   Interrogative pronouns   57
4.7   Relative pronouns   58

5 Adjectives   62
5.1   The declension of adjectives   62
5.2   Adjective-nouns   66
5.3   Adjectives used with particular cases   69
5.4   Adjectives used with particular prepositions   70
5.5   Adjectival phrases   72

6 Adverbs 73
6.1 Adverbs of time 73
6.2 Adverbs of manner 76
6.3 Adverbs of place 76
6.4 Adverbs of comment/attitude 79
6.5 Adverbs of degree 79
6.6 Adverbs of reason 80
6.7 Interrogative adverbs 81

7 Modal particles 82
7.1 Characteristics of modal particles 82
7.2 Modal particles 83

8 Comparative and superlative of adjectives and adverbs 87
8.1 The comparative and superlative forms of adjectives 87
8.2 The comparative and superlative forms of adverbs 90
8.3 Using the comparative and superlative 90

9 Prepositions 93
9.1 Prepositions followed by the accusative 94
9.2 Prepositions followed by the dative 97
9.3 Prepositions followed by the accusative or dative 103
9.4 Prepositions followed by the genitive 108
9.5 The translation of *to* with places, countries and people 110
9.6 Contraction of prepositions with the definite article 112

10 Verbs: the indicative tenses – formation 113
10.1 The present tense 114
10.2 The simple past tense 117
10.3 The perfect tense 118
10.4 The pluperfect tense 121
10.5 The future tense 122
10.6 The future perfect tense 122

11 Verbs: the indicative tenses – uses 123
11.1 The present tense 124
11.2 The perfect and simple past tenses 125
11.3 The pluperfect tense 128
11.4 The future tense 128
11.5 The future perfect tense 129

12 Verbs: other types and forms 130
12.1 Mixed verbs 131
12.2 Modal verbs 131
12.3 The uses of modal verbs 135
12.4 Irregular verbs 139
12.5 Verbs with different transitive and intransitive forms 140

12.6   Impersonal verbs   141
12.7   Reflexive verbs   144

13   Verbs with prepositional objects or unexpected cases   148
13.1   Verbs followed by prepositional objects   149
13.2   Prepositional adverbs   156
13.3   Verbs used with unexpected cases   156

14   The infinitive and participles   160
14.1   The infinitive   161
14.2   The past participle   165
14.3   The present participle   166
14.4   The translation of English -ing forms   166

15   The passive voice   169
15.1   The passive voice: formation and use   170
15.2   Alternatives to the passive   174

16   The imperative mood   176
16.1   The imperative: formation and use   177
16.2   The infinitive in general and official instructions   179
16.3   Other ways of expressing commands   179

17   The subjunctive mood   181
17.1   Subjunctive 1/*Konjunktiv I*: formation and summary   182
17.2   Subjunctive 2/*Konjunktiv II*: formation and summary   183
17.3   Subjunctive 1/*Konjunktiv I*: use   184
17.4   Subjunctive 2/*Konjunktiv II*: use   187
17.5   'Conditional in the past': uses   191

18   Word order   192
18.1   The position of the verb   193
18.2   Conjunctions   196
18.3   The position of elements within the clause   202
18.4   The position of **nicht**   205
18.5   Word order with infinitive clauses   206

19   Word formation   207
19.1   General points   207
19.2   Formation of nouns   209
19.3   Formation of adjectives   215
19.4   Formation of adverbs   218
19.5   Formation of verbs   219

20   Numbers, spelling and punctuation   227
20.1   Numbers   227
20.2   Spelling   230

20.3   One word or two?   232
20.4   **ss** or **ß**?   234
20.5   Punctuation   234

21   List of strong and irregular verbs   237

22   Guide to tenses   243

Glossary   247
Further study   253
Index   255

'TIP' boxes

Cases	Deciding which case to use	*page* 4
Cases	What are direct and indirect objects?	8
Nouns	The gender of compound nouns	12
Nouns	Noun plurals	19
Nouns	Collective nouns with singular verbs	26
Nouns	How to recognise a weak masculine noun in a dictionary	28
Determiners	*some* or *any* + noun	31
Determiners	When to add case endings to all	39
Pronouns	How to remember the 3rd person pronouns	46
Pronouns	du/ihr or Sie?	47
Pronouns	The relative pronoun cannot be omitted	58
Adjectives	How to recognise an adjective-noun in a dictionary	68
Adjectives	Adjective-noun or adjective referring to a noun?	69
Comparative	als or wie in comparisons?	91
Prepositions	How to remember the accusative prepositions	94
Prepositions	How to remember the dative prepositions	97
Prepositions	*from*: aus or von?	97
Prepositions	The prepositions for *to* with places	110

Verbs	Transitive and intransitive verbs	114
Verbs	Present tense endings common to all verbs	117
Verbs	Verbs which take sein	121
Indicative tenses	Continuous action in German – *I am reading, I was reading*	125
Verbs: other types	How to remember the present tense of modal verbs	132
Verbs: other types	können or dürfen?	135
Verbs: other types	Avoiding es gibt and es ist/es sind	143
Verbs with cases	Accusative or dative with 'double case' prepositions?	149
Infinitives/ participles	Finite verb + zu + infinitive, or omit zu?	161
Infinitives/ participles	*-ing* words: gerund (=verbal noun) or present participle?	167
Subjunctive	Remembering the Subjunctive 1/ *Konjunktiv I* forms for reported speech	184
Subjunctive	German makes clear when speech is being reported	185
Subjunctive	Simple (one-word) Subjunctive 2 or würde + infinitive?	188
Subjunctive	Conditional in both wenn clause and main clause	189
Word order	Keep clauses separate	196
Word order	Verb position in clauses joined by co-ordinating conjunctions	197
Word formation	Understanding a new compound noun	214
Word formation	What sort of prefix is it?	219
Numbers, spelling	Deutsch with a capital or a small letter?	231

Acknowledgements

I should like to thank Dr Christopher Young of Pembroke College, Cambridge, for his advice and many helpful suggestions at various stages in the writing of this book. Thanks also must go to the numerous friends and colleagues who have responded to innumerable questions and have made many wise comments on the work in progress. In particular, I should mention Elke Baden-Harrington for her help in the final stages of the manuscript. As always, some of the best critics have been those I have taught over the years. If there is any practical wisdom in this book it is to them that I owe it.

Helen Barton at Cambridge University Press has been my unfailingly cheerful and helpful editor. Special thanks must go to my copy-editor, Caroline Drake, whose many perceptive questions have removed inconsistencies and helped to improve layout.

And last but not least, my thanks go to my wife for her support, encouragement and patience during the writing of this book.

Introduction

German is a language of huge cultural and economic significance. It is the language of some of the greatest writers, scientists, composers, theologians and philosophers. Those who gain fluency in German gain access to cultural and academic riches beyond measure. It is also the language of one of the world's most vibrant and important economies and is an official language of the European Union. The ability to speak and write German with precision is essential for those who wish to be influential and effective in European business and political spheres. And, indeed, the greater the fluency in a language, the easier and more pleasurable it is to communicate with native speakers. Approximately 100 million people speak German as their first language, and many more across Eastern Europe speak it as a lingua franca. Linguistic competence is one thing, but real confidence and effectiveness come with the ability to understand the subtleties of a language and to express one's ideas accurately.

Grammar is not usually associated with glamour, though the two words have the same root. Getting to grips with the complexities of a language may feel at times like trying to master a never-ending and definitely unglamorous maze of new structures. The user of this volume will be relieved to know that the author's aim is, if not to make German grammar glamorous, then at least to make it as straightforward and accessible as possible. Learners are often surprised to discover that the grammar of German is simpler than that of many other languages and has fewer exceptions to the 'rules'. Its main structures can be gathered under just three headings:

- verbs and tenses
- prepositions and cases
- word order (especially verb position).

Almost everything else is a subdivision of one of these.

This book, which covers all the grammar required by undergraduates and other intermediate and advanced learners, has been written to help the student of the language to develop fluency and accuracy. It takes as its basis modern standard German (*Hochdeutsch*), but it also includes differences between spoken and written language, as well as variations found in German-speaking countries such as Austria and Switzerland, where these differences are significant and common. Although the emphasis is on contemporary usage, older forms that may still be encountered with some regularity are also noted.

The main features of *A Student Grammar of German* are as follows:

- **Overview** Each chapter starts with an outline of the contents, and with definitions and examples of the terms and structures described in the following pages.
- **'TIP' boxes** Short summaries of difficult points, or useful ways of remembering patterns appear throughout the text.
- **The main rules** are printed in **bold**, to highlight the key points.
- **Examples** Each point is illustrated by several examples, with translations, to enable the reader to get a feel for current usage. They are drawn from a wide variety of sources, including the press and the internet.
- **List of strong and irregular verbs**
- **Summary of tenses**
- **Glossary** A list of grammatical terms used, with brief definitions and examples.

1

Cases

> **What are cases?**

Cases show how certain classes of words, such as nouns, pronouns and determiners (such as articles) function within a sentence or clause. In English, case is unmarked on nouns and determiners, but is clearly marked on the forms of the pronoun:

> **She** likes **me**   I like **her**   but not: **Her** like **I**

◆ The group (or **case**, to give it its proper name) of personal pronouns we can use in the subject (or 'doer') position is

I, you, he, it, she, we, they

They are said to be in the **nominative** case.

◆ The group of pronouns we can use in the object (or 'done to') position is

me, you, him, her, it, us, them

These are said to be in the **accusative** case. Only *you* and *it* have identical forms in both nominative and accusative cases.

> **Cases in German**

The marking of case is vital to the structure of German. Changes to the forms of words affect not only personal pronouns, as in English, but also articles (der, die, das; ein, eine, ein), adjectives and other words. There are four cases: nominative, accusative, genitive and dative.

However, it is not quite as complicated as it at first looks.

◆ There are many similarities between the endings in each group of words:

e.g. masculine accusative: d**en**, ein**en**, mein**en**, ihn, welch**en**?

◆ Because the role of a pronoun or noun phrase is usually clear from its case ending, other aspects of the language, such as word order, are often more flexible than in English (once some basic rules have been mastered).

> ### The four cases

Here is a summary of the main functions of cases (excluding their use with prepositions):

Case	Function	Example
Nominative	Subject ('doer') of the verb	**Der Mann** läuft über die Straße *The man* is crossing the street
Accusative	Object ('done to') of the verb	Ich kenne **den Mann** *I know* **the man**
Genitive	Possession between two nouns	Das Haus **meines Freundes** **My friend's** house
Dative	Indirect (additional) object of the verb	Ich schicke **meinem Freund** einen Brief *I'm sending a letter* **to my friend**

1.1 The cases

You will find grids of the case endings in the chapters on determiners (Chapter 3), pronouns (Chapter 4) and adjectives (Chapter 5).

> **TIP** **Deciding which case to use**
> * Whenever a noun phrase or a pronoun is used, a decision must be made about which case it is in.
> * If the noun phrase or pronoun is not in the plural, you will need to know the gender of the noun.
> * For the plural, there is a single set of endings for all genders.
>
> Then ask yourself this question, which will serve in most instances:
>
>
>
> *Does the noun or pronoun*
> *come after a <u>preposition</u> (e.g.* auf, in)?
>
>
>
> | If YES – | If NO – |
> |---|---|
> | *the preposition*
determines the case | *check whether it is the*
***subject** (Nominative)*
or the
***object** (Accusative)*
of the verb |

Other factors which determine the case

* Certain verbs and adjectives are used with a particular case; see 13.3 (verbs) and 5.3 (adjectives).

▶ 1.1.1   The nominative case

a   The nominative case indicates the subject of the verb (the 'doer' of the action)

Meine Mutter hört Musik	*My mother is listening to music*
Der Lehrer unterrichtet Deutsch	*The teacher teaches German*
Was hat **er** gesagt?	*What did he say?*
Woher kommst **du**?	*Where do you come from?*

Remember that the subject does not necessarily stand before the verb (as happens in English); see 18.1.

Diesen Wein finde **ich** nicht so gut	*I don't think this wine is all that good*

b   The nominative is used after certain verbs

The nominative is used after the 'copular' verbs: **sein** (*to be*), **werden** (*to become*), **bleiben** (*to stay, remain*) and a few other verbs. This is because the noun phrase after the verb refers to the same person (or thing) as the subject.

Peter ist **mein bester Freund**	*Peter is my best friend*
Er ist **ein berühmter Politiker** geworden	*He became a famous politician*
Sie ist und bleibt **die Größte**	*She is and will remain the best*

Note Other verbs require **als** before the nominative – (see also 1.1.2e):

Er erwies sich als **ein guter Freund**	*He proved himself a good friend*
Er bezeichnet sich als **freier Photograph**	*He describes himself as an independent photographer*

▶ 1.1.2   The accusative case

a   The accusative case indicates the direct object (the thing or person on the receiving end of the action)

Ich kenne **ihn** seit Jahren	*I've known him for years*
Sie hat **den Ball** hart geschlagen	*She hit the ball hard*
Ich suche **meinen Schlüssel**, aber ich finde **ihn** nicht	*I'm looking for my key, but I can't find it*

Note The direct object does not have to stand after the verb. (See also the note about the position of the subject in 1.1.1a above.)

Diesen Wein finde ich nicht so gut	*I don't think **this wine** is all that good*

b   The accusative is used after certain prepositions (see 9.1 and 9.3)

Dieser Brief ist für **dich**	*This letter is for you*
Sie ist ohne **ihn** in Urlaub gefahren	*She went on holiday without him*
Ich gehe in **die Stadt**	*I'm going into town*
Bitte stell die Flasche auf **den Tisch**	*Please put the bottle on the table*

c   The accusative is used with certain adjectives (see 5.3)

Endlich sind wir den Hund **los**	*At last we're rid of the dog*
Ich bin die Arbeit **satt**	*I'm fed up with work*
Ich bin das Stadtleben nicht **gewohnt**	*I'm not used to city life*

d Certain verbs, sometimes of naming and calling, have a second accusative (see 13.3.3)

Ich nannte **ihn einen Idioten**	I called him an idiot
Sie schimpfte **ihn einen Faulpelz**	She called him a lazybones
Das hat **ihn das Leben** gekostet	It cost him his life

e The accusative after als is used with certain verbs of regarding, considering, etc.

Damals sah ich ihn als **meinen besten Freund**	At that time I saw him as my best friend
Jetzt betrachte ich **ihn als meinen Feind**	Now I regard him as my enemy
But halten für to consider to be	
Ich halte ihn für einen Faulpelz	I think he's a lazybones

f The accusative is used in certain phrases

+ After es gibt:

In meinem Zimmer gibt es **einen Tisch** und **einen Fernseher**	In my room there's a table and a television

+ Greetings and wishes (i.e. short for „Ich wünsche dir/Ihnen …" 'I wish you …'):

Gut**en** Tag!	Hello!
Herzlich**en** Glückwunsch!	Congratulations!
Schön**en** Tag noch!	Have a nice day!

+ **Many phrases of time** which denote a definite period of time or a point in time (cf. 1.1.3d below) not governed by a preposition:

Sie blieb **den ganzen Tag** zu Hause	She stayed at home all day
Hast du **nächsten Dienstag** Zeit?	Are you free next Tuesday?
Ich war nur **einen Tag** in München	I only spent one day in Munich
Einen Augenblick mal, bitte!	Just a moment, please!

+ **Distance covered or direction** with verbs denoting motion, and prices and measures:

Sie ging **einen Schritt** weiter	She went a step further
Er stieg **den Berg** hinauf	He climbed the mountain
Dieses Stück ist **einen Meter** lang	This piece is one metre long
Das hier kostet nur **einen Euro**	This one only costs a euro

▶ 1.1.3 The genitive case

a The genitive indicates possession (= whose?) between two nouns

Das ist das Büro **meines** Vaters	That's my father's office
Dieser Teil **der** Aufgabe ist leicht	This part of the task is easy
Peter**s** Haus; Goethe**s** Werke	Peter's house; Goethe's works

b The genitive is used after certain prepositions (see 9.4)

während **der** Sommerferien	during the summer holidays
trotz **des** Wetters	despite the weather
fünf Kilometer außerhalb **der** Stadt	five kilometres outside town

Note Colloquial German often prefers the dative (often after von) both to indicate possession and after prepositions:

das Büro **von meinem** Vater
trotz **dem** Wetter
fünf Kilometer außerhalb **von der** Stadt

c The genitive is used with certain adjectives and verbs (see 5.3.2 and 13.3.4)

Ist er dieses Verbrechens **fähig**?	*Is he capable of this crime?*
Es ist nicht der Mühe **wert**	*It's not worth the trouble*
Haustiere **bedürfen** der täglichen Pflege	*Animals require daily care*

But simpler constructions or vocabulary are often preferred:

Ist er zu diesem Verbrechen fähig?	*Is he capable of this crime?*
Haustiere brauchen tägliche Pflege	*Animals require daily care*

d The genitive is used in certain expressions

• Phrases of indefinite time not governed by a preposition (cf. 1.1.2f above):

eines Tages	*one day*
eines schönen Morgens	*one beautiful morning*
dieser Tage	*recently; soon*

Note Nacht, though feminine, takes masculine/neuter genitive endings:

eines Nachts	*one night*
Des Nachts konnte er nicht schlafen	*He couldn't sleep at night*

• Other phrases, often involving opinions:

Ich bin der Meinung, dass …	*I'm of the opinion that …*
Ich bin der Ansicht, dass …	*It's my view that …*
meines Erachtens	*in my opinion*
Ich fahre erster Klasse	*I travel first class*

▶ 1.1.4 Genitive replaced by dative

Even in formal German, there are instances when the genitive cannot be used; invariably, its place is taken by the dative, often after von.

a The genitive cannot be used with personal pronouns and some other constructions

ein Freund von mir	*a friend of mine*
viele von ihnen	*many of them*
Welches von diesen Bildern gefällt dir am besten?	*Which of these pictures do you like best?*

But a genitive construction is possible if no pronoun is used:

einer meiner Freunde	*one of my friends*

Note also the genitive construction:

viele derer, die …	*many of those who …*

b The genitive cannot be used if the case of the noun would be unclear
(because it or the word it stands with does not add a case ending):

der Verkauf **von** Häuser**n**	*the sale of houses*

(der Verkauf Häuser would be so unclear as not to make sense)

c The genitive cannot be used in consecutive genitive noun phrases
(because it is regarded as clumsy):

die Karosserie **vom** Auto meines Vaters	*the bodywork of my father's car*
(rather than die Karosserie des Autos meines Vaters)	
Sie streiten sich wegen des neuen	*They're arguing about her*
Spielzeugs **von ihrem** Bruder	*brother's new toy*
(rather than … wegen des neuen Spielzeugs ihres Bruders)	

▶ 1.1.5 The dative case

a The dative indicates the indirect object of the verb (see 13.3.2)

Er schickte **seinem Bruder** das Buch	*He sent his brother the book*
Reichst du **mir** bitte das Salz?	*Could you please pass me the salt?*
Ich habe **meiner Schwester** eine CD gekauft	*I bought my sister a CD*
Du musst es **mir** kaufen!	*You must buy it for me!*
Sie hat **mir** Geld gestohlen	*She stole money from me*

> ### ▶ TIP What are direct and indirect objects?
>
> - Think of the sentence as a sequence, with the action passing from the subject to the object. In this sentence
>
> | | |
> |---|---|
> | Er schickte **seinem Bruder** das Buch | *He sent his brother the book* |
>
> *the book* has to be sent before *his brother* can receive it; it is therefore the direct object of the verb, and is in the accusative case. *His brother* is the indirect object and is in the dative case.
> - Another 'test' for the indirect object is that the word *to* or *for* (or even *from*) can be placed in front of it (*I bought a CD for my sister*). In fact, the third example in 1.1.5a could be expressed (especially in spoken German) as:
>
> | | |
> |---|---|
> | Ich habe eine CD für meine Schwester gekauft | *I bought my sister a CD/a CD for my sister* |
>
> - The indirect object is an additional object, and even if it is left out, the sentence still makes sense: *I bought a DVD* makes sense; *I bought my sister* does not.

b The dative is used with some prepositions (see 9.2 and 9.3)

Ich habe **bei** Freunden gewohnt	*I stayed with friends*
seit meinem Besuch	*since my visit*
Die Kirche steht unserem Haus **gegenüber**	*The church stands opposite our house*
Ich arbeite in **der** Stadt	*I'm working in town*
Die Flasche ist auf **dem** Tisch	*The bottle is on the table*

c The dative is used after certain verbs (see 13.3.1)

Verbs such as danken, folgen, gefallen and helfen are followed by the dative; their English equivalents are followed by the accusative:

Dieser Musik gefällt **meinem** / *My father really likes this music*
Vater gut, aber nicht **mir** / *but I don't*
Kann ich **Ihnen** helfen? / *Can I help you?*

d The dative is used after certain adjectives (see 5.3.3)

The adjective usually follows the noun or pronoun in these constructions:

Kann ich **Ihnen** behilflich sein? / *May I help you?*
Ist es **dir** klar? / *Is that clear to you?*

e The dative object is often used to indicate possession

For the possessive, especially with parts of the body or items of clothing, German often uses a dative pronoun (as an indirect object) plus the definite article, where English usually uses a possessive determiner (see also 3.2.3a):

Ich habe **mir** das Bein gebrochen / *I broke my leg*
Sie haben **sich** die Hände gewaschen / *They washed their hands*
Sie hat **ihm** die Hände gewaschen / *She washed his hands*
Er schlug **dem Mann** ins Gesicht / *He hit the man in the face*

f The dative is also used to indicate the person affected by the verb

This is often an event to their advantage or disadvantage. This is sometimes called a 'free dative', meaning that the dative pronoun or phrase, though still an indirect object, is not essential to the construction of the predicate:

Die Tasse ist **ihm** beim Abwaschen zerbrochen / *The cup broke while he was washing it*
Der Bus ist **ihr** vor der Nase weggefahren / *She missed the bus by a whisker*

g Other expressions with the dative

Wie geht es **Ihnen/dir**? / *How are you?*
Mir geht's gut/schlecht / *I'm fine/not so good*
Es geht **mir** gut/schlecht / *I'm fine/not so good*
Es ist **mir** viel zu warm/kalt / *It's much too warm/cold for me*
Es ist **mir** egal / *It's all the same to me*
Mir ist, als ob ich ihm schon mal begegnet wäre / *I have the feeling that I may have met him somewhere before*

1.2 Apposition

a A noun or noun phrase in apposition explains or adds information about the noun or pronoun which precedes it; it therefore appears in the same case to establish the grammatical link

Helmut Schmidt, **der große Staatsmann** / *Helmut Schmidt, the great statesman*
Ich besuchte Richard, **meinen Freund** aus Berlin / *I visited Richard, my friend from Berlin*
Sie wohnen in Lübeck, **einer schönen Stadt** an der Ostsee / *They live in Lübeck, a pretty town on the Baltic*

Besucher bestaunen die Fossilien eines *Argentinosaurus huinculensis*, **des größten Sauriers** aller Zeiten	*Visitors marvel at the fossil remains of an* Argentinosaurus huinculensis, *the largest dinosaur of all time*

Note The case use in the noun phrase in apposition is often ignored in colloquial German:

„Er wohnt im Adler, **ein bescheidenes Hotel**"	*'He's staying at the Adler, a modest hotel'*

b **Days and dates: phrases with am + weekdays may be followed by the dative or the accusative**

am Mittwoch, **dem** (or **den**) 19. Juli	*on Wednesday 19 July*

c **With names and titles that include an article, the article does not change its case in apposition**

in der Zeitschrift **Der** *Spiegel*	*in* Der Spiegel *magazine*
in Manns Roman **Der** *Zauberberg*	*in Mann's novel* Der Zauberberg

d **With geographical and other names, German often uses apposition where English uses *of***

die Hansestadt Lübeck	*the Hanseatic city of Lübeck*
die Universität Tübingen	*the University of Tübingen*
die Insel Poehl	*the Island of Poehl*
die Regierung Angela Merkel	*the government of Angela Merkel*

2

Nouns

OVERVIEW

Nouns are naming words – they identify animals, people, places, things and concepts.

- German nouns always begin with a **capital letter**, which makes recognition simple.
- Nouns always have a **gender** – masculine (der), feminine (die), neuter (das). A few nouns exist only in the plural (e.g. die Leute – *people*). A very few nouns change their meaning depending on the gender.
- The noun is usually (but not always) preceded by a **determiner** (e.g. der or ein), and often by an **adjective**; the adjective may take the form of an adjectival phrase.

Determiner + noun:	der Mann
Determiner + adj. + noun	ein neues Auto
Determiner + adj. phrase + noun	das soeben erschienene Buch
	the recently published book

- The **plurals** of German nouns do not usually end in -s, as is the case with most English nouns. Nonetheless, there are certain patterns to the system of plurals.

  der Arm – zwei Arme
  das Buch – einige Bücher
  das Auto – viele Autos

- A few nouns take case endings (apart from the common genitive singular -s on masculine and neuter nouns). They are weak masculine nouns (2.3.2) and adjective nouns (5.2).
- If you get the gender or plural wrong in conversation, it will affect the meaning only in very rare instances; the context will make things clear. However, German speakers set great store by getting genders and plural forms correct!

2.1 The gender of nouns

2.1.1 Which gender?

a Nouns denoting masculine people and animals are usually masculine; feminine persons and animals are usually feminine

- There are some strange (to the eyes of English-speakers, at any rate) exceptions to this pattern, e.g.:

die Geisel	*hostage*	das Genie	*genius*
das Mädchen	*girl*	der Mensch	*human being*
das Mitglied	*member*	die Person	*person*
das Pferd	*horse*	die Waise	*orphan*

+ The reasons for this are often historical: der Mensch is from der Mann, for instance. Or the reason may be grammatical: Mädchen is neuter, as are all nouns ending with the diminutive -chen (Magd = *young girl*).
+ Usually, there is no apparent logic behind genders, especially for things and concepts; they simply need to be learned with the noun and its plural.

b New nouns entering German often gain their gender in different ways, e.g.
+ by association with the type of thing to which they refer:

die E-Mail by association with die Post
das Notebook by association with das Buch
das Handy by association with das Telefon
das Baby by association with das Kind

+ or because they have the grammatical ending of a German noun:

der Computer has a masculine -er ending
die Hotline has a feminine -e ending
das Mobbing *bullying* is akin to a neuter infinitive noun.

> **TIP** **The gender of compound nouns**
> The gender of a compound noun is always the gender of the last element:
> **der** Kinder**garten**   **der** Welt**krieg**   **die** Brief**marke**

2.1.2 Masculine nouns

a Nouns with these meanings are normally masculine

Meaning	Examples			Exceptions
Male persons/professions	der Junge	der Vater	der Arzt	die Wache *sentry*
Male animals[1]	der Hund	der Kater *male cat*	der Stier *bull*	
Days of the week, months, seasons	der Montag	der Juli	der Herbst	
Many non-German rivers **These German rivers:**[2]	der Amazonas der Rhein	der Ganges der Main	der Nil der Neckar der Inn	*See feminine nouns*
Compass points, many aspects of weather	der Norden	der Schnee	der Wind	e.g. das Wetter, das Gewitter, die Brise
Makes of car[3]	der Mercedes	der Porsche	der Nissan	
Alcoholic and many other drinks	der Kaffee der Tee	der Wein der Schnaps	der Saft	das Bier

[1] i.e. as opposed to the generic words for animals, which may be any gender (die Katze, die Kuh/das Rindvieh, das Pferd).
[2] Most German river names are feminine – see below.
[3] Masculine by association with the generic term der Wagen.

b Nouns with these endings are usually masculine

Ending	Examples	Ending	Examples
-ant	Konsonant, Brillant	-ig	Käfig, Honig
-ast	Kontrast	-ismus	Idealismus, Egoismus
-ent	Dirigent, Student	-ist	Polizist, Kommunist
-er (people)[1]	Lehrer, Autofahrer	-ling	Frühling
-ich	Teppich, Rettich	-or	Katalysator, Reaktor, Motor

[1] Exceptions: die Mutter, die Schwester, die Tochter, das Opfer.
Nouns ending in -er that refer to things may be any gender: die Butter, das Wetter, das Messer, das Fenster, das Wasser).

2.1.3 Feminine nouns

a Nouns with these meanings are usually feminine

Meaning	Examples			Exceptions
Female persons/ professions[1]	die Mutter	die Oma	die Lehrerin	das Mädchen das Fräulein
Female animals	die Kuh	die Sau		
All rivers that are not masculine	die Donau	die Themse	die Elbe	
Fruits and trees, and many flowers	die Rose	die Eiche	die Pflaume	der Apfel; trees ending in -baum, e.g. der Eichenbaum
Names of ships, motorbikes, planes[2]	die *Titanic*	die BMW	die Boeing	der Airbus
Names of numerals	die Eins	die Million	die Milliarde	

[1] Many feminine nouns for professions are formed by adding -in to the masculine noun.
[2] Feminine by association with the generic term for bikes and planes, which is die Maschine; der BMW, on the other hand, designates a car made by BMW.

b Nouns with these endings are usually feminine

Ending	Examples	Ending	Examples
-a	Aula, Pizza	-schaft	Landschaft, Freundschaft
-anz, -enz	Konferenz, Eleganz	-ion	Station, Qualifikation, Region
-ei	Partei, Bücherei	-sis	Dosis, Skepsis
-heit, -keit	Faulheit, Schönheit	-tät	Universität, Qualität
-ie	Industrie (but das Genie)	-ung	Meinung, Einstellung

Ending	Examples	Ending	Examples
-ik[1]	Musik, Physik, Fabrik	**-ur**	Kultur, Temperatur
		-e[2]	Liebe, Nähe

[1] But der Atlantik, der Pazifik (from der Ozean).

[2] This applies to about 90 per cent of nouns ending in -e, but there are some common exceptions, such as:

- **weak masculine nouns**, e.g. der Junge, der Affe, der Name (see 2.3.2)
- **adjective-nouns**, e.g. der Alte, der Deutsche, das Gute (see 5.2)
- **neuter nouns beginning with Ge-** (see below), e.g. das Gebirge, das Gemüse
- **a few other nouns**, e.g. der Käse, das Auge, das Ende, das Interesse

▶ 2.1.4 Neuter nouns

a Nouns with these meanings are neuter

Meaning	Examples			Exceptions
Young humans/animals	das Baby	das Kind	das Kalb	
Continents, most towns/countries[1]	das schöne Deutschland	das alte Berlin	das neue Europa	*See below*[1]
Letters, musical notes	das A, B, C	das H-Moll *B minor*		
Metals, scientific units, many elements[2]	das Eisen	das Silber	das Kilo das Volt das Atom	der Stahl, die Bronze, der Wasserstoff
Infinitives, adjectives, pronouns, etc. used as nouns	das Aussehen	das Blau	das eigene Ich	
Many product names[3]	das Mars	das Aspirin	das Persil	die/das Nutella

[1] The article is used with countries only when:
- there is an adjective before the noun or some other qualification:
  das wiedervereinigte Deutschland; das Berlin des Kaisers
- the country is one of the very few feminine countries and regions; these are *always* used with the definite article:
  die Schweiz, die Türkei, die Bretagne, die Normandie, die Arktis, die Antarktis
- the noun is one of the very few masculine countries; these are *sometimes* used with the definite article:
  der Irak, der Iran, der Jemen, der Kongo, der Libanon, der Sudan

[2] A few elements are masculine; they are the 'atmospheric' nouns ending in -stoff (Wasserstoff *hydrogen*, Sauerstoff *oxygen*, Stickstoff *nitrogen*), plus Kohlenstoff *carbon*, along with der Phosphor, der Schwefel *sulphur*.

[3] The gender is often decided by what the product is: die Aspirin designates an individual tablet (= die Tablette) as opposed to the generic term above, die Nivea (= die Crème), das Warsteiner (= das Bier), die Colgate (= die Zahnpasta). See also note on die BMW in 2.1.3 above.

b Nouns with these endings are neuter

Ending	Examples	Ending	Examples
-chen	Mädchen, Brötchen	-tel	Viertel, Drittel
-lein	Ringlein	-tum[1]	Datum, Eigentum
-ma	Klima, Komma	-um	Studium, Gremium
-ment[2]	Parlament, Abonnement	-o[3]	Büro, Konto

[1] But der Irrtum *error*, der Reichtum *wealth*.

[2] But der Moment, der Zement.

[3] About 30 per cent of nouns ending in -o are exceptions to this rule, e.g. der Euro, die Avocado and abbreviated forms of nouns, e.g. die Disko (Diskothek), die Limo (Limonade), der Zoo (der zoologische Garten).

2.1.5 Other endings and prefixes

Apart from the endings listed above, there are some other indicators of gender.

a Nouns with the prefix Ge- are mostly neuter

das Gebäude	*building*	das Gebirge	*(range of) mountains*
das Gelächter	*laughter*	das Gepäck	*luggage*
das Gesetz	*law*	das Geschirr	*crockery*

Exceptions:

+ A few masculine nouns, e.g. der Gebrauch *use*, der Gefallen *favour*, der Gehorsam *obedience*, der Geruch *smell*
+ A few feminine nouns, e.g. die Gebühr *fee*, die Geduld *patience*, die Gefahr *danger*, die Geschichte *history*

b Nouns formed from the infinitives of verbs and ending in -en are almost all neuter

das Autofahren *motoring, driving*	das Einkaufen *shopping*
das Lesen *reading*	

Exceptions:

der Braten *roast joint*	der Gefallen *favour*

c Nouns ending with -nis or -sal are mostly neuter

das Ereignis *event*
das Gefängnis *prison*
das Schicksal *fate*

Exceptions:

+ Some nouns ending in **-nis** or **-sal** are feminine, e.g. die Erkenntnis *realisation*, die Erlaubnis *permission*

2.1.6 Homonyms: identical nouns with different genders/meanings

a A few nouns may look and sound identical, but have different meanings, genders and, usually, different plurals

Note In English, homonyms sound the same, but have different meanings and may have different spellings, e.g. *to / too / two*

der Band[1] (⁻er) *volume, book*	das Band (⁻er) *ribbon, conveyor belt*
	das Band (-e) *bonds, ties (of friendship)*
der Bund (⁻e) *union*	das Bund (-e) *bunch*
der Ekel (no pl) *disgust, loathing*	das Ekel (–) *obnoxious person*
der Erbe (-n) *heir*	das Erbe (no pl) *inheritance*
der Golf (-e) *gulf*	das Golf (no pl) *golf*
der Hut (⁻e) *hat*	die Hut (no pl) *guard, watch*
der Junge (-n) *boy*	das Junge (adj.n.) *young (animal)*
der Kiefer (–) *jaw(-bone)*	die Kiefer (-n) *pine-tree*
der Kunde (-n) *customer*	die Kunde (no pl) *knowledge, study of e.g. Erdkunde*
der Leiter (–) *manager*	die Leiter (-n) *ladder*
der Marsch (⁻e) *march*	die Marsch (-e) *marsh, fen*
der Messer (–) *gauge*	das Messer (–) *knife*
der Pack (-e *or* ⁻e) *stack, pile*	das Pack (-s) *package*
	das Pack (no pl) *rabble*
der Pony (no pl) *(hair) fringe*	das Pony (-s) *pony*
der Schild (-e) *shield*	das Schild (-er) *sign*
der See (-n) *lake*	die See (-n) *sea*
die Steuer (-n) *tax*	das Steuer (–) *steering-wheel, helm*
der Tau (no pl) *dew*	das Tau (-e) *rope, hawser*
der Verdienst (-e) *earnings*	das Verdienst (-e) *merit, contribution*
der Weise (adj.n.) *wise man*	die Weise (-n) *way, means*

[1] Note also die Band (-s) pronounced [bɛnt] *rock group*.

◆ A few other nouns look and sound identical, and have the same gender, but different meanings and different plurals (see 2.2.7 below).

b In addition, there are a few nouns (mostly of foreign origin) where more than one gender may be used, but where the meaning does not vary

der/das	Bonbon	sweet
der/das	Cartoon	
der/das	Curry	
das/die	Elastik	
der/das	Fakt	
der/das	Filter	
der/die	Gischt	*spray (e.g. on road)*
der/das	Joghurt	
der/das	Keks	*biscuit, cookie*
der/das	Ketchup	
der/das	Liter	
der/das	Teil[1]	*part*
der/das	Virus[2]	
der/das	Zubehör	*accessories*

[1] Mostly masculine, except in technical uses: das Ersatzteil *spare part*.
[2] Originally neuter, but colloquially masculine, by analogy with other nouns ending in -us.

c **There are some regional variations in gender, including**

das Foto (Germany, Austria)	die Foto (Switzerland)
der Keks (Germany, Switzerland)	das Keks (Austria)
das Match (Germany)	der Match (Austria, Switzerland)
das Radio (Germany, Austria)	der Radio (Switzerland)
der Sakko *jacket* (Germany, Switzerland)	das Sakko (Austria)
das Taxi (Germany, Austria)	der Taxi (Switzerland)

2.1.7 Gender agreement with nouns and pronouns

If the gender of the noun is not the same as the natural gender of the person or animal, German-speakers will often use a pronoun that is in keeping with the natural gender. Determiners and adjectives always agree with the grammatical gender.

a **In formal German, the pronoun referring back to the noun reflects the gender of the noun**

Sie ist ein unartiges Kind	*She's a naughty child*
Er ist eine starke Person	*He's a strong person*

But

Er ist **eine** Person, **die** alles kann	*He's a person who can do anything*
Er blickte nach dem Kind; **es** schlief noch	*He looked at the child; it was still asleep*

b **In colloquial German, this rule is often ignored, and the natural gender is used, especially if the speaker has in mind the person rather than the noun**

Wenn ich **sie** (dieses Mädchen) wäre …	*If I were her (that girl), I'd …*
Er wusste, dass er das Mädchen nie wieder sehen wird, und er umarmte **sie** das letzte Mal	*He knew that he'd never see the girl again, and he embraced her for the last time*

2.1.8 Gender issues with nouns and pronouns

Just as in English, where certain nouns, particularly those which end in *-man* (e.g. *chairman*), may be thought to lack inclusivity towards women, a number of ways have come into use to render the German language more egalitarian, some more readily accepted than others.

a **Some nouns, especially adjective-nouns, can be used with either gender:**

der/die Jugendliche	*young person*
der/die Vorsitzende	*chairman/chairwoman*
der/die Deutsche	*German*

b **Feminine forms of other nouns may be distinguished in several ways**

• By natural gender:

der Bruder/die Schwester	*brother/sister*
der Neffe/die Nichte	*nephew/niece*

| der Krankenpfleger/die Krankenschwester | *male nurse/(female) nurse* |
| meine Damen und Herren | *ladies and gentlemen* |

+ By adding a feminine suffix:

der Arzt/die Ärztin	*doctor*
der Cousin/die Cousine	*cousin*
der Verkäufer/die Verkäuferin	*salesman/saleswoman*

c **With other nouns, German-speakers sometimes try to avoid apparent sexism, especially in formal language and in the media, in several ways**

+ By referring to both masculine and feminine forms, where in the past the masculine plural would have been used for mixed groups:

| Kollegen und Kolleginnen | *colleagues* |
| Mitbürger und Mitbürgerinnen | *citizens* |

+ By combining the masculine and feminine forms into one word, sometimes with an upper-case 'I' for emphasis; this, of course, only works in print:

KollegInnen, MitbürgerInnen (**or** Kolleg/innen, Mitbürger/innen)

+ This can occasionally lead to verbose formulations, especially in lists, and bizarre inventions which, however, have not come into general use:

| Frauschaft (**for** Mannschaft) | Gästin (*female guest*) |
| Menschin (*female human*) | |

+ However, some speakers point out that the gender of many nouns does not indicate the gender of the designated person or animal (see 2.1.1.b):

die Giraffe, das Kind, die Person, das Pferd, die Wache (*sentry*)

While the issue still arouses controversy, most people now accept that it is unnecessary to use clumsy double nouns repeatedly, or invented gender-neutral forms such as Lesende (instead of Leser), or Studierende (instead of Student). Instead, a writer may

+ use **a gender-neutral noun** if one is available (such as das Mitglied *member*)
+ use **an adjective-noun**, as in 2.1.8a above, if one is available; see 5.2
+ make it clear at the outset that where one form is used, both males and females are designated.

d **Indefinite pronouns such as jeder, man, niemand and wer have to be used with masculine forms of the possessive**

This can appear odd, but can only be avoided by using, for instance, the definite or indefinite article; the writer must judge whether the change in meaning is acceptable.

Jemand hat seinen Lippenstift auf den Boden fallen lassen (**or**: einen Lippenstift)	*Someone's dropped their* (**lit**: *his*) *lipstick on the floor*
Man muss seine BHs nicht immer im teuersten Geschäft kaufen	*You don't always have to buy your bras at the most expensive shop*
Wer kann seinen Rock nicht finden?	*Who can't find their* (**lit**: *his*) *skirt?*

2.2 The plural of nouns

As mentioned at the start of the chapter, the plural should be learned along with the noun and its gender. It may help to realise that there are only a limited number of patterns for forming the plurals for each gender of noun.

> ▶ **TIP** **Noun plurals**
> A rough guide to the commonest plural endings:
> • **Masculine nouns** often add **-e**, and an umlaut to one-syllable words with a, o, u. Beware weak nouns! They add **-en**.
> • **Feminine nouns** mostly add **-en**, or **-n** if they end with an -e.
> • **Neuter nouns** usually add **-e** with many of the rest adding **-er** (and an umlaut if possible).

▶ 2.2.1 Summary of plural endings

Plural	Masculine	Feminine	Neuter
-e *or* **ːe**	Many nouns, often single-syllable Kriege Sinne Romane Arme Bälle Füsse	Some single-syllable nouns add **ːe** Hände Städte Mäuse Wände Kenntnisse	Many nouns, often single-syllable, add **-e** Beine Schafe Geschenke Meere Jahre Systeme Erlebnisse
-en *or* **-n**	Weak nouns (see p. 000) Studenten Affen Menschen Jungen	Most nouns Blumen Taschen Brücken Gabeln Kartoffeln Flaschen Uhren Türen Lehrerinnen	A few nouns Betten Ohren Hemden Augen
–	Most nouns ending in -el, -en, -er Onkel Arbeiter Kuchen Fehler		Nouns ending in -el, -en, -er, -chen Fenster Opfer Segel Zimmer Zeichen Mädchen
ːer	A few nouns ending in -el, -en, -er Väter Läden Vögel Brüder		
-er *or* **ːer**	A few nouns (add ¨ if possible) Skier Wälder Reichtümer Männer		Most nouns which don't add **-e** (add ¨ if possible) Eier Kinder Lichter Bilder Häuser Länder Räder Schlösser

-s	Nouns borrowed from other languages
	  Autos Pizzas Babys Abonnements
	
	Plurals of abbreviations and family names
	  LKWs PKWs Schmidts		

Misc	Words from Latin, Greek, etc. Viren Dramen Museen Praktika Materialien		

▶ 2.2.2 Masculine nouns

a Many masculine nouns add -e

der Arm – Arm**e** *arm*	der Ingenieur – Ingenieur**e** *engineer*

Other examples:

der Abend *evening*	der Krieg *war*
der Bleistift *pencil*	der Monat *month*
der Brief *letter*	der Schuh *shoe*
der Film *film, movie*	der Tag *day*
der Freund *friend*	der Tisch *table*
der Hund *dog*	der Unterschied *difference*

Note der Bus – Bu**sse**

b Many, mostly single-syllable, nouns with a, o or u add ̈e

der Fuß – Fü**ß**e	der Zahn – Z**äh**n**e**

Other examples:

der Arzt *doctor*	der Grund *reason*
der Ball *ball*	der Gruß *greeting*
der Baum *tree*	der Plan *plan*
der Entschluss *decision*	der Sohn *son*
der Fall *case, matter*	der Stuhl *chair*
der Flug *flight*	der Traum *dream*
der Fluss *river*	der Vorwand *excuse*

c A small number of masculine nouns add -(e)n, including weak masculine nouns (see 2.3.2)

der Mensch – Mensch**en**	der Junge – Jung**en**

Other examples:

der Buchstabe *letter*	der Präsident *president*
der Gedanke *thought*	der Schmerz *pain*
der Muskel *muscle*	der Staat *state*

d Most masculine nouns ending in -el, -en or -er (like their neuter equivalents) remain unchanged in the plural

der Finger – Finger	der Lehrer – Lehrer

Other examples:

der Fehler *mistake*	der Löffel *spoon*
der Gipfel *summit, peak*	der Schlüssel *dish*
der Koffer *suitcase*	der Teller *plate*
der Kuchen *cake*	

• A very few nouns ending in -el, -en or -er simply add an umlaut:

der Apfel – **Ä**pfel	der Bruder – Br**ü**der

Other examples:

der Garten *garden*	der Mantel *coat*
der Hafen *harbour*	der Schaden *damage*
der Laden *shop, shutter*	der Vater *father*
der Mangel *lack*	der Vogel *bird*

e A few masculine nouns add -er or ˸er (with the umlaut if possible)

    der Mann – Männer   der Ski – Skier *skis*

Other examples:

    der Geist *spirit*   der Wald *forest*

    der Gott *god*   der Wiking *Viking*

    der Irrtum *mistake*   der Wurm *worm*

    der Rand *edge*

2.2.3 Feminine nouns

a Most feminine nouns add the plural -(e)n

    die Familie – Familie**n**   die Frau – Frau**en**

Other examples:

    die Antwort *answer*   die Gefahr *danger*

    die Apotheke *chemist's shop*   die Kartoffel *potato*

    die Bank *bank*   die Mauer *wall*

    die Birne *pear*

Note Feminine nouns ending in **-in** double the **n** before the **en** to form the plural:

    die Dozentin – die Dozentin**nen** *lecturer*

    die Lehrerin – die Lehrerin**nen** *teacher*

b A few single-syllable feminine nouns add ˸e

    die Hand – H**ä**nd**e**   die Maus – M**äus e**

Other examples:

    die Angst *fear, anxiety*   die Nuss *nut*

    die Bank *bench*   die Stadt *town*

    die Faust *fist*   die Wand *wall*

    die Kuh *cow*   die Wurst *sausage*

    die Nacht *night*

Also nouns ending in **-kunft**, e.g.

    die Ankunft *arrival*   die Auskunft *information*

c There are a few other possible (but rare) feminine noun plurals

♦ Add ¨ – only two feminine nouns: die Mutter (M**ü**tter) and die Tochter (T**ö**chter)

♦ Add **-(s)e**: die Kenntnis (Kenntnis**se**)

♦ Change in ending (see 2.2.6): die Firma – Firm**en**

2.2.4 Neuter nouns

a Most neuter nouns (about 75 per cent) add the plural ending -e

    das Boot – Boot**e** *boat*   das Haar – Haar**e** *hair*

Other examples:

    das Bein *leg*   das Paar *pair*

    das Ding *thing*   das Paket *packet, parcel*

    das Gebet *prayer*   das Pferd *horse*

    das Gedicht *poem*   das Problem *problem*

    das Gefühl *feeling*   das Schaf *sheep*

    das Geschäft *shop, business*   das Schiff *ship*

    das Geschenk *present*   das Spiel *game*

    das Jahr *year*   das Tier *animal*

    das Konzert *concert*   das Ziel *aim, destination*

Note Nouns ending in -**is** double the **s** before the **e**:

> das Ereignis – Ereigni**sse** *event*
> das Gefängnis – Gefängni**sse** *prison*
> das Verhältnis – Verhältni**sse** *relation(-ship)*

b Most of the remainder add -er/-̈er, with umlaut added if possible

> das Kind – Kind**er** *child*   das Buch – Büch**er** *book*

Other examples:

> das Bild *picture*   das Glas *glass*
> das Blatt *leaf*   das Glied *limb*
> das Dach *roof*   das Haus *house*
> das Dorf *village*   das Lied *song*
> das Ei *egg*   das Land *country*
> das Fach *subject*   das Rad *wheel*
> das Gespenst *ghost*   das Schloss *castle, palace*

c Neuter nouns ending in -el, -en, -er, like their masculine equivalents, and with those ending in -chen and -lein do not change in the plural

This includes infinitives used as nouns, though most of these are not used in the plural.

> das Fenster – Fenster *window*   das Mädchen – Mädchen *girl*

Other examples:

> das Gebäude *building*   das Segel *sail*
> das Leiden *suffering*   das Theater *theatre*
> das Märchen *fairy story*   das Ufer *bank*
> das Messer *knife*   das Wunder *miracle*
> das Mittel *means*   das Zeichen *sign*
> das Opfer *victim*   das Zimmer *room*

* Two neuter nouns do not change their endings, but add an umlaut:

> das Kloster – Kl**ö**ster *monastery*   das Wasser – W**ä**sser *water, fluid*

d A few common neuter nouns add -(e)n

> das Auge – Auge**n** *eye*   das Bett – Bett**en** *bed*

Other examples:

> das Ende *end*   das Insekt *insect*
> das Fakt *fact*   das Interesse *interest*
> das Hemd *shirt*   das Ohr *ear*
> das Herz *heart*   das Verb *verb*

e One neuter noun takes the plural ⸚e

> das Floß – Flöße *raft*

▶ 2.2.5 Plurals ending with -s

a The plural ending -s is usually used with words which have been borrowed from other languages

Note that the -**y** ending does not change to -**ies** in the plural as in English:

> das Auto – Auto**s** *car*   das Hobby – Hobby**s** *hobby*

Other examples:

der Balkon *balcony*	das Komma *comma*
das Büro *office*	das Labor *lab*
das Café *café*	die Party *party*
der Chef *boss*	die Pizza *pizza*
das Deck *deck (of ship)*	das Pony *pony*
das Handy *mobile, cell-phone*	das Restaurant *restaurant*
das Hotel *hotel*	der Streik *strike*
der Karton *carton*	das Team *team*

b The ending -s is also often used with abbreviations or shortened words, especially in colloquial or slang use

Azubi**s**	*trainees (= Auszubildende)*
Jung**s** und Mädel**s**	*guys and girls*
LKW**s** und PKW**s**	*lorries/trucks and cars*
Opa**s** und Oma**s**	*granddads and grandmas*
Ossi**s** und Wessi**s**	*East and West Germans*
Profi**s**	*pros (professionals)*
Promi**s**	*VIPs*

c The -s plural is also used with surnames

bei Neitzel**s**	*at the Neitzels' house*

▷ 2.2.6 Other plural forms

a Other plural forms mostly concern words of foreign origin, especially those ending in -um, -us or -ma

+ -um, -us

das Album	Alb**en**	*album*
das Antibiotikum	Antibiotik**a**	*antibiotic*
das Gymnasium	Gymnasi**en**	*grammar school*
das Museum	Muse**en**	*museum*
das Praktikum	Praktik**a**	*practical training*
das Virus	Vir**en**	*virus*
das Zentrum	Zentr**en**	*centre*

+ -ma

das Drama	Dram**en**	*drama*
die Firma	Firm**en**	*firm, company*
das Thema	Them**en**	*subject*

b Other plural forms

das Adverb	Adverb**ien**	*adverb*
der Atlas	Atlas**se**/Atlan**ten**	*atlas*
das Fossil	Fossil**ien**	*fossil*
der Kaktus	Kakt**een**/Kaktus**se**	*cactus*
das Konto	Kont**en**/Konto**s**	*(bank) account*
das Lexikon	Lexik**a**	*encyclopaedia*
das Material	Material**ien**	*material*
das Mineral	Mineral**ien**	*mineral*
das Prinzip	Prinzip**ien**	*principle*

das Privileg	Privileg**ien**	*privilege*
das Risiko	Risik**en**	*risk*
das Stadion	Stadi**en**	*stadium*
die Villa	Vill**en**	*villa, large house*

c Some German nouns do not have their own plural form, and add another noun in order to make the plural

das Gemüse[1]	Gemüse**sorten**	*vegetables*
der Käse	Käse**sorten**	*cheese*
das Obst	Obst**sorten**	*fruit*
der Sport	Sport**arten**	*sport*
der Stock	Stockwerk**e**	*storey (of building)*
der Tod	Todes**fälle**	*death*
das Unglück	Unglücks**fälle**	*accident*
also: das Essen	Mahlzeiten	*meal*

[1] Gemüsesorten is used to emphasise variety; otherwise use singular Gemüse:

Im Supermarkt sind viele	*In the supermarket you can find lots*
Gemüsesorten zu finden	*of (sorts of) vegetables*
Man sollte viel Gemüse essen	*One should eat lots of vegetables*

▶ 2.2.7 Nouns which have two plural forms

a A very few nouns look and sound identical, and have the same gender, but have different meanings and different plurals

die Bank	*bank*	Banken
	bench	Bänke
der Block	*block (e.g. stone)*	Blöcke
	notepad (paper)	Blocks (Wohnblocks *blocks of flats*)
die Mutter	*mother*	Mütter
	nut (for bolts)	Muttern
der Strauß	*bunch of flowers*	Sträuße
	ostrich	Strauße
das Wort	*individual word*	Wörter (as in Wörterbuch)
	speech	Worte (as in Churchills Worte)

This list does not include words from 2.1.6 above (homonyms).

▶ 2.2.8 Nouns which are plural in German but singular in English

die Flitterwochen	*honeymoon*
die Haare	*hair*
die Immobilien	*property, real estate*
die Lebensmittel	*food, groceries*
die Möbel	*furniture*
die Schmerzen	*pain*
die Trümmer	*rubble*
die Zinsen	*interest (on bank account)*

Note die Eltern *parents* has no singular form; however, die Einelternfamilie *single parent family*, and ein Elternteil *a parent* are used (the latter in official German especially).

▶ **2.2.9** Nouns which are usually plural in English but singular in German

a These nouns do have plural forms for more than one item

die Brille (-n)	(a pair of) spectacles
das Fernglas (-̈er)	binoculars
die Hose (-n)	(a pair of) trousers
die Kaserne (-n)	barracks
das Mittel (–)	means
der Pyjama (-s)	pyjamas
die Schere (-n)	(a pair of) scissors
das Spielzeug (-e)	toy(s)
die Treppe (-n)	stairs
die Umgebung (-en)	surroundings
die Waage (-n)	scales

b Some other nouns are not normally used in the plural in German

das Aussehen	looks, appearance
das Benehmen	manners, behaviour
der Inhalt	contents
die Politik	politics

▶ **2.2.10** Nouns which have singular and plural forms in German

These nouns are singular in English, but are often used in the plural in German

die Auskunft (-̈e)	(piece of) information
die Hausaufgabe (-n)	(piece of) homework
die Information (-en)	(piece of) information
die Kenntnis (-se)	(piece of) knowledge
die Nachricht (-en)	(piece of) news
der Rat (Ratschläge)	(piece of) advice
Ich habe eine Nachricht für Sie	I have (a piece of) news for you

Examples:

Seine Deutschkenntnisse sind besser als meine	His knowledge of German is better than mine
Bitte schicken Sie weitere Informationen	Please send further information

▶ **2.2.11** Plural agreement

There are a few instances where German uses a singular where English usage might lead one to expect a plural.

a Parts of the body/items of clothing are often used in the singular when referring to groups of people

The noun is singular because each person has only one of the designated items!

Ich sah auf **das Gesicht** der Passanten	I looked at the faces of the passers-by
Zwei Spieler hatten sich **am Kopf** verletzt	Two players had injured their heads
Sie schüttelten sich **die Hand**	They shook hands

> **Das Leben** der Anderen   The Lives of Others (film title)
> Alle Angestellten tragen **einen**   *All the employees wear suits*
>   **Anzug**

b Weights, measures, values

Masculine and neuter nouns usually stay in the singular; feminine nouns take a plural. See also 20.1.4.

Masculine / neuter	Feminine
zwei **Glas** Wein	zwei **Tassen** Kaffee
mehrere **Stück** Kuchen	einige **Scheiben** Brot
dreißig **Euro**	ein paar **Flaschen** Bier
viele **Paar** Schuhe	

c Festivals: Weihnachten and Ostern

While Weihnachten *Christmas* and Ostern *Easter* are followed by a verb in the singular, they are preceded by an adjective in the plural:

> Frohe Weihnachten!   Bald ist Weihnachten
> letzte Ostern   Ostern fällt nächstes Jahr früh

> **TIP** **Collective nouns with singular verbs**
>
> Some collective nouns in English, although singular, are often used with a plural verb. In German, a singular noun must always be used with a singular verb:
>
> Die Polizei **will** den Verbrecher   *The police want to arrest the criminal*
>   festnehmen
> Nach dem Training **duscht** sich die   *After the training session the whole team*
>   ganze Mannschaft   *take(s) a shower*

2.3 The declension of nouns

2.3.1 Case endings on nouns

Apart from the plural endings described above, there are few changes to the endings of German nouns. For most nouns, the endings are as follows:

a Dative plural forms (all genders) add -n if possible

> mit den Männer**n**, in den Städte**n**

But not if the noun already ends with -n, or adds -s in the plural:

> in den Büros, bei seinen Eltern

b Genitive singular of masculine and neuter nouns add -s or -es

Whether to use -s or -es is mostly a matter of common sense and 'feel' regarding ease of pronunciation, style and rhythm. As a rough guide:

* **-s** is often used with words of more than one syllable

> des Abend**s**, des Ingenieur**s**, des Problem**s**, des Wagen**s**, des Auto**s**, des Monat**s**, and also, for instance, des Wein**s**, des Film**s**

♦ **-es** is frequently used with single-syllable nouns

> des Kopf**es**, des Hem**des**, des Arzt**es**, des Fluss**es**, des Freun**des**, des Kin**des**, des Mann**es**, des Jahr**es**

c Dative singular -e on the dative singular of masculine and neuter nouns is now found in only a few set phrases
Even here it is often regarded as unnecessary:

nach Hause	*home(-wards)*
zu Hause	*at home*
im Lauf(e) des Abends	*in the course of the evening*
im Grund(e) genommen	*basically*
zu Grunde gehen	*to decay*
aus diesem Grund(e)	*for this reason*

d Adjective-nouns. Adjectives may often be used as nouns, taking the gender and case endings of adjectives (see 5.2)

2.3.2 Weak masculine nouns

a Weak masculine nouns add -(e)n in all forms except the nominative singular
'Weak' masculine nouns (there is no real reason for the designation 'weak') add -(e)n not only in the plural, but in all singular forms except the nominative. Almost all refer to male humans or animals. Do not confuse these with adjective-nouns, which are all based on adjectives or participles of verbs (see 5.2).

	Singular	Plural	Singular	Plural
Nom.	der Mensch	die Mensch**en**	der Herr	die Herr**en**
Acc.	den Mensch**en**	die Mensch**en**	den Herr**n**	die Herr**en**
Gen.	des Mensch**en**	der Mensch**en**	des Herr**n**	der Herr**en**
Dat.	dem Mensch**en**	den Mensch**en**	dem Herr**n**	den Herr**en**

Some of these nouns are masculine nouns which end with **-e**; others are foreign words which end with **-at, -ent, -ist, -krat, -nom.**, and others. However, there are many other weak masculine nouns which do not fall into either of these categories. Common examples are:

der Affe	*ape*	der Graf	*count*
der Architekt	*architect*	der Held	*hero*
der Bär	*bear*	der Herr[1]	*gentleman*
der Bauer	*farmer*	der Hirt	*shepherd*
der Bayer	*Bavarian*	der Jude	*Jew*
der Chinese	*Chinese*	der Junge	*boy*
der Chirurg	*surgeon*	der Kamerad	*comrade*
der Christ	*Christian*	der Kunde	*customer*
der Demokrat	*democrat*	der Lieferant	*supplier*
der Elefant	*elephant*	der Löwe	*lion*
der Experte	*expert*	der Mensch	*human being*
der Franzose	*Frenchman*	der Nachbar	*neighbour*
der Fürst	*prince*	der Neffe	*nephew*

[1] Herr takes -n in the singular and -en in the plural – see grid above.

der Papagei	*parrot*	der Sklave	*slave*
der Photograph	*photographer*	der Soldat	*soldier*
der Präsident	*president*	der Spatz	*sparrow*
der Psycholog	*psychologist*	der Student	*student*
der Riese	*giant*	der Zeuge	*witness*
der Schotte	*Scot(-sman)*		

> **TIP** **How to recognise a weak masculine noun in a dictionary**
> + When referring to a dictionary, a weak masculine noun can be recognised by the genitive and plural forms given immediately after it, e.g.
>   der Junge (-n, -n)   der Mensch (-en, -en).
> + Other masculine nouns will have the genitive -s and the appropriate plural.

b The feminine forms of these nouns are formed in the usual way by adding -in, and sometimes an umlaut

die Bäuerin	die Französin
die Kundin	die Löwin
die Sklavin	die Studentin

Note Herr and Mensch have no feminine forms.

c There are a few weak masculine nouns which refer to things, e.g.

der Automat	*cash machine*
der Diamant	*diamond*
der Komet	*comet*
der Paragraph	*paragraph*
der Planet	*planet*

d There are a few weak nouns which add not only -(e)n in all forms but also -s to the genitive singular

	Singular	Plural
Nom.	der Name	die Namen
Acc.	den Namen	die Namen
Gen.	des Namens	der Namen
Dat.	dem Namen	den Namen

There are only eight nouns in this group:

der Buchstabe	*letter (alphabet)*	der Glaube	*belief*
der Friede[1,2]	*peace*	der Name	*name*
der Funke	*spark*	der Same	*seed*
der Gedanke	*thought*	der Wille[2]	*will* (as in *will-power*)

[1] May also be found with the nominative der Frieden.
[2] Friede and Wille are rarely used in the plural.

e One weak noun, das Herz, is neuter. It may also be declined as a normal noun especially in medical communications and colloquial German

das Herz	*heart*
schweren Herzens	*with a heavy heart*
But Sie hat ein schwaches Herz	*She has a weak heart*

▶ 2.3.3 Declension of names and proper nouns

a In the genitive singular, most names and proper nouns add -s

Goethe**s** Werke	*Goethe's works*
Christa Wolf**s** Romane	*Christa Wolf's novels*
die Novellen Theodor Storm**s**	*the novellas of Theodor Storm*
das Reich Karl**s des** Großen	*the empire of Charlemagne*
die Frauen **des** König**s** Heinrich **des** Achten	*The wives of King Henry VIII*
Richard**s** Haus; Anna**s** Familie	*Richard's house; Anna's family*
die Schönheit **des** Rhein**s**	*the beauty of the Rhine*
But das Wort Gott**es**	*God's Word*

b Personal names preceded by adjectives or articles are not usually declined

die Siege **des** Alten Fritz	*The victories of 'Old Freddy'* *(=Frederick the Great)*
But die Siege König Friedrich**s** *(no article or adjective)*	*King Frederick's victories*

c Nouns which end with a sibilant (-s, -ß, -ss, -x, -z) use an apostrophe, or von

Felix' Mutter (*or* die Mutter von Felix)
Brahms' Werke (*or* die Werke von Brahms)

d Titles of books, magazines, etc. take case endings unless the full title is given in quotation marks

Ich lese **den** *Spiegel*	**or**	Ich lese *Der Spiegel*
in Kleists *Zerbrochenem Krug*	**or**	in Kleists *Der zerbrochene Krug*
die Hauptfigur des *Lebens* des Galilei	**or**	die Hauptfigur des Stücks *Das Leben des Galilei*

e Geographical names, if masculine or neuter, add -s in the genitive

This may be omitted if there is an adjective:

die Schönheit **des** Rhein**s**	*the beauty of the Rhine*
die Grenzen des neuen Deutschland(**-s**)	*the borders of the new Germany*

♦ If the place name ends with a sibilant, **von** must be used:

die Alleen von Paris   **but**   die Alleen Berlin**s**/die Alleen von Berlin

f The plural of surnames is usually shown by adding -s (or -ens if a sibilant)

die Schmidt**s**, die Fischer**s**, die Schulz**ens**

3

Determiners

OVERVIEW

Determiners are words used *with* nouns. They fall into the following groups:

+ **definite and indefinite articles**

e.g.	der, die, das, die	*the*
	ein, eine, ein	*a, an*
	kein, keine, kein	*not a, not an, not any*

+ **demonstratives**

e.g.	dieser	*this*
	jener	*that*

+ **possessives**

e.g.	mein, meine, mein	*my*
	unser, unsere, unser	*our*

+ **interrogatives**

e.g.	welcher?	*which?*
	was für (ein)?	*what sort of?*

+ **indefinites**

e.g.	einige	*several*
	viel, viele	*a lot, many*

Note

1 Unlike English, the endings of German determiners change according to gender, number and case; the only exceptions are some singular indefinites such as viel and mehr.
2 Many determiners can also be used as pronouns (words used *in place of* noun phrases) – see Chapter 4 and the summary at the end of this chapter.

3.1 The definite and indefinite articles

▶3.1.1 The definite article: der, die, das

	Masc.	Fem.	Neuter	Plural
Nom.	der	die	das	die
Acc.	den	die	das	die
Gen.	des	der	des	der
Dat.	dem	der	dem	den

▶3.1.2 The indefinite article: ein, eine, ein, and kein, keine, kein, plural keine

	Masc.	Fem.	Neuter	Plural (kein only)
Nom.	(k)ein	(k)eine	(k)ein	keine
Acc.	(k)einen	(k)eine	(k)ein	keine
Gen.	(k)eines	(k)einer	(k)eines	keiner
Dat.	(k)einem	(k)einer	(k)einem	keinen

a **Like its English equivalent *a, an*, the German indefinite article ein has no plural**

Indefinite plural nouns are used without an article, or with an indefinite determiner (see 3.6):

Hast du Orangen gekauft?	*Did you buy (any) oranges?*
Brötchen sollen immer frisch sein	*Rolls should always be fresh*

b **Ein has a negative form, kein (*not a, not any*) which has both singular and plural forms**

Er hat **eine** Schwester, aber **keinen** Bruder	*He has a sister, but not a brother*
Wir haben Äpfel, aber **keine** Bananen	*We have (some) apples, but no bananas*

Note The English *not a* is never translated by nicht ein.

▶**TIP**   *some* or *any* + noun

• German normally omits the article altogether where English uses the indefinite determiners *some* or *any*:

Hast du Geld?	*Have you got any money?*
Er kaufte Brötchen	*He brought some rolls*
Möchtest du Kaffee?	*Would you like some coffee?*
Ich möchte noch Tee	*I'd like some more tea*

• To emphasise the idea of a limited number or quantity, determiners such as **etwas** (with singular nouns), **einige** (with plural nouns), or **manche** (with plural nouns, to emphasise 'certain') may be used:

einige Bücher	*some (=a number of) books*
Manche Leute glauben …	*Some (=certain) people believe*
Manche Fragen sind leicht	*Some questions are easy*

| Möchtest du (etwas) Milch? | Would you like some milk? |
| Sie spricht etwas Englisch | She speaks some (=a little) English |

◆ *Some* may also be used in English as an intensifier:

| Es ist ziemlich weit von hier | It's some distance from here |
| Es könnte einige Zeit dauern | It could take some time |

See also einige (3.6.4, 4.5.5), etwas (3.6.7, 4.5.6), irgendeiner (3.6.8, 4.5.7), manche (3.6.10, 4.5.11) and welcher (4.6.2).

3.2 The use of the article

◆ **Mostly, English and German use and omit the definite and indefinite articles in the same way**

Ein Buch liegt auf dem Tisch	A book is lying on the table
Bücher und Zeitschriften lagen	Books and magazines were lying
überall	everywhere

There are some variations to this pattern, however, and sections 3.2.1, 3.2.2 and 3.2.3 explain these.

▶ 3.2.1 Article used in German but omitted in English

a The article is often used with abstract nouns

der Krieg; **die** Schönheit	war; beauty
die erste Liebe	first love
die moderne Kunst	modern art
das Christentum	Christianity
So ist **das** Leben!	Life's like that!
Die Zeit vergeht	Time flies

See also 3.2.2.d below.

b The article is used with infinitives used as nouns

| Sie hat ihm **das** Lesen beigebracht | She taught him to read |
| **beim** Einkaufen | (while) shopping |

c The article is used with the names of feminine, masculine or plural countries and regions

der Iran; **der** Irak	Iran; Iraq
die Schweiz; **die** Türkei	Switzerland; Turkey
die USA; **die** Niederlande	the USA; the Netherlands
die Bretagne; **die** Toskana	Brittany; Tuscany
das Elsass	Alsace

Note Most countries are neuter and are used without the article:

England, Deutschland, Amerika

d The article is used with mountains, lakes, streets, squares, buildings

der Mount Everest	Mount Everest
der Bodensee	Lake Constance
der Alexanderplatz	(name of square in Berlin)

der Kölner Dom	*Cologne Cathedral*
Er wohnt in **der** Bahnhofstraße	*He lives in Bahnhofstraße*

But Er wohnt Bahnhofstraße 27

e The article is used with seasons, months, days, etc. after the prepositions an, bis zu, in, and when referring to meals

der November	*November*
im Frühling; **im** Juli	*in spring; in July*
am Montag	*on Monday*
nach **dem** Mittagessen	*after lunch*
zum Frühstück	*for breakfast*
einmal **im** Monat	*once a month*
im Jahre 2000	*in 2000*

But months and seasons omit the article in other constructions:

Ende Juni	*at the end of June*
letzten/nächsten Sommer	*last/next summer*
Anfang nächsten Jahres	*at the beginning of next year*

f The article is used with names preceded by an adjective

die arme Franzi!	*Poor Franzi!*
das heutige Deutschland	*modern Germany*

g The article is used colloquially with names

Kennst du **den** Klaus auch?	*Do you know Klaus too?*
„Ist **die** Frau Neitzel zu sprechen?"	*'Can I speak to Mrs Neitzel?'*

h The article is always used with the adjective meist (*most*)

die meisten Deutschen	*most Germans*
die meisten meiner Lehrer	*most of my teachers*
die meiste Zeit	*most (of the) time*

i The article is used in many idiomatic phrases, usually after a preposition

in **der** Schule	*in school*
nach **der** Schule	*after school*
mit **dem** Bus, mit **dem** Auto	*by bus, by car*
Ich gehe in **die** Stadt	*I'm going into town*
im Allgemeinen	*in general*
in **der** Tat	*indeed*
in **der** Praxis	*in practice*

▶ 3.2.2 Article omitted in German but used in English

a The article is omitted before nouns of nationality, profession, religion and rank used after the verbs sein, werden, bleiben

Er ist Deutscher, Amerikaner	*He's (a) German, (an) American*
Ich bin Christ. Sie ist Muslimin	*I'm a Christian. She's a Muslim*
Sie wurde Lehrerin	*She became a teacher*
Er ist Offizier geblieben	*He remained an officer*

But the article is used if there is an adjective before the noun:

Er ist **ein** guter Lehrer	*He's a good teacher*

b **The article is omitted after als (*as*) and ohne (*without*)**

Seine Aufgabe als Arzt ist es …	*His job as a doctor is to …*
Sie arbeitet als Krankenschwester	*She's working as a nurse*
Er benutzte seine Mappe als Regenschirm	*He was using his briefcase as an umbrella*
Geh nicht ohne Jacke aus dem Haus!	*Don't leave the house without a jacket!*

c **The article is omitted in some set phrases**

Ich habe Fieber, Schnupfen	*I've got a temperature, a cold*
mit lauter Stimme	*with a loud voice*

d **The article is omitted in German with nouns (including abstract nouns) used in pairs or groups**

Sie hat ihm Lesen und Schreiben beigebracht	*She taught him to read and write*
Es geht um Leben und Tod	*It's a matter of life and death*

e **The article is omitted in certain constructions, mostly set phrases, and always with haben**

Ich habe Hunger; er hat Angst	*I'm hungry; he's frightened*
Höflichkeit kostet nichts	*Courtesy costs nothing*

▶ 3.2.3 Other variations

a **The article is used rather than a possessive determiner with clothing and parts of the body where these belong to the subject of the sentence**

Ich zog **den** Pullover aus	*I took off my pullover*
Er hat **den** Arm gebrochen	*He broke his arm*
Sie sanken sich in **die** Arme	*They fell into one another's arms*
Er schüttelte **den** Kopf	*He shook his head*
Mach **die** Augen zu!	*Close your eyes!*
Das habe ich mit eigenen Augen gesehen!	*I saw it with my own eyes!*

But a dative pronoun or a possessive is used to avoid ambiguity, or where the relevant person is not the subject of the sentence, or where there is a preposition before the clothing or part of the body:

Mein Bein tut weh	*My leg hurts*
Er hat **sich** am Kopf verletzt	*He has injured his head*
Sie schüttelte **mir** die Hand	*She shook my hand*
Er küßte **ihren** Mund	*He kissed her mouth*

See also 1.1.5e.

b **The definite article is used with certain measures or amounts, where English may use the indefinite article**

3 Euro **die** Flasche	*3 Euros a bottle*
zweimal in **der** Woche	*twice a week*

c **ein used to mean *a* or *one***

Ein can mean both *a* and *one* in number when followed by a noun; the distinction between them is made by emphasis:

| Hast du **einen** Euro dabei? | Have you got a euro? |
| Ich habe nur noch **einen** Euro | I've only got one euro left |

3.3 Demonstrative determiners

3.3.1 dieser *this, these*; jener *that, those*

	Masc.	**Fem.**	**Neuter**	**Plural**
Nom.	dieser	diese	dieses	diese
	jener	jene	jenes	jene
Acc.	diesen	diese	dieses	diese
	jenen	jene	jenes	jene
Gen.	dieses	dieser	dieses	dieser
	jenes	jener	jenes	jener
Dat.	diesem	dieser	diesem	diesen
	jenem	jener	jenem	jenen

- **dieser and jener can be used both as determiners and as pronouns with no change of form**
- **jener is uncommon except in formal written German; dieser (or, colloquially, der/die/das) is used almost without exception for both meanings:**

Dieses Auto kostet viel mehr als das andere	This car costs a lot more than that one/the other
Diese Idee kannst du dir gleich aus dem Kopf schlagen	You can put that idea out of your mind straight away
Von **jenem** Tage an …	From that day onwards …
Das Haus würde ich gerne kaufen!	That's the house I'd like to buy!
Den Kerl will ich nie wieder sehen	I never want to see that guy again

3.3.2 solcher *such (a)*

a Solcher declines like dieser (see 3.3.1), and is usually used in the plural

| in **solchen** Fällen | in such cases |
| **Solche** Leute finde ich doof | I find people like that stupid |

Note It may also be used in the singular, but this sounds formal:

| **solches** herrliche Wetter | such wonderful weather |

b Solcher may also be used as an ordinary adjective after the indefinite article ein in the singular

| Sie arbeitet mit einer **solchen** Hektik | She works at such a hectic pace. |
| Eine **solche** Frau würde ich auch gern heiraten | I'd like to marry a woman like that too |

c A more colloquial way of expressing *such a* is so ein

| **So eine** Frau würde ich auch gern heiraten | I'd like to marry a woman like that too |

So ein Mist!	*What a pain/nuisance!*
So einen tollen Film habe ich seit langem nicht gesehen	*I haven't watched such a good film for ages*

▶3.3.3 derjenige/diejenige/dasjenige *the one who/which*

	Masc.	Fem.	Neuter	Plural
Nom.	derjenige	diejenige	dasjenige	diejenigen
Acc.	denjenigen	diejenige	dasjenige	diejenigen
Gen.	desjenigen	derjenigen	desjenigen	derjenigen
Dat.	demjenigen	derjenigen	demjenigen	denjenigen

a derjenige has the forms of a definite article + adjective, but is written as one word

It may be used as a determiner or as a pronoun (see 4.3.4).

b derjenige is usually followed by a relative pronoun

derjenige Schauspieler, **der** …	*the actor who …*
diejenigen Studenten, **die** sich für Kunst interessieren	*those students who are interested in art*

c derjenige is often replaced by der, die, das in colloquial German

der Schauspieler, der die Rolle von Faust spielte	*the actor who played the role of Faust*

▶3.3.4 derselbe/dieselbe/dasselbe *the same*

	Masc.	Fem.	Neuter	Plural
Nom.	derselbe	dieselbe	dasselbe	dieselben
Acc.	denselben	dieselbe	dasselbe	dieselben
Gen.	desselben	derselben	desselben	derselben
Dat.	demselben	derselben	demselben	denselben

a derselbe, like derjenige, has the forms of a definite article + adjective, but is written as one word

It can be used as a determiner or as a pronoun:

Er fährt immer **dasselbe** Auto	*He always drives the same car*
Es handelt sich um ein und **dieselbe** Person	*It's about one and the same person*
Ihr PIN-Code bleibt **derselbe**	*Your PIN code remains the same*

b derselbe can be used with a preposition which has a contracted form; the two words are then written separately

im selben Gebäude	*in the same building*
zur selben Zeit	*at the same time*

c Note that derselbe means *the (very) same*; der gleiche (which is not written as one word) means *the same (similar)*

Er trägt **dieselbe** Krawatte jeden Tag	*He wears the same tie every day*

Beide Männer tragen die **gleiche** Krawatte	*Both men are wearing the same tie*

Note In colloquial German this distinction is often ignored:

Sie sind auf **derselben**/der **gleichen** Wellenlänge	*They're on the same wavelength*

3.4 Possessive determiners

a The possessives mein, dein, sein, etc. are often called possessive adjectives
However, the designation sometimes used in German – *Possessivartikel* (possessive articles) – is a better description in terms of how they work grammatically.

	Singular			Plural	
ich	**mein**	*my*	wir	**unser**	*our*
du	**dein**	*your*	ihr	**euer**	*your*
er	**sein**	*his*	sie	**ihr**	*their*
sie	**ihr**	*her*	Sie	**Ihr**	*your (polite)*
es	**sein**	*its*			
man	**sein**	*one's*			

- The polite form **Sie** *you* and its possessive **Ihr** *your* are used for one person or any number of people.
- Possessives may also be used, with some changes to endings, as pronouns (see 4.4).

b All the possessives take the same endings as ein (3.1.2)
The table below shows the endings for mein:

	Masc.	Fem.	Neuter	Plural
Nom.	mein	meine	mein	meine
Acc.	meinen	meine	mein	meine
Gen.	meines	meiner	meines	meiner
Dat.	meinem	meiner	meinem	meinen

sein Bruder, **seine** Schwester	*his brother, his sister*
der Freund **seiner** Schwester	*his sister's boyfriend*
mit **seiner** Schwester	*with his sister*
mit **seinen** Eltern	*with his parents*

- When **unser** and **euer** add an ending, they often lose -**e**- from the root word, especially in spoken German:

Unser Haus ist auf dem Land	*Our house is in the country*
In **uns(e)rem** Haus ist es immer kalt	*In our house it's always cold*
Eu(e)re Eltern sind lustig	*Your parents are funny*

c The genitive determiner may be used instead of the possessive to avoid ambiguity

Meine Mutter, meine Schwester und **deren** Kinder	*my mother, my sister, and her [i.e. my sister's] children*

3.5 Interrogative determiners

▶ 3.5.1 welcher/welche/welches *which*

a welcher takes the same endings as dieser (see 3.3.1 above)

Welches Buch hast du gewählt?	*Which book did you choose?*
In **welchem** Haus wohnt sie?	*Which house does she live in?*
Welcher deutsche Sportler hat die Medaille gewonnen?	*Which German sportsman won the medal?*

b welcher may also be used in exclamations

This occurs mostly in formal German, sometimes without case endings if followed by ein or an adjective:

Welcher Blödsinn!	*What nonsense!*
Welch traurige Geschichte!	*What a sad tale!*
Welch ein Glück!	*What good luck!*
Welches Glück!	*What good luck!*

Note Spoken German usually prefers was für (ein) or so ein:

Was für ein Glück! / **So ein** Glück!	*What good luck!*

▶ 3.5.2 was für *what kind of*

. The case of the following noun phrase is decided not by für but by the rest of the clause

In **was für** einem Haus wohnst du?	*What sort of a house do you live in?*
(einem is dative because of the preposition in)	
Was für ein Mann ist er?	*What sort of a man is he?*
(ein is nominative because it is the complement of er ist)	
Sie hat nicht gesagt, **was für** Wein ich kaufen soll	*She didn't say what sort of wine I should buy*
Was für Bücher liest du gern?	*What sort of books do you like reading?*

3.6 Indefinite determiners

▶ 3.6.1 all, alles, alle *all, everybody*

a Inflected all takes the same endings as dieser (see 3.3.1), with the alternative masculine and neuter genitive singular form allen

	Masc.	Fem.	Neuter	Plural
Nom.	aller	alle	alles	alle
Acc.	allen	alle	alles	alle
Gen.	all**en**	aller	all**en**	aller
Dat.	alllem	aller	allem	allen

b all used as a determiner

+ It is always inflected, and is commonly used in the plural:

alle Studenten	*all (of the) students*
Die Karten **aller** Gäste wurden kontrolliert	*The tickets of all the guests were checked*

+ In the singular it is sometimes used in set phrases and with adjective-nouns:

Aller Anfang ist schwer	*The first step is always the hardest*
in **aller** Frühe	*at the crack of dawn*
Alles Gute!	*All the best!*
allen Ernstes	*in all seriousness*

Note If this inflected form of **all** is followed by an adjective, the adjective takes weak endings (i.e. as it does after der, die, das) – see 5.1.1:

alle guten Sachen	*all good things*
trotz **allen** guten Willens	*in spite of all the good will*

c all followed by a definite article or other determiner

+ both inflected and uninflected forms are used:

alle die Schuld	*all the guilt*
alle die Häuser	*all (of) the houses*
all die Studenten	*all the students*
all der Wein	*all the wine*
mit **all** dem Essen	*with all the food*
all mein Wein	*all my wine*
all dieses Bier	*all this beer*
mit **all** dem Stress	*with all the stress*
all/alle diese Teller	*all these plates*
mit **all/allen** seinen Zweifeln	*with all his doubts*

+ **all** is never followed by the genitive case to indicate *all of*:

alle meine besten Freunde	*all (of) my best friends*
alle Anwesenden	*all (of) those present*
all der Wein	*all (of) the wine*

+ **all** may itself, of course, be used *in* the genitive case:

trotz **allen** Fleißes	*despite all (of) the hard work*

+ **all** (inflected) does not have to precede the noun:

Meine Freunde sitzen **alle** draußen im Garten	*My friends are all sitting outside in the garden*

▶ **TIP** **When to add case endings to all**

There is great flexibility in deciding whether **all** used as a determiner should take case endings. If the following rules are followed, the user will make few mistakes.

+ **Do not** add endings when **all** is followed by a determiner. (Note that **all** and **alle** are never followed by the genitive):

all meine Freunde	*all (of) my friends*
mit **all** dem Geld	*with all the money*

+ **Add** endings in both singular and plural when **all** is used as a determiner:

alle Kinder	*all (of the) children*
Sie hat **allen** Grund dazu	*She has every reason to do so*
Er wünschte mir **alles** Gute	*He wished me all the best*

▶ 3.6.2 ganz *all, whole*

+ **Instead of all, Germans often use the adjective ganz**

This avoids altogether the question of whether and how **all** and any following adjective inflect. Colloquially, **ganz** may also be used with a plural noun:

Ich habe mein **ganzes** Geld ausgegeben	*I've spent all my money*
Er hat die **ganze** Zeit nur gemeckert	*He just complained all the time*
Ganz Deutschland	*all of Germany*
Den **ganzen** Sommer über war es kalt und windig	*It was cold and windy all summer*
die **ganzen** Kinder	*all the children*

▶ 3.6.3 beide *both*

a beide takes the same endings as dieser (see 3.3.1)

Ich habe **beide** Filme gesehen	*I've seen both films*
Beide älteren Schwestern leben im Ausland	*Both older sisters live abroad*

b beide can be used as an adjective

Seine **beiden** Eltern sind gestorben	*Both his parents are dead*
die ersten **beiden** Romane	*the first two novels*
or: die **beiden** ersten Romane	

▶ 3.6.4 einige *some*

+ **einige is almost always used in the plural. It takes the same endings as dieser (see 3.3.1)**

einige Autofahrer	*some car-drivers*
mit **einigen** alten Freunden	*with some old friends*
nach **einiger** Zeit	*after some time*

▶ 3.6.5 ein bisschen, ein wenig *a little, a bit*

a ein bisschen and ein wenig are invariable and always followed by a singular noun

Hast du **ein wenig** Zeit für mich?	*Can you spare a moment?*
Ich habe nur noch **ein wenig** Geld	*I only have a little money left*
mit **ein bisschen** Geduld	*with a little patience*

b bisschen is occasionally used with a determiner other than ein

Ich habe **kein bisschen** Hunger	*I'm not the least bit hungry*
mit **dem bisschen** Geld, das ich noch habe	*with the little money I still have*

▶ 3.6.6 ein paar *a few*

a ein paar does not take case endings. It is always followed by a plural noun

Ich gehe mit **ein paar** Freunden ins Kino	*I'm going to the cinema with a few friends*
nach **ein paar** Tagen	*after a few days*
ein paar Tausend Euro	*a few thousand Euros*

b paar is sometimes used with another (declinable) determiner

alle **paar** Minuten	*every few minutes*
die **paar** Euro, die es kostet	*the few Euros it costs*
mit seinen **paar** Siebensachen	*with his few belongings*

▶ 3.6.7 etwas *some, any*

+ **etwas does not take case endings. It is often used with a neuter adjective-noun (see 5.2e)**

Wir brauchen noch **etwas** Zeit	*We need some more time*
Etwas frische Sahne dazugeben	*Add some fresh cream*
etwas Interessantes	*something interesting*

▶ 3.6.8 irgendeiner, irgendwelcher *some ... or other*

+ **irgend is added to emphasise vagueness**

Irgendein Passant muss das gesehen haben	*Some passer-by or other must have seen it*
aus **irgendeinem** Grund	*for some reason or other*
Hat jemand **irgendwelche** gute Ideen?	*Does anyone have any good ideas?*

▶ 3.6.9 jeder *each, every*

+ **jeder is always singular, and is inflected like dieser (see 3.3.1)**

Wie **jede** moderne Frau weiß ...	*As every modern woman knows ...*
Jeder Jugendliche will sein eigenes Auto	*Every young person wants their own car*
Er rief **jeden** Tag an	*He phoned every day*
Jedes Mal, wenn ich ihn sehe ...	*Every time I see him ...*

▶ 3.6.10 manche(r) *some, many a*

+ **manche(r) can be singular or plural and is usually inflected like dieser (see 3.3.1)**

When it precedes the indefinite article ein, manch remains uninflected:

Mancher Student/**manch ein** Student	*Many a student*
manch eine Nacht	*many a night*
Manche junge Leute sehen nicht ein, dass ...	*Some young people just don't realise that ...*

▶ 3.6.11 mehrere *several*

+ **mehrere is used in the plural and is inflected like dieser (see 3.3.1 above)**

Er war **mehrere** Tage bei uns	*He was with us for several days*
mehrere nagelneue Autos	*several brand new cars*
Mütter mit **mehreren** kleinen Kindern	*Mothers with several small children*

▶ 3.6.12 sämtliche *all*

+ **sämtliche is used in the plural and indicates all the members of a particular group or set**

It takes the same endings as dieser (see 3.3.1 above):

sämtliche Jungen in dieser Klasse	*all the boys in this class*
die Meinung **sämtlicher** anwesenden Mitglieder	*the opinion of all the members present*
Schillers **sämtliche** Werke	*Schiller's complete works*

▶ 3.6.13 viel/viele *lots/many*, wenig/wenige *a little/a few*

a Both viel and wenig add endings in the plural (where they take the same endings as dieser, see 3.3.1), but not in the singular

Er hat **wenig** Geduld	*He doesn't have much patience*
Es nimmt zu **viel** Zeit in Anspruch	*It takes up too much time*
Sie hat **viele/wenige** Verwandte	*She has lots of/few relatives*
Er hat nur **wenige** gute Bücher	*He only has a few good books*
die Meinungen **vieler** Wähler	*the opinions of many voters*

b viel and wenig are also used with adjective-nouns

Ich habe **viel** Gutes von ihm gehört	*I've heard many good things about him*
Sie hat nur **wenig** Schönes gesehen	*She saw only a little that was beautiful*

c viel and wenig can be used as a normal adjective after a determiner

die **vielen** Bücher, die er gelesen hat	*the many books he's read*
seine **wenigen** Freunde	*his few friends*
das **wenige** Geld, das wir noch haben	*the little money we still have*

▶ 3.6.14 welcher/welche/welches *which*

+ See Interrogative determiners (3.5.1 above).

▶ 3.6.15 Indefinite determiners + adjectives + noun

Although there is considerable flexibility with the endings of indefinite determiners and following adjectives, the following patterns often apply.

a Where indefinite numbers (or 'quantifiers') are followed by an adjective and a noun, both the determiner and the adjective take the same Group 3 (strong) ending (see 5.1.3)

einige	einige **alte** Freunde; mit einigen **alten** Freunden
einzelne	einzelne **kurze** Regenchauer
etliche	die Taten etlicher **guter** Menschen
manche (*pl*)	manche **junge** Leute
mehrere	trotz mehrerer **langer** Arbeitstage
viele	viele **tolle** Geschenke

Note Singular quantifiers (e.g. viel, wenig, etwas) are usually invariable, but any adjectives which follow them take Group 3 endings:

viel	viel **guter** Wein
wenig	mit wenig **wirklichem** Interesse

b Other indefinite determiners, including a few indefinite numbers (or 'quantifiers'), work like Group 1 determiners, and the following adjective takes the appropriate weak ending (see 5.1.1)

These occur most frequently in the plural:

alle	alle **interessanten** Nachrichten; mit aller **möglichen** Eile
beide	beide **alten** Nachbarn
folgende	folgendes **erstaunliche** Ereignis; folgende **erstaunlichen** Ereignisse
manch (*sing*)	mancher **junge** Mann
sämtliche	sämtliches **vorhandenes** Material; sämtliche **deutschen** Politiker
solche	bei solcher **täglichen** Hektik; solche **interessanten** Bücher

c These rules also apply to indefinite determiners used with plural adjective-nouns (see 5.2)

♦ Indefinite numbers (3.6.15a above):

einig**e** Arbeitslos**e**	*several unemployed (people)*
mit mehrer**en** Bekannt**en**	*with several acquaintances*
viel**e** Jugendlich**e**	*many young people*

♦ Other indefinite determiners (3.6.15b above):

all**e** Arbeitslos**en**	*all (the) unemployed*
solch**e** Deutsch**en**	*such Germans; Germans like that*

3.7 Determiners and pronouns: a summary

The table below summarises the use of determiners and pronouns, and provides cross-references between Chapter 3 (Determiners) and Chapter 4 (Pronouns).

♦ Mostly, these words decline in an identical way, and any variations concern their use rather than their form.

◆ The reference is <u>underlined</u> if there is some variation in the way the two forms are declined; these variations are always minor, however.

Used as pronouns and determiners		Determiner	Pronoun
Definite article/demonstrative	der, die, das	3.1.1	<u>4.3.1</u>
Demonstratives	dieser, jener	3.3.1	4.3.2
	derjenige	3.3.3	4.3.4
	(ein) solcher	3.3.2	4.3.3
Indefinite article	ein, eine, ein; kein, keine, kein	3.1.2	<u>4.5.4</u>
Possessives	mein, meine, mein	3.4	4.4
Interrogatives	welcher	3.5.1	4.6.2
	was für (ein-)	3.5.2	
Indefinites/pronouns	all-/ganz	3.6.1, 3.6.2	4.5.1
	beide	3.6.3	4.5.2
	einige	3.6.4	4.5.5
	ein bisschen, ein wenig	3.6.5	4.5.3
	ein paar	3.6.6	4.5.3
	etwas	3.6.7	4.5.6
	irgendeiner	3.6.8	4.5.7
	jeder	3.6.9	4.5.8
	manche(r)	3.6.10	4.5.11
	mehrere	3.6.11	4.5.12
	sämtliche	3.6.12	
	viel/viele, wenig/wenige	3.6.13	4.5.14
Used as pronouns only			
	jemand/niemand		4.5.9
	man		4.5.10
	nichts		4.5.13
Interrogatives	wer(?), was(?)		4.6.1/4.6.3
Personal pronouns	ich, mich, mir		4.1/4.2
Relative pronouns	..., der; ..., die; ..., das		4.7

4

Pronouns

OVERVIEW

Pronouns are words *in place of* a noun phrase which is known or understood. They include:

+ **personal** pronouns

    e.g.   ich, mich, mir   *I, me*

+ **reflexive** pronouns

    e.g.   sich   *himself, herself, itself*

+ **demonstrative** pronouns

    e.g.   dieser, der, jener   *this one, that one, these, those*

+ **possessive** pronouns

    e.g.   meiner, unserer   *mine, ours*

+ **indefinite** pronouns

    e.g.   jemand, man   *someone, one*

+ **interrogative** pronouns

    e.g.   wer?, was?   *who?, what?*

+ **relative** pronouns

    e.g.   der Mann, **der** ...   *the man who*

The forms of most pronouns change according to gender, number and case. It is important to choose the form carefully, as these words are vital to the structure of the language

    e.g.   er, ihn, ihm   du, dich, dir

The English pronoun *it* is expressed by the given form of er, sie, es depending on gender, number and case.

Many pronouns are identical in use and form with the corresponding determiners – see Chapter 3.

4.1 Personal pronouns

▶ 4.1.1 The forms of the personal pronouns

Singular/plural	Person	Nom.	Acc.	Dat.
Singular	1st	ich	mich	mir
	2nd	du	dich	dir
	3rd	er	ihn	ihm
		sie	sie	ihr
		es	es	ihm
Plural	1st	wir	uns	uns
	2nd	ihr	euch	euch
	3rd	sie	sie	ihnen
		Sie	Sie	Ihnen

▶ TIP **How to remember the 3rd person pronouns**
Note that both singular and plural forms of the 3rd person pronouns have the
same endings as the parallel case forms of **der, die, das,** and plural **die.**

	Masc.	Fem.	Neuter	Plural
Nom.	der – er	die – sie	das – es	die – sie
Acc.	den – ihn	die – sie	das – es	die – sie
Dat.	dem – ihm	der – ihr	dem – ihm	den – ihnen

▶ 4.1.2 The use of the personal pronouns

a **It is not always expressed by es; the pronoun depends on the gender and case
of the noun referred to**

der Wagen > *er*   die Garage > *sie*   das Haus > *es*

Der Wagen ist neu – ich habe **ihn** gestern gekauft	*The car is new – I bought it yesterday*
Kennst du die Brücke im Dorf? **Sie** ist 400 Jahre alt!	*Do you know the bridge in the village? It's 400 years old!*
Das alte Haus da drüben – **es** gehörte früher meiner Oma	*The old house over there – it used to belong to my grandma*

b **Some nouns have a gender which is different from the 'natural' gender of the
person or animal referred to**

e.g. das Mädchen, die Person, der Hund. See 2.1.7 for more details.

Wir haben einen Hund – **sie** (formal: er) ist 6	*We've got a dog – she's 6*
„Kennst du das Mädchen?" „Ja, **sie** (formal: es) heißt Alex"	*'Do you know the girl?' 'Yes, she's called Alex'*

c **The definite article (der, die, das) is often used colloquially in place of a personal pronoun**
   It is often placed first for emphasis; the genitive form cannot be used in this way:

Der Richard? **Den** habe ich seit langem nicht mehr gesehen	*Richard? I haven't seen him for ages*
Kathrin? **Die** ist aber doof!	*Kathrin? She's really stupid!*

d **The genitive forms of personal pronouns (meiner, deiner, seiner, ihrer, unser, euer, ihrer, Ihrer) exist, but are rarely used**
   - This applies even in formal written language, and an alternative construction is almost always preferred.
   - With prepositions which take the genitive, the dative pronoun is often used instead, when referring to persons; if things are being referred to, adverbs such as **stattdessen**, **trotzdem** or **deswegen**, are used:

wegen dir	*because of you*
Er hat eine Panne gehabt; **deswegen** kann er nicht kommen	*He's had a breakdown; because of that he can't come*

▶ **TIP**   **du/ihr or Sie?**

du and its plural **ihr** are used between relatives, close friends, fellow students at school or university, work colleagues (though not in the professions), and when talking to God, children and animals.

Sie is used when addressing all adult strangers, whether singular or plural, and colleagues in the professions.

   - It is quite common for people to work in the same office for years and still address one another as Sie; it does not denote a lack of friendliness. Even insults can be traded using the Sie form:

   Sie Sau! *You bastard!*

   - Outside the workplace, Germans are quick to suggest replacing siezen (calling someone Sie) with duzen, and the person's first name:

   Wollen wir uns duzen?   *Shall we call each other du?*

▶ **4.1.3   The pronoun es – some special uses**

As well as its use in referring to a neuter noun, the following less obvious uses of **es** should be noted:

a **To refer to a preceding noun or adjective (used with sein, werden, bleiben)**

Du bist müde? Ich bin **es** auch	*You're tired? I am too*
„Wer ist das?" „**Es** ist mein Sohn"	*'Who's that?' 'It's my son'*
„Wer ist da?" „Ich bin'**s**"	*'Who's there?' 'It's me'*
„Was sind das für Bücher?" „**Es** sind Romane"	*'What sort of books are those?' 'They're novels'*
Ihr Vater ist Anwalt, und sie wird **es** auch	*Her father's a lawyer, and she's going to become one too*

b To refer to a preceding clause or action

Sie kann schwimmen; ich kann **es** auch	*She can swim, and so can I*
Kommt sie mit? Ich hoffe **es**	*Is she coming too? I hope so*
Jemand hat das Fenster zerbrochen, aber keiner will **es** getan haben	*Somebody broke the window, but nobody will own up to it*

c As a temporary subject (or 'placekeeper'); its role is to ensure that the finite verb stands in second position

The real subject often follows the verb, and is also in the nominative:

Es wartet jemand auf ihn	*There's someone waiting for him*
Es standen viele Leute an der Tür	*There were lots of people standing at the door*
Es freut mich sehr, dich wieder zu sehen	*I'm really pleased to see you again*
Es hat sich niemand gemeldet	*Nobody has volunteered*
Es geschah ein Unfall	*An accident occurred*
Es war einmal ein schöner Prinz…	*Once upon a time there was a handsome prince…*

But if another element is placed first, es is usually not required:

Jemand wartet auf ihn
Viele Leute standen an der Tür
Bisher hat sich niemand gemeldet

d As the subject of many impersonal or passive constructions (where, as in 4.1.3c above, it acts as a 'placekeeper' to keep the verb in second position)

Es regnet	*It's raining*
Es ist kalt/Freitag/8 Uhr	*It is cold/Friday/8 o'clock*
Es klopfte an der Tür	*There was a knock at the door*
Hier wohnt **es** sich gut	*It's great living here*
Es wird heute Abend gefeiert	*There will be a celebration this evening*
Es darf nicht geraucht werden	*No smoking is allowed*

But if another element is placed first in a passive construction, es is not needed:

Heute Abend wird gefeiert
Hier darf nicht geraucht werden

See also 12.6 (impersonal constructions), and 12.6.3 (es ist/sind, es gibt).

e As an indeterminate object

Hier habt ihr **es** gut!	*You've got it good here!*
Ich habe **es** eilig	*I'm in a hurry*
Ich finde **es** unfair, dass …	*I think it's unfair that …*
Ich finde **es** nicht gut, dass du so viel Geld ausgegeben hast	*I don't think it's good that you've spent so much money*

▶ 4.1.4 Pronouns used with prepositions

. If the pronoun refers to **a person or persons**, use preposition + pronoun.

• If the pronoun refers to **a thing** or **things**, use **da(r)-** + preposition. (This form is called the prepositional adverb.)

Note außer, gegenüber, ohne and seit cannot be used with da(r)- ; they are used with a pronoun.

Pronoun refers to *person*	Pronoun refers to *thing*
Use preposition + pronoun	Use **da-/dar-** in front of preposition
Mein Freund:	Der Wagen:
Dieser Brief ist von **ihm**	Ich kaufe Öl **dafür**
Das Geschenk ist für **ihn**	Ich fahre **damit** nach Salzburg
Ich gehe mit **ihm** ins Kino	Meine Schlüssel sind **darin** (*inside it*)
	But Ohne **ihn** komme ich nicht zur Arbeit

4.2 Reflexive pronouns

▷ 4.2.1 Reflexive object pronouns

• A reflexive object pronoun is used when the object refers to the same person as the subject. See 12.7 (reflexive verbs).
• The reflexive pronouns are, with one exception, the same as the direct and indirect object pronouns (e.g. **mich/mir**).
• The exception is in the third person (**er**, **sie**, **es**, **sie/Sie**); to avoid ambiguity, the pronoun **sich** is used for both accusative and dative of all three genders and the plural.

Accusative pronoun	**Dative** pronoun
ich wasche **mich**	ich wasche **mir** die Hände
du wäschst **dich**	du wäschst **dir** die Hände
er/sie/es wäscht **sich**	er/sie/es wäscht **sich** die Hände
wir waschen **uns**	wir waschen **uns** die Hände
ihr wascht **euch**	ihr wascht **euch** die Hände
sie/Sie waschen **sich**	sie/Sie waschen **sich** die Hände

Ich habe **mich** gewaschen	*I had a wash*
Ich will **mir** einen Laptop kaufen	*I want to buy myself a laptop*
Er hat **sich** gewaschen	*He had a wash*
Sie will **sich** einen Laptop kaufen	*She wants to buy herself a laptop*
Ich singe vor **mich** hin	*I sing to myself*
Sie haben keine Kreditkarte bei **sich**	*They haven't got a credit card on them*

See also 1.1.5e–f (for object pronoun used in place of possessive determiner).

▶ 4.2.2 selbst/selber *myself, yourself, himself*

* **selbst/selber are emphatic**

Den Kuchen habe ich **selbst/ selber** gebacken	*I baked the cake myself*
Small children say „**Selber** machen!!"	*'Me do it!!'*

▶ 4.2.3 sich/einander *each other, one another* (the reciprocal pronoun)

* **sich is more common in speech; einander is the only possibility after a preposition**

Sie lieben **sich/einander**	*They love one another*
Sie denken oft **aneinander**	*They often think of each other*
Cf. Sie denken nur an sich	*They only think of themselves*

4.3 Demonstrative pronouns

Most demonstrative pronouns are also used as determiners. Notes on the declensions of these (apart from the pronouns der, die, das – see below) can be found in 3.3.

▶ 4.3.1 der, die, das *that*

* **In spoken German, der is commonly used as a demonstrative determiner or pronoun in place of dieser**
* It is always pronounced stressed.
* Its forms are mostly identical to the definite article, except in the genitive singular and plural and the dative plural (shown in bold below). It is completely identical to the relative pronoun (see 4.7.1 below).

	Masc.	Fem.	Neuter	Plural
Nom.	der	die	das	die
Acc.	den	die	das	die
Gen.	**dessen**	**deren**	**dessen**	**deren**
Dat.	dem	der	dem	**denen**

Käse? – Also, ein Stück von **dem** hier, bitte	*Cheese? – Er, a piece of this one, please*
So was kann nur **die** gemacht haben	*Only she could have done something like that*
Sein Computer ist besser als **der**, den ich gekauft habe	*His computer is better than the one I've bought*
Das sind alles Sachen, die nicht gut sind	*Those are all things which aren't good*
Doch **das** sind Details	*But those are (just) details*

▶ **4.3.2** dieser *this* (one), jener *that* (one)

> **a dieser and jener used as pronouns have the same declensions as the determiners**

	Masc.	Fem.	Neuter	Plural
Nom.	dieser	diese	dieses	diese
	jener	jene	jenes	jene
Acc.	diesen	diese	dieses	diese
	jenen	jene	jenes	jene
Gen.	dieses	dieser	dieses	dieser
	jenes	jener	jenes	jener
Dat.	diesem	dieser	diesem	diesen
	jenem	jener	jenem	jenen

> ◆ jener is uncommon except in formal written German.
> ◆ dieser or, colloquially, der/die/das (see 4.3.1 above), is used almost without exception to mean both *this* and *that*:
>
> | Die Polizei fand einen Schuh. | *The police found a shoe. This* |
> |---|---|
> | **Dieser** stamme von dem | *belonged to the missing man* |
> | Vermissten, erklärte sie | *they said* |
> | Sie wollte nicht dieses Kleid | *She didn't want to try this dress* |
> | anprobieren, sondern **jenes** | *on, but that one* |

> **b dieses used as a pronoun is often shortened to dies**
>
> | **Dies** *war jedoch wegen des Sturms* | *However, this was impossible* |
> |---|---|
> | *nicht möglich* | *owing to the storm* |

▶ **4.3.3** solcher *such* (a)

> ◆ **solcher declines like dieser (see 4.3.2 above). In the singular it is usually replaced with so einer**
>
> | Das Problem als **solches** | *The problem as such* |
> |---|---|
> | Lehrer gibt es **solche** und **solche** | *There are teachers and teachers* |
> | **So eines** wollte ich schon immer | *I always wanted one like that* |
> | haben | |

▶ **4.3.4** derjenige/diejenige/dasjenige *the one who/which*

> **a derjenige has the forms of a definite article + adjective, but is written as one word**
>
> See 3.3.3 for its declension; it may be used as a determiner or as a pronoun.

> **b derjenige is usually followed by a relative pronoun**
>
> | **diejenigen**, die mitkommen | *Those who would like to come* |
> |---|---|
> | möchten | |
> | Er ist **derjenige**, der … | *He is the one who …* |

Diese Straftaten kosten **diejenigen** Geld, denen Graffiti an die Hauswand gesprüht wird		These criminal acts cost those who find graffiti sprayed on the walls of their houses a lot of money

c **derjenige is colloquially often replaced by der, die, das**

Der, der angerufen hat, sollte … *The one who phoned up should …*
Der, den du mir gegeben hast … *The one you gave me …*

4.4 Possessive pronouns

a **The possessive pronoun is used when no noun follows the possessive**
It must agree with the number and gender of the noun to which it refers.

b **The forms of the possessive pronoun are identical to the possessive adjectives/articles (3.4) except in the basic masculine and neuter forms (shown in bold in the table below)**

	Masc.	Fem.	Neuter	Plural
Nom.	**meiner**	meine	**mein(e)s**	meine
Acc.	meinen	meine	**mein(e)s**	meine
Gen.	meines	meiner	meines	meiner
Dat.	meinem	meiner	meinem	meinen

Das ist mein Buch – das hier ist **dein(e)s** — *That's my book – here's yours*
Die zwei Kulis – **meiner** ist rot, **seiner** ist blau — *Those two pens – mine's red, his is blue*
Wenn du keinen Taschenrechner hast, gebe ich dir **meinen** — *If you haven't got a calculator, I'll give you mine*

c **The e in mein(e)s etc. is often dropped in speech and informal writing**

4.5 Indefinite pronouns

◆ **An indefinite pronoun refers to a non-specific person or thing**
Note Many indefinite pronouns are also used as determiners. Notes on the declensions of these may be found in 3.6; a summary is in 3.7. The notes below describe the differences encountered when these words are used as pronouns.

▶ **4.5.1 all, alles** *all, everything, everyone*

a **all used as a pronoun inflects like dieser (see 4.3.2 above), though there is no genitive singular form. English *everything* is translated by alles**

Alles wurde gegessen — *Everything was eaten*
Das sind **alles** Sachen, die nicht gut sind — *All of those are things which aren't good*

Warst du mit **allem** zufrieden?	Were you satisfied with everything?
Sind **alle** da?	Is everybody here?
Die Spiele waren toll – wir waren bei **allen** dabei	The matches were great – we went to all of them
zu **aller** Erstaunen (genitive plural)	to everyone's amazement

b all is often used inflected with a personal pronoun

Er kannte uns **alle** bei Namen	He knew us all by name
Wir **alle** bleiben hier	We're all staying here
Seid ihr **alle** bescheuert?	Are you all crazy?

4.5.2 beide, beides *both*

a beide is used in the plural and takes the same endings as dieser (4.3.2). It may stand before or after the verb

Wir sahen zwei Filme – **beide** waren interessant	We saw two films – both were interesting
Sie gingen **beide** ins Haus	They both went into the house

b beides refers to two things and is singular

Beides ist teuer	They're both expensive
„Was trinkst du lieber, Wein oder Bier?" „**Beides**!"	'What do you prefer drinking – wine or beer?' 'Both!'

4.5.3 ein bisschen, ein wenig *a little, a bit*, ein paar *a few*

♦ None of these phrases changes its endings

Er verlangt **ein bisschen** viel, finde ich	He's asking for a bit much, I think
„Hast du Geld dabei?" „Nur noch **ein wenig**"	'Have you any money with you?' 'Only a little'
Ich hatte früher sehr viele davon; jetzt habe ich nur noch **ein paar**	I used to have a lot of those; now I only have a few left

4.5.4 einer *one (of them)*

a einer takes the same endings as the possessive pronouns meiner, meine, meines (see 4.4 above), though of course there is no plural

Its negative is keiner *none*, which does have a plural.

Die zwei Kulis – **einer** gehört mir	Those two pens – one of them is mine
Ich habe keinen Taschenrechner – leihst du mir bitte **einen**?	I don't have a calculator – can you lend me one, please?
Er ist **einer** meiner besten Freunde	He's one of my best friends
Keiner meiner Freunde war zu Hause	None of my friends was at home

b einer is often used as a synonym for jemand

Einer muss ihn gesehen haben!	*Someone must have seen him!*
Für so **eine** würde ich das nicht machen	*I wouldn't do that for somebody (a woman) like her*

c *one of my ..., one of the ... ; a ... of mine*

- Note that the second part of the phrase is always in the genitive plural:

einer meiner Freunde	*one of my friends*
mit **einem** meiner Freunde	*with one of my friends*
Das ist **eines** der besten Restaurants, die ich kenne	*That's one of the best restaurants I know*

- In spoken German, von + dative is often used instead:

ein Freund **von** mir	*a friend of mine*
eine Bekannte **von** uns	*an acquaintance of ours*

▶ 4.5.5 einige *some*

- **einige takes the same endings as dieser (see 4.3.2 above)**

Er hat noch **einiges** zu erledigen	*He's still got a few things to*
Da spricht **einiges** dafür	*There's quite a lot in favour of it*
Hast du schon **einige** gefunden?	*Have you found some already?*

▶ 4.5.6 etwas *some(-thing)/any(-thing)*

- **etwas is invariable and is often abbreviated to was**

Sonst noch **etwas**?	*Anything else?*
Suchen Sie sich **etwas** aus!	*Take your pick!*
Er wird es nie zu **etwas** bringen	*He'll never get anywhere*
Kann ich dir **was** helfen?	*Can I do anything to help you?*

▶ 4.5.7 irgend- *some ...or other*

- **irgend can be added to emphasise vagueness**

irgendetwas *something (or other)* irgendjemand *someone (or other)*
irgendein *some (sing.) ... (or other)* irgendwelche *some (pl.) ... (or other)*

Er ist nicht **irgendwer**	*He's not just anybody*
Irgendetwas hat mich geweckt	*Something (or other) woke me up*
Vermisst **irgendjemand** einen Schlüssel?	*Has someone lost a key?*

▶ 4.5.8 jeder *each/every, everybody*

- **jeder is always singular and declines like dieser (see 4.3.2)**
- If used in a general way to mean *everyone*, the masculine form is used.
- If a possessive is required, forms of sein are used, where English uses *their* to avoid *his/her*.

Er gab **jedem** von beiden 20€	*He gave each of them 20€*
Jeder will sein eigenes Auto	*Everybody wants their own car*
Hier kennt **jeder jeden**	*Here everyone knows everyone else*

▶ 4.5.9 jemand/niemand *somebody/nobody*

a jemand and niemand may be used with or without case endings in both spoken and written German
The endings are as follows:

Nom.	jemand	niemand
Acc.	jemand**en**	niemand**en**
Gen.	jemand**es**	niemand**es**
Dat.	jemand**em**	niemand**em**

Niemand glaubt dir!	*Nobody believes you!*
Hast du **jemand**(en) im Gebäude gesehen?	*Did you see anyone in the building?*
Erinnert Sie der Name an **jemand**(en)?	*Does that name remind you of someone?*
Das habe ich bisher **niemand**(em) erzählt	*I've never told anyone that before*
Außer mir ist **niemand** zu Hause	*Apart from me there's nobody at home*
Es ist **niemand** da	*There isn't anybody there*

b If followed by an adjective, jemand and niemand usually add no endings
The adjective itself is treated as a noun, and can add the ending -es in all cases:

War er **jemand** Berühmtes?	*Was he someone famous?*
Seine Freundin hat **jemand** Neues/Neuen kennengelernt	*His girlfriend has met someone new*
Ich habe soeben mit **jemand** sehr Interessantes/Interessantem gesprochen	*I've just been talking to somebody really interesting*
Jemand anders hat es gefunden	*Someone else found it*

▶ 4.5.10 man *one*

a man is equivalent to *one* in English, but is much more commonly used
English often prefers *you, we, they,* or *people* (German does not use Leute or another noun in this sense), or a passive construction (see 15.2). The possessive form of man is sein.

Man sagt, er sei stinkreich	*People say (It's said) he's rolling in it*
Vom Dach hat **man** eine schöne Aussicht	*From the roof you have a lovely view*
Man darf seine Tischmanieren nie vergessen	*People should always remember their table manners*
Wenn **man** auf ihren Vorschlag eingeht …	*If we consider her suggestion …*
Das tut **man** einfach nicht	*That just isn't done*
Man kann nicht bestreiten, dass …	*There's no denying that …*

b man is also used as a polite form of address

Darf **man** fragen, was	*May one/well ask*
Sie damit genau sagen wollen?	*exactly what you meant by that?*

c man exists only in the nominative

In the accusative and dative the pronouns einen and einem are used:

Das würde er **einem** nie vergeben! *He'd never forgive someone for that!*

▶4.5.11 manche(r) *some, many*

+ **manche(r) is used in the singular or plural and is inflected like dieser (see 4.3.2 above)**

Manche sehen nicht ein, dass …	*Some (people) just don't realise that …*
Ich habe noch **manches** zu tun	*I've still got a number of things to do*
Mancher lernt's nie	*Some people never learn*
Die Qualität **mancher** ihrer Waren ist hervorragend	*The quality of many of their goods is excellent*

▶4.5.12 mehrere *several*

+ **mehrere is used in the plural and is inflected like dieser (see 4.3.2 above)**

Mehrere meiner Freunde können nicht kommen	*Several of my friends can't come*
mehrere hundert Autos	*several hundred cars*

▶4.5.13 nichts *nothing, not …anything*

+ **nichts never inflects**

Alles oder **nichts**!	*It's all or nothing!*
Mir fällt **nichts** ein	*I can't think of anything*
Das macht **nichts**	*That doesn't matter*

▶4.5.14 viel/viele *lots/many*, wenig/wenige *a little/a few*

+ **Both viel and wenig decline in the plural, but not normally in the singular**

However, viel may add -es in more formal writing:

Ich habe **viel/wenig** gegessen	*I've eaten a lot/a little*
Vieles deutet darauf hin, dass …	*There's (plenty of) evidence to suggest that …*
Es waren nicht **viele** im Kino	*There weren't many (people) in the cinema*
in **vielen** dieser Fälle	*in many of these cases*
Ihr Buch enthält **viel** Interessantes	*Her book contains much that is interesting*

4.6   Interrogative pronouns

▶ 4.6.1   was *what*

a   was does not change its endings

Was ist los?	*What's up?*
Was suchst du?	*What are you looking for?*
Sage, **was** du willst!	*Say what you like!*
Na, so **was**!	*Well, I never!*

b   was is not used with prepositions

In place of was plus a preposition, wo(r)- + preposition is used. This is called an interrogative adverb (see 4.1.4 – prepositions with da(r)-).

Note that the preposition is not left at the end of the sentence or question as in English:

Wofür interessierst du dich?	*What are you interested in?*
Wovor hat sie Angst?	*What is she frightened of?*
Ich weiß nicht, **wozu** er das alles macht	*I don't know what he's doing all that for*
Worüber schreibt sie?	*What is she writing about?*
Worauf wartest du?	*What are you waiting for?*

c   In colloquial language, the preposition + was is often used instead of the interrogative adverb

Um was (for **Worum**) handelt es sich?	*What's it about?*
An was (for **Woran**) denkst du?	*What are you thinking about?*

• For wofür, worauf, etc. as relative pronouns, see 4.7.2d.

▶ 4.6.2   welcher *some, any*

a   welcher takes the same endings as dieser (see 4.3.2 above). It is more colloquial than einige, manche, etwas

„Ich habe keinen Wein mehr. Ist noch **welcher** im Kühlschrank?"	*'I've run out of wine. Is there some in the fridge?'*
„Nein, ich muss morgen noch **welchen** kaufen"	*'No, I've got to get some more tomorrow'*
Diese Kulis – **welcher** gehört dir?	*These pens – which (one) is yours?*

b   welcher may also be used as a relative pronoun (see 4.7.1f) and as an interrogative determiner (see 3.5.1)

▶ 4.6.3   wer *who*

a   The endings on wer change depending on its case, but there is only one set of endings for all genders

Nom.	wer	who
Acc.	wen	who(m)
Gen.	wessen	whose
Dat.	wem	(to) who(m)

Wer möchte ins Kino gehen?	*Who would like to go to the cinema?*
Wer sind die Männer da drüben?	*Who are the men over there?*
Für **wen** hast du die CD gekauft?	*Who did you buy the CD for?*
Wen sollten wir fragen?	*Who should we ask?*
Wessen Auto ist das?	*Whose car is that?*
Wessen Idee war das?	*Whose idea was that?*
Mit **wem** geht sie ins Kino?	*Who is she going to the cinema with?*
Ich möchte wissen, **wer** dahinter steckt	*I'd like to know who's behind it*

b **Wessen is often avoided in modern German, and another way of expressing the idea is found**

Wem gehört das Auto?	*Whose car is that?*
Wer ist auf diese Idee gekommen?	*Whose idea was that?*

. For other uses of **was** and **wer**, see 4.7.2 and 4.7.3 (relative pronoun) and 18.2.2f (conjunctions).

4.7 Relative pronouns

▶ 4.7.1 der, die, das *who, which*

e.g.	der Mann, **der**…	*the man who*
	die Bücher, **die** …	*the books which*

a **The forms of the relative pronoun are mostly identical to the definite article, except in the genitive singular and plural and the dative plural; these forms are in bold below. It is completely identical to those of the demonstrative pronoun (see 4.3.1 above)**

	Masc.	Fem.	Neuter	Plural
Nom.	der	die	das	die
Acc.	den	die	das	die
Gen.	**dessen**	**deren**	**dessen**	**deren**
Dat.	dem	der	dem	**denen**

▶ **TIP** **The relative pronoun cannot be omitted**
It is often dropped in spoken English but never in German:

das Auto, **das** ich letztes Jahr gekauft habe…	*the car (which) I bought last year…*
der Mann, **den** du kennst …	*the man (whom) you know …*

b **Gender and number (singular or plural) are determined by the noun to which the relative pronoun refers**

♦ **The case is decided by the role of the relative pronoun in its own clause**

Der Mann, **der** gestern ankam, … *The man who arrived*
(masculine; subject of verb ankam) *yesterday …*
Der Mann, **den** ich sah, … *The man (whom) I saw…*
(masculine; object of verb sah)
Der Mann, **dem** ich geholfen habe, … *The man (whom) I helped …*
(masculine; dative object of verb helfen)
Der Mann, **dessen** Eltern in Ulm *The man whose parents live in*
wohnen, … *Ulm …*
(masculine; genitive of possession)
das ideale Auto für Sportfans, **denen** … *The ideal car for sports car fans for*
Lamborghini zu protzig ist *whom …Lamborghinis are too*
(plural; dative indirect object of verb sein) *showy*

c **A preposition before the relative pronoun determines its case**

Der Mann, neben **dem** ich saß, … *The man I sat next to/**next to***
***whom** I sat…*
Der Mann, für **den** ich arbeite, … *The man I work for/**for whom** I*
work…

d **When the relative pronoun refers to a first person pronoun, it is usually followed by the personal pronoun in the nominative**

Sie mochte ihren Hund, ganz im *She liked her dog, quite unlike me,*
Gegensatz zu mir, **die ich** mir *who often wished to myself*
oft gewünscht hatte, er wäre *that it was dead*
tot

e *whose* **(genitive case) is always expressed by a genitive relative pronoun, even after a preposition**

Der Mann, **dessen** Tochter ich *The man **whose** daughter I*
kenne, … *know …*
Der Mann, **mit dessen** Tochter *The man **with whose** daughter*
ich ins Kino gehe, … *I'm going to the cinema…*

f **welcher, welche, welches, etc. are found very occasionally as a synonym of der, die, das, but only in formal written language**

Firmen, **welche** unsere Dienste in Anspruch *companies which utilise our services*
nehmen

g **Word order in relative clauses**

♦ A relative pronoun introduces a subordinate clause; the verb therefore stands at the end.

◆ The relative clause stands as close as possible to the noun it refers to, though other elements (usually verbs) may interpose so that they are not isolated:

Kennst du den Mann, der gestern ankam?	*Do you know the man who arrived yesterday?*
Der Mann, der gestern ankam, ist ein Freund von meinem Vater	*The man who arrived yesterday is a friend of my father's*
Ich habe den Mann **gesehen**, von dem du mir nur erzählt hast	*I've seen the man you've only told me about*
Wenn ich die E-mail **finden kann**, die sie mir geschickt hat, …	*If I can find the e-mail which she sent me…*

▶ 4.7.2 was as a relative pronoun

a was is used as a relative pronoun when referring back to an indefinite pronoun such as nichts, alles, etwas, vieles or a demonstrative pronoun such as das

Es gibt nichts, **was** ich lieber tun würde	*There's nothing I'd rather do*
Ich kaufte alles, **was** ich brauchte	*I bought everything I needed*
Etwas, **was** er gesagt hat, hat mich tief beeindruckt	*Something he said impressed me deeply*
Ich sehe etwas, **was** du nicht siehst	*I spy with my little eye* (children's game)
Vieles, **was** wir gesehen haben, war nicht zu kaufen	*Much of what we saw wasn't for sale*
Sie haben nichts, außer dem, **was** sie am eigenen Leibe tragen	*They have only what they stand up in* (i.e. *their clothes*)

b was can also refer back to a whole clause, whereas der, die, das, etc. refer back to a specific noun

Compare these two sentences:

Ich arbeite in einem Büro, **was** ich langweilig finde	*I work in an office, which I find boring* (i.e. it's the whole idea of working in an office which bores me)
Ich arbeite in einem Büro, **das** ich langweilig finde	*I work in an office that I find boring* (i.e. it's this specific office that bores me)

c was is also used after neuter adjective-nouns

Das ist das Einzige, **was** wir noch machen können	*That's the only thing we can do now*
Das Allerbeste, **was** mir je passiert ist, war …	*The very best thing that ever happened to me was …*

d If was requires a preposition, a wo(r)- construction is used

Etwas, **wovon** ich geträumt habe …	*Something I've dreamed of …*
Alles, **worauf** ich mich gefreut habe …	*Everything I've been looking forward to …*

▶ 4.7.3 wer anyone who, those who; was that which

Wer schweigt, stimmt zu	*Silence equals consent*

Wer das glaubt, ist dumm	*Anyone who thinks that is stupid*
„Nur **wer** die Sehnsucht kennt,	*'Only those who know longing*
weiß, was ich leide" (Goethe)	*understand what I suffer'*
Was Preis und Qualität betrifft, …	*As far as price and quality are*
	concerned…

▶ 4.7.4 Relative pronouns with places and times

a For places, a form of wo is often used

das Haus, **wo** (*or* **in dem**) ich wohne	*the house where I / in which I live*
die Stadt, **wohin** (*or* **in die**) ich fahren sollte	*the town I was supposed to go to*

b With time expressions, a preposition + der, etc. is usual; however, als (past time) or wenn (present, future), or (colloquially) wo may be used

der Tag, **an dem** Kennedy ermordet wurde	*the day when Kennedy was murdered*
am Tag, **als** er ermordet wurde	*on the day he was murdered*
die Zeit, **in der** wir leben	*the time in which we live*
eine Zeit, **wo** die Risiken steigen	*a time in which the risks are increasing*
Das erinnert an eine Zeit, **als** …	*It reminds us of a time when …*
eine Zeit in der Zukunft, **wenn** Roboter alles machen	*a time in the future when robots will do everything*
Jetzt, **wo** wir nichts mehr machen können, …	*Now, when there's nothing more we can do,…*

5

Adjectives

OVERVIEW

An **adjective** describes a noun – a ***red*** *car; the book is* **interesting**.
- The adjective can be used, as in English, in one of two positions:
  - **before the noun ('attributive')**.
    Adjectives used in this way add endings depending on the gender, case and number of the noun:

das rot**e** Auto	ein klein**es** Kind
gut**er** Wein	mein ält**erer** Bruder

  - **after the verb sein**, or occasionally **werden** or **bleiben** ('predicative').
    Adjectives used in this way never add endings:

Das Auto ist **rot**	Das Wetter bleibt **warm**

Note The adjective never stands after the noun, as it may in French or Spanish.
- There are no irregular adjectives in German. However, there are a few small variations in spelling, and a few irregular comparative and superlative forms:

alt, älter, älteste	*old, older, oldest/eldest*
gut, besser, beste	*good, better, best*

- A few adjectives are indeclinable – that is, they do not add endings, even when they stand before a noun:

lila, rosa	*purple, pink*
in einer live Sendung	*in a live broadcast*

5.1 The declension of adjectives

a Adjectives add case endings only when they stand before the noun; in this position they are called *attributive* adjectives.

b There is a logical pattern to the endings and a very limited number of variations.

Note how, in the examples below, the nominative masculine -er ending, or the nominative neuter ending -s is present in one element each time, either the article or the adjective.

Masculine	Neuter
der gute Wein	**das** gute Buch
ein gut**er** Wein	ein gut**es** Buch
gut**er** Wein	kalt**es** Wasser

c Adjective endings do not affect the meaning of the following noun, and while it is important to check their accuracy in written German, they are often unemphasised in colloquial spoken German

„Ich habe einen kleinen Bruder" usually sounds more like „Ich hab ein klein Bruder", or even „Ich hab 'n' klein Bruder."

5.1.1 Group 1: weak endings

a The adjectives are said to have 'weak' endings because they do not show the gender and case clearly; that is the role of the definite article

• The adjectives have only two possible endings: **-e** with the basic forms, **-en** with the rest.

Case	Singular			Plural
	Masculine	**Feminine**	**Neuter**	
Nom.	der alte Mann	die junge Frau	das gute Buch	die jungen Frauen
Acc.	den alten Mann	die junge Frau	das gute Buch	die jungen Frauen
Gen.	des alten Mannes	der jungen Frau	des guten Buchs	der jungen Frauen
Dat.	dem alten Mann	der jungen Frau	dem guten Buch	den jungen Frauen

b Group 1 declensions are used when the noun phrase starts with the definite article (der, die, das) and determiners which decline like it

dieser	*this, these/that, those*	manch- *(sing)*	*many a*
welcher?	*which?*	all-[1]	*all*
irgendwelcher	*some … or other*	sämtlich-	*all*
jeder	*each, every (+ sing noun)*		
jener	*that, those (formal)*		

[1] When inflected (see 3.6.1).

Bei welcher deutsch**en** Firma arbeitet er?	*Which German company does he work for?*
irgendwelches dumm**e** Zeug	*some rubbish or other*
Dieses neu**e** Auto gehört mir	*This new car belongs to me*
Mancher jung**e** Mann …	*Many a young man …*

5.1.2 Group 2: mixed endings

a The adjectives are said to have 'mixed' endings because they clearly show the gender in the nominative singular forms but not elsewhere

• The adjectives end with -en in all forms apart from with the basic ein, eine, ein.

	Singular			Plural
Case	Masculine	Feminine	Neuter	
Nom.	ein alter Mann	eine junge Frau	ein gutes Buch	keine alten Männer
Acc.	einen alten Mann	eine junge Frau	ein gutes Buch	keine alten Männer
Gen.	eines alten Mannes	einer jungen Frau	eines guten Buchs	keiner alten Männer
Dat.	einem alten Mann	einer jungen Frau	einem guten Buch	keinen alten Männern

b Group 2 declensions are used when the noun phrase starts with the indefinite article (ein, eine) and its negative (kein), and after the possessive adjectives

These are sometimes more accurately called possessive articles:

mein	*my*	unser	*our*
dein	*your*	euer	*your*
sein	*his*	ihr	*their*
ihr	*her*	Ihr	*your*
sein	*its*		

Wir haben euren letzten Brief erst gestern bekommen	*We received your last letter only yesterday*
Er arbeitet bei irgendeiner kleinen Firma in Bonn	*He works for some little company (or other) in Bonn*
Ich habe keine guten Freunde	*I have no close friends*

5.1.3 Group 3: strong endings

a The adjectives are said to have 'strong' endings because they show the gender, case and number of the noun

* **all** as a determiner can be declinable or invariable (see 3.6.1).
* Group 3 endings are essentially the same as those on the article **der/die/das**, with the exception of the genitive singular of the masculine and neuter forms.

	Singular			Plural
Case	Masculine	Feminine	Neuter	
Nom.	guter Wein	frische Milch	kaltes Wasser	gute Weine
Acc.	guten Wein	frische Milch	kaltes Wasser	gute Weine
Gen.	guten Weins	frischer Milch	kalten Wassers	guter Weine
Dat.	gutem Wein	frischer Milch	kaltem Wasser	guten Weinen

b Group 3 declensions are used when there is no article before the adjective, and after numbers (including indefinite determiners – see list below), except ein

guter Rat	*good advice*
zwei schöne Häuser	*two lovely houses*
viele alte Autos	*lots of old cars*
Sie trinkt viel frische kalte Milch	*She drinks lots of fresh cold milk*
trotz dichten Nebels	*despite (the) thick fog*

c Common examples of these indefinite determiners (see 3.6) are

+ invariable; followed by singular noun:

ein bisschen	*a little, a bit*
ein wenig	*a little*
etwas	*some, a little*
viel	*a lot, much*
wenig	*little*

+ declinable; followed by plural noun:

andere	*other*
ein paar	*a few*
einige	*several*
einzelne	*individual*
etliche	*several*
manche (*pl*)	*a good number of*
mehrere	*several*
sonstige	*other, further*
verschiedene	*various*
viele	*many, lots of*
wenige	*few*

▶ 5.1.4 Indeclinable adjectives

A few adjectives do not change their endings, even when they stand before a noun.
They fall into the following categories.

a Some adjectives which are foreign in derivation; many refer to colour

beige	*beige*	creme	*cream*	klasse; prima; spitze	*great*
lila	*mauve*	live	*live (broadcast)*	orange *orange* purpur	*purple*

Ich habe ein klasse Buch gelesen	*I've read a great book*
Sie trug ein lila Kleid	*She was wearing a purple dress*

b Adjective + noun compounds

Some adjectives have become attached (without case ending) to the noun to form
new compound nouns; these are best learned as individual vocabulary items:

die Altstadt	*the old (part of the) town*
die Fremdsprache	*foreign language*
die Großstadt	*the big town, city*
der Neubau	*new building*
die Privatschule	*private school*
der Rotwein	*red wine*

c Noun prefixes

Some adjectives in English are noun prefixes in German. The commonest are
Haupt- *main* and Lieblings- *favourite*:

mein **Lieblings**film	*my favourite film*
der **Haupt**bahnhof	*the main station*

d **Adjectives from place names or decades (e.g.** *the twenties*) **add -(e)r and are invariable**

die *Frankfurter* Allgemeine Zeitung	(*name of newspaper*)
der Kölner Dom	*Cologne Cathedral*
im Kölner Dom	*in Cologne Cathedral*
die Berliner Polizei	*the Berlin police*
Karlsruher Einwohner	*inhabitants of Karlsruhe*
die sechziger Jahre	*the sixties*
Mitte der siebziger Jahre	*in the mid 1970s*

Note

Sie ist in den Sechzigern	*She's in her sixties*
Er ist Mitte vierzig	*He's in his mid forties*

5.1.5 Adjectives in titles

+ **Adjectives in titles, as in the names of kings and queens, are declined 'weak' (see 5.1.1 above) and written with a capital letter**

Nom.:	Karl	der	Große	*Charlemagne*
Acc.:	Karl	den	Großen
Gen.:	Karls	des	Großen
Dat.:	Karl	dem	Großen

5.1.6 Irregular adjectives

a **There are no irregular adjectives in German (i.e. ones which have different feminine or neuter forms), although there are several irregular comparative and superlative forms (see 8.1.2)**

b **A few adjectives modify slightly when they are used with an ending**
This change reflects the pronunciation:
+ Adjectives which end in **-el** or **-er** lose the -e- before an ending.
+ **hoch** *high* becomes **hoh-** when followed by a vowel.

hoch:	der Berg ist hoch	ein **hoh**er Berg
dunkel:	die Nacht ist dunkel	eine dunk**le** Nacht
teuer:	das Auto ist teuer	ein teu**res** Auto

5.2 Adjective-nouns

a **Almost any adjective or participle can be used as a noun. The masculine and feminine forms refer to people, while the neuter refers to abstract ideas**

der Gute *the good man*	die Gute *the good woman*
das Gute *goodness; the good thing*	die Guten *good people*

Other common examples:

der/die Angestellte	*employee*
der/die Arbeitslose	*unemployed (person)*
der Beamte	*civil servant*
But die Beamtin (**not**: die Beamte)	

der/die Bekannte	*acquaintance*
der/die Deutsche	*German*
der/die Erwachsene	*adult*
der/die Fremde	*stranger*
der/die Gefangene	*prisoner*
der/die Jugendliche	*young person*
der/die Kranke	*patient*
der/die Reiche	*rich (man)*
der/die Reisende	*traveller*
der/die Verwandte	*relative*
der/die Verlobte	*fiancé(e)*
der/die Vorsitzende	*chair(man)*
das Äußere	*exterior*
das Interessante	*the interesting thing*
das Böse	*evil*
das Neue	*(what's) new*
das Alte	*(what's) old*

Note ◆ Because neuter adjective-nouns refer to abstract ideas, they have no plural.

◆ Die Linke *The Left* (name of political party) is a feminine adjective-noun which refers to a thing (die Partei) rather than a person.

b German does not usually require a noun such as Ding *thing*, Mann *man* or Leute *people* after an adjective

etwas Gutes	*a good thing*
das Gute daran	*the good thing about it*
die Jugendlichen	*(the) young people*

c Adjective-nouns decline as though there were a following noun (see sections 5.1.1, 5.1.2 and 5.1.3 above)

The example in the table below is for the noun der Blinde *the blind man*, die Blinde *the blind woman*; the neuter noun is das Neue *the new (thing), that which is new.*

	Singular						Neuter
	Masc.			**Fem.**			**Neuter**
Nom.	der Blinde	ein	Blinder	die Blinde	eine	Blinde	das Neue
Acc.	den Blinden	einen	Blinden	die Blinde	eine	Blinde	das Neue
Gen.	des Blinden	eines	Blinden	der Blinden	einer	Blinden	des Neuen
Dat.	dem Blinden	einem	Blinden	der Blinden	einer	Blinden	dem Neuen

	Masc./Fem. plural			Neut. singular[1]
Nom.	die Blinden		Blinde	Neues
Acc.	die Blinden		Blinde	Neues
Gen.	der Blinden		Blinder	Neuen
Dat.	den Blinden		Blinden	Neuem

[1]When no article present; see also 5.2e below.

Sie half dem Blind**en**	*She helped the blind man*
ein Verwandt**er** von mir	*a relative of mine*
Was ist das Neu**e** an diesem Buch?	*What's new about this book?*
von Neu**em**	*from the beginning, from scratch*
Er ist Deutsch**er**	*He's German*
Es waren keine Deutsch**en** unter	*There were no Germans among*
den Fluggästen	*the passengers*
meine Bekannt**en**	*my acquaintances*

d If an adjective-noun is preceded by an adjective, both have the same ending

This is because both words are adjectives, even though one is used as a noun:

ein alt**er** Deutscher	*an old German (man)*
bei einer alt**en** Deutschen	*at the house of an elderly German (lady)*
mit einem jung**en** Deutschen	*with a young German (man)*
Es waren keine jung**en** Deutschen	*There were no young Germans*
unter den Fluggästen	*among the passengers*
berühmt**e** Deutsch**e**	*famous Germans*

TIP **How to recognise an adjective-noun in a dictionary**

An adjective-noun will be shown in the dictionary as:
- ending in -e or -e(r)
- dual gender: der/die or **MF** (depending on the dictionary)
  - e.g. Jugendliche(r) MF; Alte(r) MF

Do not confuse adjective-nouns with weak masculine nouns (see TIP on p. 28):
- adjective-noun: der/die Jugendliche, ein Jugendlicher
- weak noun: der Junge, den Jungen, ein Junge

---

e After etwas, nichts, wenig, viel, allerlei, neuter adjective-nouns are used (see above); after alles they take Group 1 (weak) neuter endings (see 5.1.1)

	Group 3 endings (after nichts, viel, etc.)	Group 1 endings (after alles)
Nom.	nichts Neu**es**	alles Gute
Acc.	nichts Neu**es**	alles Gute
Gen.	nichts Neu**en**	alles Gut**en**
Dat.	nichts Neu**em**	allem Gut**en**

Nom. *Im Westen nichts Neu**es***	All Quiet on the Western Front
(title of novel)	*(literally: Nothing New…)*
Acc. Das Buch enthält viel	*The book contains much of*
Interessant**es**	*interest/many interesting ideas*
Was gibt's Neu**es**?	*What's new?*
Gen. anstatt etwas Neu**en**	*instead of something new*
Dat. Er ist immer auf der Suche	*He's always on the lookout for*
nach etwas Neu**em**	*something new*
Wir wünschen dir alles Gute	*We wish you all the best*

> **TIP**   **Adjective-noun or adjective referring to a noun?**
> * Take care not to confuse an adjective-noun with an adjective used alone because the noun is understood (and therefore does not need to be repeated).
>
> | | |
> |---|---|
> | Das **Beste** an ihrem Roman ist … | *The best thing about her novel is …* |
> | Dieser Apfel ist sauer – hast du noch einen **süßen**? | *This apple is sour – have you got another sweet one?* |
> | „Welches Auto gefällt dir am besten?" „Das **blaue**." | *'Which car do you like best?' 'The blue one.'* |

5.3   Adjectives used with particular cases

* **A number of adjectives can be used with a dependent noun in the accusative, genitive or dative case**

The adjectives used in this way usually follow the noun:

Acc.	Sie war das Stadtleben nicht **gewohnt**	*She was unused to city life*
Gen.	Er war des Kämpfens **überdrüssig**	*He was weary of fighting*
Dat.	Es ist mir **bewusst**, dass …	*I'm aware that …*

▶ 5.3.1   Adjectives governing the accusative

gewohnt	*used to*	schuldig	*to owe*
los	*rid of*	wert	*worth*
satt	*sick of, fed up with*		

Ich habe die Büroarbeit satt	*I'm fed up with working in an office*
Erst nach drei Stunden wurde ich ihn los	*I couldn't get rid of him for three hours*

▶ 5.3.2   Adjectives governing the genitive

bewusst	*aware of*
fähig	*capable of*
gewiss	*certain of*
müde	*tired of*
schuldig	*guilty of*
sicher	*certain of*
überdrüssig	*weary of*
wert	*worthy of*
würdig	*worthy of*

Er war mehrer**er** Straftaten schuldig	*He was guilty of several crimes*
Nicht **der** Rede wert!	*Don't mention it!*
Sie ist **des** Lebens müde	*She's tired of life*

* **Several of these adjectives have alternatives to the genitive which are often preferred in colloquial German**

Er ist **zu** keinem Gedanken fähig	*He's incapable of thought*
Es ist nicht **die** Mühe wert	*It's not worth the trouble*

▶ 5.3.3 Adjectives governing the dative

This list contains a selection of common adjectives used with the dative:

ähnlich	*similar*
behilflich	*helpful*
bekannt	*familiar*
bequem	*comfortable*
bewusst	*aware*
böse	*cross, angry*
dankbar	*thankful*
fern	*distant*
fremd	*strange*
gehorsam	*obedient*
gemeinsam	*general*
gerecht	*just, fair*
heilig	*sacred*
klar	*clear*
leicht	*easy*
möglich	*possible*
nahe	*near, close*
nötig	*necessary*
nützlich	*useful*
peinlich	*embarrassing*
schwer	*hard*
teuer	*expensive*
treu	*loyal*
überlegen	*superior*
verständlich	*comprehensible*
wichtig	*important*
widerlich	*disgusting*
willkommen	*welcome*
zugänglich	*accessible*

Sei mir nicht böse!	*Don't be cross with me!*
Sie ist ihrer Mutter ähnlich	*She's like her mother*
Es wurde mir langsam klar, dass …	*It gradually became clear to me that …*
Wie dir wohl bewusst ist, …	*As you are well aware …*
Diese Nachricht ist mir willkommen	*This piece of news is welcome to me*

But willkommen heißen *to welcome* (a normal verb construction + accusative):

Ich heiße Sie herzlich willkommen bei unserer Firma	*I'd like to welcome you to our company*

5.4 Adjectives used with particular prepositions

♦ **Some adjectives are used with particular prepositions; these need to be learned with the adjective**

▶ 5.4.1 Adjective + preposition + pronoun or noun phrase

a **The adjective may stand before or after the prepositional phrase**

Sie war ganz **böse auf** ihn	*She was cross at him*
Er war **in** sie **verliebt**	*He was in love with her*

b auf and über take the accusative when used with an adjective; an and in usually take the dative – but beware of exceptions!

This list contains a selection of common adjectives and their prepositions:

abhängig von	*dependent on*
allergisch gegen	*allergic to*
arm an (+ dat.)	*poor in, lacking in*
aufgeregt über (+ acc.)	*excited about*
bedeckt mit	*covered with*
begeistert von/über	*enthusiastic about*
bekannt wegen	*known for*
bereit zu	*ready for*
besorgt um	*worried about*
böse auf (+ acc.)	*angry at*
charakteristisch für	*characteristic of*
eifersüchtig auf (+ acc.)	*jealous of*
einverstanden mit	*in agreement with*
empfindlich gegen	*sensitive to*
empört über (+ acc.)	*indignant about*
enttäuscht von	*disappointed by*
erstaunt über (+ acc.)	*astonished by*
fähig zu	*capable of*
fertig mit	*finished with*
freundlich zu	*friendly towards*
geeignet für	*suitable for*
gespannt auf (+ acc.)	*very curious about*
gewöhnt an (+ acc.)	*used to*
gierig nach	*greedy for*
gut in (+ dat.)	*good at*
höflich zu/gegenüber	*polite to*
neidisch auf (+ acc.)	*envious of*
neugierig auf (+ acc.)	*curious about*
reich an (+ dat.)	*rich in*
schuld an (+ dat.)	*at fault*
schlecht in (+ dat.)	*good at*
stolz auf (+ acc.)	*proud of*
typisch für	*typical of*
überzeugt von	*convinced by*
umgeben von	*surrounded by*
verglichen mit	*compared to*
verheiratet mit	*married to*
verliebt in (+ acc.)	*in love with*
verwandt mit	*related to*
vorbereitet auf (+ acc.)	*prepared for*
wütend auf (+ acc.)	*furious with*

So einer ist **zu** allem fähig	*People like that are capable of anything*
Sie sind stolz **auf** ihre Kinder	*They're proud of their children*
Ich bin allergisch **gegen** Nüsse	*I'm allergic to nuts*

▶ 5.4.2 Adjectives + preposition followed by a clause

+ **Where there is a clause instead of a noun, the preposition becomes a prepositional adverb beginning with da(r)- (see 13.2)**

Ich bin **davon** überzeugt, dass …	*I'm convinced that …*
Sie ist **darauf** gespannt, ihn wiederzusehen	*She's really keen to see him again*
Wer ist **daran** schuld, dass …?	*Whose fault is it that …?*
Er war **dazu** fähig, sich durchzusetzen	*He was capable of asserting himself*

5.5 Adjectival phrases

+ **Long adjectival phrases, which in English would often have to be expressed using a relative clause, may precede the noun in formal German; they are most often found in the printed news media**

Similar phrases may be based on participles, also used as adjectives (see 14.2.2b, 14.3.2a).

Der **erst seit 10 Jahren unabhängige** Staat hat …	*The state, which has only been independent for ten years, has …*
In seinem **über die Wirtschafts-prognosen eher pessimistischen** Bericht…	*In his report, which is rather pessimistic regarding the economic outlook …*

6

Adverbs

OVERVIEW

+ **Adverbs** tell us the *when, where, how* and *why* of the verb. Adverbs consist of a single word, while adverbial phrases contain several words, often starting with a preposition:

Er spricht **schnell**	*He speaks quickly*
Ich fahre **mit dem Bus**	*I'm going by bus*

+ They may also qualify (i.e. give information about) adjectives, or other adverbs, or the sentence as a whole:

Er spricht **furchtbar** schnell	*He speaks terribly quickly*
ein **sehr** spannender Film	*a very exciting film*
Natürlich kannst du hier bleiben	*Of course you can stay here*

+ Adjectives and adverbs are usually (but not always) identical in German; only rarely is there an equivalent of the *-ly* ending routinely used on English adverbs:

Das Essen ist **gut**	*The food is good* (adjective)
Er singt **gut**	*He sings well* (adverb)
Er war ganz **normal**	*He was quite normal* (adjective)
Normalerweise darf man …	*Normally one can …* (adverb)

+ Adverbs may be classified in different ways. In this chapter they have been grouped as follows:

Time	(= *when*)	gestern, um 7 Uhr, manchmal
Manner	(= *how*)	mit dem Auto, schnell, irgendwie
Place	(= *where*)	in die Stadt, dort, überall
Comment	(= *attitude*)	natürlich, leider
Degree	(= *to what extent*)	sehr, ziemlich, äußerst
Reason	(= *why*)	deshalb, folglich
Interrogative	(= *questions*)	wie? wann? woher?

+ The order of adverbs when used together is dealt with in 18.3.3; however, the order Time–Manner–Place provides a useful basic rule.

6.1 Adverbs of time

+ Adverbs of time indicate **when**, or **how often**, or **for how long** the action takes place

▶ 6.1.1 One-word adverbs of time

a Common one-word adverbs of time

bald	*soon*
damals	*then, at that time*
dann	*then, next*
endlich	*at last*
früher	*formerly (used to…)*
gestern	*yesterday*
heute	*today*
jetzt	*now*
manchmal	*sometimes*
morgen	*tomorrow*
neulich	*recently*
nie	*never*
oft	*often*
noch einmal	*again*
noch nicht	*not yet*
schließlich	*finally*
schon	*already*
sofort	*immediately*
vorher	*beforehand*
wieder	*again*

b One-word adverbs of time may be formed by adding a suffix to a noun

- adding -s to a noun (indicating '*every …*')
  morgens, nachmittags, abends, nachts, sonntags, mittwochs, wochentags
- adding -lang to a plural noun (indicating '*for…*', '*for … on end*')
  stundenlang, tagelang, wochenlang, sekundenlang, jahrelang

▶ 6.1.2 Prepositional phrases of time

• Many of these phrases begin with the preposition an, in or zu

am Montag, am Abend	*on Monday, in the evening*
am Wochenende, am 19. Juli	*at the weekend, on 19 July*
an Sonn- und Feiertagen	*on Sundays and public holidays*
in der Nacht, im Winter	*in/during the night, in winter*
in den Sommerferien	*in the summer holidays*
heute in einer Woche	*a week today*
zu Weihnachten, zu Ostern	*at/for Christmas, at Easter*
zum Geburtstag	*for one's birthday*
zur Zeit	*at the moment*
um 7 Uhr	*at 7 o'clock*
gegen 7 Uhr	*at about 7 o'clock*
nach dem Essen	*after the meal*
vor dem Spiel	*before the match*
vor zwei Wochen	*two weeks ago*

▶ 6.1.3 Adverbial phrases without prepositions

These may be in the accusative or the genitive.

a Accusative

jeden Morgen	*every morning*
jeden Tag, jeden Samstag	*every day, every Saturday*
letzten Montag	*last Monday*
den ganzen Tag	*all day*
den ganzen Monat	*the whole month*
den ganzen Sommer	*all summer*

Note Feminine and neuter nouns do not vary in the accusative, of course:
   jede Woche, das ganze Jahr

b Genitive

eines Tages	*one day*
eines Abends	*one evening*
eines Nachts	*one night* (feminine, but case ending by correlation with eines Abends, etc.)

6.1.4 *'For'* + time

a Starting now (i.e. at the point of speaking) and continuing: für + accusative
As well as a period of time, this may also refer to a point in time:

Ich fahre **für** zwei Tage nach Köln — *I'm going to Cologne for two days*
   (i.e. that's how long I'm going to stay there; without für it implies that
   the driving (fahren) will take two days)

Ich bin **für** zwei Tage nach Köln gefahren — *I went to Cologne for two days*
   (i.e. I went to Cologne; it was for a two-day visit)

Sie ist **für** ein paar Tage verreist — *She has gone away for a few days*

b Referring to the completed past: 'for' is not translated, but lang may be added to the phrase

Ich war zwei Tage (**lang**) in Köln — *I spent two days in Cologne*
Er hat ein Jahr (**lang**) dort gelebt — *He lived there for a year*

c Starting in the past and continuing at the time of speaking: seit + dative
+ schon may be used as an alternative to seit, or together with it.
+ Note that the German verb is one tense further forward than in English: the emphasis is on the continuing action rather than on time elapsed.

Seit wann wohnst du hier? — *How long have you been living here?*

Ich wohne **seit zwei Jahren** hier — *I've been living here for two years*
Ich wohne **(schon) seit 2009** hier — *I've been living here since 2009*
Ich wohnte **seit zwei Jahren** dort, als ich sie kennenlernte — *I had been living there for two years when I met her*

But **seit** is used with the perfect tense in negative statements, unless they describe a state of affairs. Compare these two sentences:

Ich **habe** ihn seit Oktober nicht mehr **gesehen** — *I haven't seen him since October*
   (i.e. the action hasn't taken place)

Seit seiner Operation **geht** er nicht mehr aus dem Haus (i.e. that's how things are)	Since his operation he hasn't left the house

6.2 Adverbs of manner

+ Adverbs of manner indicate *how* an action takes place

▶ 6.2.1 Common one-word adverbs of manner

anders (als)	differently (to)
auswendig	by heart
ausnahmsweise	as an exception
gut	well
hoffentlich	hopefully
schnell	quickly
schön	nicely, beautifully
so	like this
teilweise	partly
toll	well
traurig	sadly
umsonst	in vain

Das hast du **gut** gemacht!	You did that well!
Sie kann **schön** singen	She can sing beautifully

▶ 6.2.2 Adverbial phrases of manner

mit dem Auto	by car
mit Freunden	with friends
zu Fuß	on foot
mit viel Geduld	with a lot of patience

6.3 Adverbs of place

+ **Adverbs of place indicate the *place* or *direction* of an action**

▶ 6.3.1 One-word place/direction adverbs

geradeaus	straight on
heim	home (direction)
herum	round/around
unterwegs	on the way
weg	away
zurück	back
zusammen	together

▶ 6.3.2 Prepositional adverbs of place

in die Stadt/in der Stadt	into town/in (the) town
aufs Land/auf dem Land	into the country/in the country
an die Küste/an der Küste	to the coast/on the coast

▶ 6.3.3 The suffixes -**hin** and -**her**, and the prepositions **nach** and **von**

a These are common ways used to indicate direction

Place		Direction	
dort	there	dorthin/dorther	(to) there/from there
da	there	dahin/daher	(to) there/from there
draußen[1]	outside	nach draußen	outside
drinnen[1]	inside	nach drinnen	inside
oben	upstairs	nach/von oben	(to)/from upstairs
unten	downstairs	nach/von unten	(to)/from downstairs
hinten	at the back	nach/von hinten	to/from the back
vorn	at the front	nach/von vorn	to/from the front
links	to/on the left	nach/von links	to/from the left
rechts	to/on the right	nach/von rechts	to/from the right
mitten in / auf etc			
	in the middle of		
überall	everywhere	überallhin	(to) everywhere
		überallher	from everywhere
irgendwo	somewhere	irgendwohin	(to) somewhere (or other)
		irgendwoher	from somewhere
anderswo	somewhere else	anderswohin	(to) somewhere else
		anderswoher	from somewhere else

oben auf dem Berg	at the top of the mountain
unten rechts auf dem Foto	at the bottom right in the photo
Er musterte mich **von oben bis unten**	He looked me up and down
Ich fahre **irgendwohin**, wo es warm ist	I'm going somewhere where it's warm
Ich würde so gern mit dir **dorthin** fahren	I'd really like to go there with you
Ich arbeite **mitten in** der Stadt	I work in the middle of town

[1] **Compare** draußen/drinnen *(inside/outside)* with außen and innen *(on the outside/on the inside)*:

Der Becher war **draußen** im Garten	The mug was outside in the garden
Außen ist der Becher ganz sauber	On the outside the mug is quite clean

b hin and her are directional adverbs

hin indicates direction *away from*, and **her** direction *towards* the speaker (or point of reference).

• **hin** and **her** are often used with the interrogative adverb **Wo?** or with the separable prepositional prefixes of verbs to emphasise movement:

Woher kommen Sie? ⎫ **Wo** kommen Sie **her**? ⎭	*Where do you come from?*
Wohin fährst du in Urlaub? ⎫ **Wo** fährst du in Urlaub **hin**? ⎭	*Where are you going on holiday?*
Er ging aus dem Zimmer **hinaus**	*He went out of the room*
Er kam in das Zimmer **herein**	*He came into the room*
Sie steigt den Berg **hinauf**	*She's climbing the mountain*
Sie steigt den Berg **herunter**	*She's coming down the mountain*

Note The prepositions which are commonly used in this way are **ab**, **auf**, **aus**, **ein** (from in), **über** and **unter**.

• **hin** and **her** may stand alone (for instance when used as a separable prefix):

Er deutete auf das Schild **hin**	*He pointed at the sign*
Sie legte sich **hin**	*She lay down*
Halte dein Glas **her**!	*Hold your glass out!*

• **hin** and **her** may be used with adverbs of place such as irgendwo, überall (see others in 6.3.3a above):

Die Kinder laufen **überallhin**	*The children run around everywhere*
Irgendwoher muss ich das Geld kriegen	*I've got to get the money from somewhere*

c hin and her are often used with figurative meanings

Er gab sich seinen Studien **hin**	*He devoted himself to his studies*
Sie machten sich über die Arbeit **her**	*They got on with their work*
In Stuttgart stellt man Autos **her**	*In Stuttgart they manufacture cars*
Er rief großes Erstaunen **hervor**	*He caused great astonishment*

d In colloquial German, hin and her are often abbreviated to r-

Komm **rein**!	*Come in!*
Sie ging zu ihren Freunden **rüber**	*She went over to her friends*

e Some other constructions use hin and her

hin und **her**	*to and fro*
hin und wieder	*now and again*
Die Katze kam unter dem Sofa **hervor**	*The cat came out from under the sofa*
Sie sah zum Fenster **hinaus**	*She looked out of the window*
Ich singe gern **vor** mich **hin**	*I like singing to myself*
Sie sah **vor** sich **hin**	*She looked straight in front of her*
Er kam **hinter** mir **her**	*He walked along behind me*
Seine Kindheit ist schon lange **her**	*His childhood was a long time ago*
auf seinen Rat **hin**	*on his advice*

6.4 Adverbs of comment/attitude

+ **Adverbs of comment indicate an <u>attitude</u> to the rest of the statement.**
+ See also Chapter 7 (Modal particles).
  Common examples include:

eigentlich	*actually*
freilich	*admittedly*
gern	*= to like*
glücklicherweise	*fortunately*
hoffentlich	*hopefully, I (etc.) hope so*
leider	*unfortunately, I'm afraid that*
möglicherweise	*possibly*
natürlich	*naturally, of course*
normalerweise	*normally*
selbstverständlich	*of course*
sicher	*certainly*
vielleicht	*perhaps*
wahrscheinlich	*probably*
zum Glück	*fortunately*
zweifellos	*undoubtedly*

Dazu habe ich **wahrscheinlich** keine Zeit	*I probably won't have time for that*
Leider ist sie nicht zu Hause	*I'm afraid she's not at home*
Ich spiele **gern** Fußball	*I like playing football*

6.5 Adverbs of degree

+ **Adverbs of degree indicate the <u>extent</u> or <u>intensity</u> of an adjective or adverb**

Common examples include:

äußerst	*extremely*
besonders	*especially*
etwas	*rather, a bit*
fast	*almost*
ganz	*quite*
gar	*at all*
keineswegs	*not at all*
nicht	*not*
sehr	*very*
total	*very*
überhaupt	*anyhow, anyway*
viel	*much*
wesentlich	*considerably, significantly*
wirklich	*really*
ziemlich	*quite*
zu	*too*

Ihr neuester Film ist **besonders** gut	Her latest film is especially good
Sie spricht **zu** schnell	She speaks too quickly
Das Essen ist **gar nicht** schlecht	The food isn't at all bad
Er hat **viel** mehr Geld als ich	He has much more money than I do

6.6 Adverbs of reason

♦ **Adverbs of reason indicate a <u>reason for</u> or a <u>qualification to</u> the rest of the clause**

▶ 6.6.1 Reason or consequence

also	
darum ⎫	
daher ⎪	*so*
deshalb ⎬	*that's why, because of that*
deswegen ⎭	
folglich	*consequently, therefore*

Ich habe kein Geld, **also** bleibe ich zu Hause	I haven't got any money, so I'll have to stay at home
Ich habe kein Geld, ich bleibe **deswegen** zu Hause	I haven't got any money, so I'll have to stay at home
Du meinst **also**, wir sollten hier bleiben?	So you think we should stay here, then?

▶ 6.6.2 Qualification or contrast

a One-word examples

allerdings	*though, mind you*
außerdem	*in addition, as well*
dennoch	*nevertheless*
jedenfalls	*in any case*
sonst	*otherwise*
trotzdem	*in spite of that, nevertheless*
übrigens	*incidentally, by the way*

Es regnet in Strömen, wir gehen **trotzdem** spazieren	It's pouring with rain, but we're going for a walk anyway
Ich rufe ihn an, ich muss **allerdings** erst seine Telefonnummer heraussuchen	I'll phone him up, but I'll need to look his phone number up first

b Prepositional phrases which fall into this category include those starting with wegen or trotz

Wegen des Wetters bleiben wir zu Hause	Because of the weather we're staying at home
Trotz seiner Probleme wollte er wieder arbeiten	In spite of his problems he wanted to work again

6.7 Interrogative adverbs

a Interrogative adverbs are used to introduce questions

This list does not include wer? or was?, which are pronouns (see 4.6), nor the determiners welcher? (see 3.5.1, 4.6.2) or was für (see 3.5.2):

wann?	*when?*	**Wann** fahren wir ab?
		Bis **wann** muss ich den Aufsatz schreiben?
		Seit **wann** lernst du Deutsch?
warum?[1]	*why?*	**Warum** hast du das gemacht?
wie?	*how?*	**Wie** geht's?
		Wie heißen Sie?
		Wie oft besuchst du ihn?
		Wie viel Geld hast du?
	what ... like?	**Wie** ist ihr neues Haus?
wieso?	*why?*	**Wieso** hast du das gemacht?
wo?	*where?*	**Wo** hast du es gefunden?
woher?	*where ... from?*	**Woher** kommen Sie?
		Woher soll ich das Wissen?
wohin?	*where... to?*	**Wohin** gehst du?
wozu?	*what... for?*	**Wozu** braucht man so was?

[1] Weshalb? and weswegen? are more formal versions of warum?

Note also these two interrogatives, which do not begin with **w-** and are largely interchangeable:

| inwiefern? | *in what way?* | **Inwiefern** hat sich die Lage verbessert? |
| inwieweit? | *to what extent?* | **Inwieweit** kann man ihr helfen? |

b Wo + preposition forms an interrogative adverb (see Pronouns 4.6.1)

| **Worauf** wartest du? | *What are you waiting for?* |
| **Wofür** interessierst du dich? | *What are you interested in?* |

c Interrogative adverbs may be used to introduce indirect questions. As such, they are subordinating conjunctions, and so send the verb to the end of the clause (see 18.2.2f)

| Er wußte nicht, bis **wann** wir den Aufsatz schreiben mussten | *He didn't know when we had to have written the essay by* |
| Ich sollte ihn fragen, **wie** lange wir hier bleiben müssen | *I ought to ask him how long we have to stay here* |

7

Modal particles

OVERVIEW

- **Modal particles** are **adverbs** such as mal, schon, doch, nun.
- They are used in spoken German to indicate something of the speaker's attitude to what she is saying – surprise, disbelief, annoyance, for instance. Modal verbs (müssen, dürfen, etc.) also help to express attitude to an action – see 12.2.
- Modal particles are sometimes difficult to translate into English, where the speaker will often use tone of voice to achieve a similar effect. But compare the following pairs of sentences:

Come on!	*Oh, do come on!*
That was fun!	*That was such fun!*
Can you pass the salt?	*Can you just pass the salt?*

  Notice the emphasis added by the use of the auxiliary *do* and the adverb *such*, and the politeness (or frustration!) added by *just*.
- Many modal particles will be familiar from other uses – aber *but* (conjunction), ja *yes* (interjection). The list in this chapter is not exhaustive, but includes all the common ones, and those words which are likely to appear unusual or difficult to English-speakers.

7.1 Characteristics of modal particles

a **Modal particles indicate something of the attitude of the speaker to the action – politeness, surprise, urgency, and so on**
Compare these pairs of statements:

Sei nicht so laut!	*Don't be so noisy!*
Sei **doch** nicht so laut!	*For goodness' sake, don't be so noisy!*
(**doch** adds emphasis)	
Kannst du mir bitte helfen?	*Can you help me, please?*
Kannst du mir bitte **mal** helfen?	*Could you just help me, please?*
(**mal** makes the request more polite)	

b **Modal particles share three main characteristics**
- They always relate to the whole sentence or clause.
- They cannot form the point of a question.
- They cannot stand in first position before the verb.

c Modal particles are often used in pairs, or occasionally even in threes

War das **aber auch** schön!	*That was absolutely fantastic!*
Das ist **ja wohl** ein Blödsinn!	*That's just complete rubbish!*
Na, hilf mir **doch mal**!	*Come on! Help me, for goodness' sake!*
Ruf **doch ruhig mal** bei mir an!	*Do feel free just to give me a call*
Sie hätte ihn **ja doch wohl** besuchen können, als er so krank war	*She really might have visited him while he was so ill*

d Individual modal particles are often associated with a particular type of expression, sometimes more than one

Statements:	aber, doch, eben, ja, halt, schon
Questions:	denn, eigentlich, mal, wohl
Commands:	doch, eben, mal, schon
Exclamations, wishes:	aber, bloß, doch, nur, vielleicht

Because they may appear in more than one category, the modal particles are dealt with individually below.

7.2 Modal particles

7.2.1 aber

a aber expresses surprise or emphasis

Das war **aber** ein toller Abend!	*That was a really good evening!*
War das **aber** schön!	*Wasn't that just fantastic!*
Oh! Das Geschenk ist **aber** schön!	*Oh! What a lovely present!*
Der Tee ist **aber** stark!	*This tea is really strong* (=more so than expected; cf. ja)

b aber expresses a contradiction (as when used as a conjunction)

Er ist nett, sein Bruder **aber** nicht	*He's nice, but his brother isn't*

7.2.2 auch

♦ auch stresses the reason for or against something

„Sie sieht nett aus." – „Sie ist es ja **auch**."	*'She looks nice.' – 'Well, she really is nice.'*
„Der ist aber **auch** dumm!"	*'Wow – he's really stupid!'*

7.2.3 bloß

♦ bloß *only, just* is identical in use to nur

Wenn er **bloß** hier bleiben würde!	*If only he would stay here!*
Gib mir **bloß** das Ding zurück!	*Just give me that thing back!*

7.2.4 denn

♦ denn *then* makes questions less direct (and therefore more polite or tentative)

OK – fangen wir **denn** an?	*OK – shall we start, then?*

Warum hast du **denn** das gesagt?	*Why did you say that, then?*
Was ist **denn** los?	*What's up then?*

7.2.5 doch

a In statements, doch *but/however* expresses disagreement

„Du bist erst 16." – „Ich bin **doch** kein Kind mehr."	*'You're only 16.' – 'But I'm not a child any more.'*

b doch invites agreement with a statement, often with nicht wahr? or oder? added – *'didn't you?', 'wasn't it?'*

Das haben Sie **doch** gesagt, oder?	*I think it was you who said that, wasn't it?*

c doch makes requests or demands more urgent – or less urgent, depending on the tone of the demand

Hört bitte **doch** endlich mit dem Lärm auf!	*Will you <u>please</u> just stop that racket!*
Ruh dich **doch** mal aus – ich hole Kaffee	*Just relax – I'll go and get some coffee*

d In exclamations, doch expresses surprise or other strong feeling (like nur, bloß)

Wenn sie **doch** nur anrufen würde!	*If only she would phone!*
Sie ist **doch** blöd!	*She's really stupid!*

7.2.6 eben

◆ eben emphasises the truth of a statement or command, often with a hint of resignation

So ist es **eben**	*Well, that's just how things are*
Na, bleib doch **eben** allein zu Hause	*Well, stay alone at home, then*

7.2.7 eigentlich

◆ In questions, eigentlich expresses *actually, in reality*

Was hältst du **eigentlich** von ihr?	*What do you really think of her?*
Wer ist denn dieser Kerl **eigentlich**?	*Who is this guy really then?*
Er sieht vielleicht dumm aus, aber er ist **eigentlich** sehr intelligent	*He may look stupid, but actually he's very intelligent*
Das Kuriose daran ist, dass sie **eigentlich** gute Freunde waren	*The strange thing about it is that they were actually good friends*

7.2.8 erst

◆ erst as a modal particle is used as an intensifier

Abends geht es **erst** recht los!	*Things really come alive in the evenings!*
Wäre er doch **erst** zu Hause!	*If only he were at home!*

7.2.9 etwa

◆ etwa emphasises the possibility of the (undesirable) statement or question

Ist dein Reisepass **etwa** schon abgelaufen?	*Has your passport really expired?*

Er sollte nicht **etwa** denken, dass
   er so etwas unbestraft tun
   darf!

*He shouldn't think that he can do
   that and get away with it!*

▶ 7.2.10 gleich

+ **gleich expresses** *just now, just then* **and often indicates resignation**

Was hast du noch **gleich** gesagt? — *What did you just say?*
Wenn du mir nicht hilfst, kann
   ich **gleich** aufgeben

*If you're not going to help me, I
   might as well give up now*

▶ 7.2.11 halt

+ **halt is identical to eben and expresses** *'just'*

So ist es **halt** — *Well, that's just how it is*
Dann kommen wir **halt** spät an — *We'll just have to arrive late then*

▶ 7.2.12 ja

+ **ja invites and expects agreement with a statement (cf. doch):**

Das haben Sie **ja** gestern gesagt — *Of course, you said that yesterday*
Ihr kennt ihn **ja** schon — *You know him already, I know*
Der Tee ist **ja** stark — *Oh, the tea is strong (= I was
   expecting it not to be. cf. aber)*

▶ 7.2.13 mal

+ **mal** *just* **makes statements and commands less blunt**

Moment **mal**! — *Just a minute!*
Ich muss **mal** kurz in den
   Supermarkt

*I just need to nip into the
   supermarket*

Besuchen Sie uns doch **mal**! — *Do come to visit us!*
Versuch's doch **mal**! — *Go on – try it!*
Gibst du mir bitte **mal** das Salz? — *Could you just pass the salt,
   please?*

▶ 7.2.14 nur

+ **nur intensifies the statement**

Vergiss **nur** nicht die Flugkarten! — *Whatever you do, don't forget the
   tickets!*

Wie kam er **nur** dazu? — *What on earth made him do that?*
Zum Geburtstag bekommt er
   alles, was er **nur** will

*For his birthday, he gets absolutely
   everything he wants*

▶ 7.2.15 schon

a schon emphasises the probability of a statement

Es wird **schon** gut gehen — *It will be fine, I'm sure*
Das hört sich **schon** besser an! — *Now you're talking!*
Das ist **schon** ein Problem — *That really is a problem*

b In commands, schon emphasises impatience

Na, komm **schon**! — *Oh, do come on!*

c schon expresses a reservation, often followed by aber

Das stimmt **schon**, aber …	*That's true, but …*
Das Geld dafür hätte ich **schon**, leider aber keine Zeit	*I might have the money for it but I just don't have the time*
Wer hätte so was **schon** erwartet?	*Well, who'd have thought it?*

7.2.16 überhaupt

♦ Used as a particle, überhaupt is similar in meaning to eigentlich, with the sense of *at all, anyhow*

Er ist **überhaupt** ein ganz seltsamer Typ	*He's a strange guy anyway*
Wie konnte er das **überhaupt** sagen?	*How could he possibly say that?*

7.2.17 vielleicht

♦ vielleicht adds emphasis

Er war **vielleicht** wütend!	*Boy, was he angry!*
Das ist **vielleicht** ein toller Wein!	*That's a really good wine!*
Du glaubst nicht **vielleicht**, dass er das getan hat, oder?	*You really don't think he did that, do you?*

7.2.18 wohl

a In statements, wohl expresses probability

Dein Vorschlag wird **wohl** der beste sein	*You're suggestion's likely to be the best*
Das mag **wohl** stimmen, aber …	*That may well be true, but …*
Wie dir **wohl** bewusst ist, …	*As you well know …*
Bei dir piept's **wohl**!	*You're crazy!*
Der Markt wird **wohl** noch einen tiefen Sturz verkraften müssen	*The stock-market is likely to have to face another steep fall*
Sie machen **wohl** Witze!	*You're kidding!*

b In questions, wohl expresses uncertainty

Wer kann es **wohl** gewesen sein?	*Who could it have been?*

7.2.19 zwar

a zwar expresses *although* when followed by aber or a similar word; indicates or concedes a level of agreement, with reservation expressed in the other clause

Das Buch ist **zwar** interessant, **aber** es ist viel zu lang	*Although the book's interesting, it's much too long*
Er ist **zwar** arm, aber ehrlich	*He may be poor, but he's honest*
Zwar gibt es die Klassiker der Weltliteratur längst zum kostenlosen Download im Internet, **trotzdem** …	*Even though the classics of world literature have been available as free downloads on the internet for quite a while, they still …*

b Used with und, zwar introduces further detail on something just mentioned

Ich habe ein Auto gekauft, **und zwar** einen nagelneuen BMW	*I've just bought a car – a brand new BMW, in fact*

8

Comparative and superlative of adjectives and adverbs

OVERVIEW

The **comparative** and **superlative** forms of adjectives and adverbs are used to draw a comparison between the attributes and qualities of people, things and actions.

. The **comparative** is used when comparing two items or people:

> This car is **better** than that one
> Can you drive a little **more slowly**? (i.e. than at present)

. The **superlative** is used when comparing more than two items or people:

> This car is better than that one but the blue one is the **best** of the three
> That was the **worst** film I've ever seen
> He drives **fastest**

. The comparative and superlative are also used in other ways:

Equality	She is **as** tall **as** her sister
Progression	Things just got **worse** and **worse**
Proportion	**The longer** they waited, **the colder** it became
Relative	an **older** lady
Absolute	She sends her **best** wishes
	At **least** it's not raining

8.1 The comparative and superlative forms of adjectives

Adjectives and adverbs form the comparative and superlative in similar ways, with the exception of the superlative of the adverb (see section 8.2 below).

▷ 8.1.1 The regular formation of the comparative and superlative

a **Adjectives form their comparative and superlative forms by adding -er and -(e)st-**

schön	schön**er**	am schön**sten**/der schön**ste**
interessant	interessant**er**	am interessant**esten**/der interessant**este**
langweilig	langweilig**er**	am langweilig**sten**/der langweilig**ste**

♦ In English, there are two ways of forming the comparative and superlative: short words add **-er** to form the comparative and **-(e)st** to one syllable words, while longer words use **more** and **most**:

long – longer – longest
interesting – more interesting – most interesting

But German has only the one form for each, however long the word.

b A number of single-syllable adjectives with the vowel -a-, -o-, or -u- (but not -au-) add an umlaut in the comparative and the superlative

alt – **älter** – am **ältesten**/der **älteste**

alt	*old*	kalt	*cold*	rot	*red*
arm	*poor*	klug	*clever*	scharf	*sharp*
dumm	*stupid*	krank	*ill, sick*	schwach	*weak*
grob	*coarse*	kurz	*short*	schwarz	*black*
hart	*hard*	lang	*long*	stark	*strong*
jung	*young*	oft	*often*	warm	*warm*

See also nah, hoch in section 8.1.2a below.

mein **jüngerer** Bruder	*my younger brother*
Das waren finanziell noch **härtere** Zeiten als jetzt	*Financially, those were even harder times than now*
In der Sonne ist es am **wärmsten**	*It's warmest in the sun*

c A few adjectives form their comparative and superlative forms sometimes with an umlaut and sometimes without (the latter are usually in written German)

bang	*scared*
blass	*pale*
fromm	*pious*
gesund	*healthy*
glatt	*smooth*
krumm	*crooked*
nass	*wet*
schmal	*narrow*
zart	*tender*

Die Nebenstraße war noch **schmaler/schmäler**	*The side street was even narrower*
das **zarteste/zärteste** Fleisch	*the tenderest meat*

d The many other single-syllable adjectives with the vowels -a-, -o- or -u- which do not add an umlaut include

bunt	*colourful*
falsch	*wrong*
flach	*flat*
froh	*glad, pleased*
hohl	*hollow*
klar	*clear*
rund	*round*
schlank	*slim*
stolz	*proud*
stumpf	*blunt*

toll	*great*
voll	*full*
wahr	*true*

Sie will noch **schlanker** sein	*She wants to be even slimmer*
Welches Glas ist **das vollste/am vollsten**?	*Which glass is the fullest?*
die **klarste** Antwort	*the clearest answer*

e Rules regarding case endings on comparative and superlative forms are identical to those for normal adjectives

+ **add** case endings if the adjective is **attributive** (i.e. stands before the noun):

eine **ruhigere** Atmosphäre	*a more peaceful atmosphere*
Das **kälteste** Wetter war im Februar	*The coldest weather was in February*
Das ist das **interessanteste** Buch	*This is the most interesting book*
Dieser See ist der **schönste** von allen	*This lake is the loveliest (lake) of all*

+ **do not add** case endings if the adjective is **predicative** (i.e. stands after the verb sein):

Der See ist schön	*The lake is beautiful*
Dieser See ist noch **schöner**	*This lake is even more beautiful*
Hier ist es etwas **ruhiger**	*This room is a bit quieter*
Hier ist der See **am schönsten**	*The lake is most beautiful here*
Ich finde dieses Buch **am interessantesten**	*I think this book is the most interesting*

8.1.2 Irregular forms of the comparative and superlative

a A few adjectives/adverbs have irregular comparative and superlative forms

groß	*big*	größer	der größte/am größten
gut	*good*	besser	der beste/am besten
hoch	*high*	höher	der höchste/am höchsten
nah	*near(by)*	näher	der nächste/am nächsten
viel	*a lot, much*	mehr	der meiste/am meisten

In addition, mehr and weniger do not decline when followed by a noun:

Ich habe **mehr/weniger** Zeit als er	*I have more/less time than he does*

b Adjectives which end in -haft, -s, -ß and -z add -e- before the superlative ending -st

This is to make for ease of pronunciation:

der zaghaft**e**ste/am zaghaft**e**sten	*the most timid*
der hilflos**e**ste/am hilflos**e**sten	*the most helpless*
der süß**e**ste/am süß**e**sten	*the sweetest*
der kürz**e**ste/am kürz**e**sten	*the shortest*

c Adjectives which end with -d, -t, or -sch, or which end with a long vowel or diphthong often add -e- before -st-

This makes the word easier to pronounce:

der breit**e**ste/am breit**e**sten	*the widest*
der bekannt**e**ste/am bekannt**e**sten	*the best known*
der neu**e**ste/am neu**e**sten	*the newest*
der genau**e**ste/am genau**e**sten	*the most exact*

But longer words ending with **-d, -t** or **-sch**, which have an unstressed final syllable, don't add -e-:

der praktischste/am praktischsten	*the most convenient*
der bedeutendste/am bedeutendsten	*the most significant*

d **The sense of a comparative or superlative is sometimes achieved by a prefix (see 19.3.4b)**

messerscharf	*as sharp as a knife*
superintelligent	*superintelligent*
ultramodern	*ultramodern*

▶ 8.1.3 Compound adjectives

♦ **Compound adjectives that are thought of as a single word form their comparative and superlative in the usual way**

das altmodisch**ste** Kleid	*the most old-fashioned dress*
Das war noch leichtsinnig**er**	*That was even more foolish*
Deutschland ist weltweit die viert**größte** Hersteller der Atomenergie	*Germany is the fourth largest producer of atomic energy in the world*
„Blizzard" ist der weltweit leistungs**fähigste** Klima-Rechner	*'Blizzard' is the world's most powerful climate computer*

8.2 The comparative and superlative forms of adverbs

a **The rules for the formation of the comparative and superlative of adverbs are largely identical to those for adjectives – see above**

♦ The only real difference is that the superlative of all adverbs is always the **am ...-sten** form:

Maria singt **lauter** als er, aber ich singe immer **am lautesten**	*Maria sings louder than he does but I always sing loudest*

b **A few adverbs have irregular comparative and superlative forms**

bald *soon*	eher	am ehesten
gern *with pleasure*	lieber	am liebsten
oft *often*	öfter	am häufigsten
viel *much, a lot*	mehr	am meisten

8.3 Using the comparative and superlative

a **Comparison (größer als ...** *bigger than ...***; weniger ... als ...** *less...than...***)**

Sie ist **größer als** ich	*She's taller than I am*
Die Donau ist ein noch **längerer** Fluß **als** der Rhein	*The Danube is an even longer river than the Rhine*
Er ist **weniger** begabt **als** seine Schwester	*He's less gifted than his sister*

einer der **weniger** interessanten Filme	*one of the less interesting films*
Er war **besser** bezahlt als ich	*He was better paid than I was*
Weil er noch **größer** ist[1] **als** ich, …	*Because he's even taller than me …*

[1] Note the position of the verb in a subordinate clause!

> **TIP** *als* or *wie* in comparisons?
>
> ✦ **als** is the equivalent of *than*; **wie** is used for *as*:
>
> | | |
> |---|---|
> | fauler als | *lazier than* |
> | so faul wie | *as lazy as* |
> | nicht so faul wie | *not as lazy as* |
>
> ✦ **wie** will occasionally be heard colloquially in place of **als**. This is, however, generally regarded as sub-standard.

---

b Superlative (der größte … / am größten *the biggest*)

✦ If the adjective is before the noun, the **der/die/das …-ste** form must be used:

Das ist der **beste** Tag der Woche	*That is the best day of the week*
die **billigsten** Karten	*the cheapest tickets*
Das ist **der beste** aller seiner Filme/von allen seiner Filme	*That's the best of all his films*
Das war der **allerbeste** Film, den ich je gesehen habe!	*That's absolutely the best film I've ever seen*
Er ist einer der **besten** in der Klasse Er ist mit[1] der **beste** in der Klasse	*He's among the best in the class*
Kafka hat mit[1] die **klarste** und **schönste** deutsche Prosa geschaffen	*Kafka was the creator of some of the clearest and most beautiful prose in the German language (or: was among the creators of)*
die **größte** je konstruierte Maschine	*the largest machine ever built*

[1] i.e. 'mit anderen'; used with following superlative.

✦ If the noun is being compared with itself, or there is no 'understood' noun, the **am …-sten** form is used:

Die Berge sind im Sommer **am schönsten**	*The mountains are (at their) most beautiful in summer*

✦ If the noun is being compared with others, or there is an 'understood' noun (i.e. the noun is omitted to avoid repetition), either form may be used:

Von allen Gebirgen sind die Alpen **die schönsten/am schönsten**	*Of all mountains, the Alps are the most beautiful*

✦ As described in 8.2a above, only the **am …-sten** form is possible for the superlative of adverbs:

Sie singt **am lautesten**	*She sings (the) loudest*
Er spricht **am leisesten**	*He speaks (the) quietest*
Sie läuft **am schnellsten**	*She runs fastest*
Am besten kommen Sie zu uns	*The best thing is for you to come to our house*

c Equality (so...wie... *as big as...*)

Du bist **so** groß **wie** er	*You're as tall as him/he is*
Wenn ich **so** alt[1] bin **wie** er, ...	*When I'm as old as him / he is ...*

> [1] Note position of verb in subordinate clause!

Er ist **genauso** groß **wie** sie	*He is just as tall as her/she is*
Ich bin **nicht so** groß **wie** du	*I'm not as tall as you*

* **Note** other ways of expressing equality:

Er ist **ebenso** dumm **wie** faul	*He's as stupid as he is lazy*
Sie sind **gleich** dumm	*They're as stupid each other*

d Progression (immer größer *bigger and bigger*)

Das Wetter wird **immer kälter**	*The weather is getting colder and colder*
Der Film wird **immer spannender**	*The film gets more and more exciting*

e Proportion (je ... desto ... *the bigger ..., the more ...*)

Je schneller man mit diesem Auto fährt, **desto/umso** gefährlicher wird es	*The faster you drive this car, the more dangerous it becomes*
Je kälter es wird, **desto** mehr Kleider muss man tragen	*The colder it gets, the more clothes you have to wear*

f Relative comparative (größere *a fairly big ... quite a big ...*)

The comparative can be used in an 'absolute' sense (i.e. where no comparison is being made with anything else):

eine **ältere** Dame	*quite an elderly lady*
eine **kleinere** Stadt	*a fairly small town*
seine **neueren** Romane	*his more recent novels*

g 'Absolute' superlative

The superlative is sometimes used in an 'absolute' sense (i.e. where no comparison is being made with anything else), mostly in the adverbial form, but occasionally, as in the first two examples, adjectivally:

Es ist **höchste** Zeit, dass ...	*It's high time that ...*
Die **wenigsten** Leute merken, dass ...	*Almost no one notices that ...*
Er lief **möglichst** schnell	*He ran as quickly as possible*
Er war **höchst** erstaunt	*He was very surprised*
Das ist **äußerst** interessant	*That's extremely interesting*
Das Schloss ist schon **längst** verschwunden	*The castle disappeared a long time ago*
Ich bin in **höchstens** einer Stunde da	*I'll be there in an hour at the latest*
Meistens fahren wir an die Küste	*Mostly we go to the coast*
Sie lässt **bestens** grüssen	*She sends her very best wishes*
Wenigstens schneit es nicht mehr	*At least it's not snowing any more*
Ich brauche **mindestens** drei davon	*I need at least three of those*

9

Prepositions

OVERVIEW

What is a preposition?

- Prepositions tell us the relationship between one noun phrase or pronoun and another – often a physical position.

  Compare
*The shoe is **on** the chair*	*The shoe is **under** the chair*
*This present is **from** my brother*	*This present is **for** my brother*

- Prepositions are so called because they stand before the pronoun or phrase to which they refer, as in the examples above. In German there are also a few postpositions (words which stand after the pronoun or phrase), such as entlang and gegenüber. These are also dealt with in this chapter.

Prepositions can indicate

- **position**

  Die Milch ist **in** dem Kühlschrank   *The milk is **in** the fridge*

- **direction**

  Sie fährt heute **nach** Berlin   *She is travelling **to** Berlin today*

- **manner**

  Wir fahren **mit** dem Bus   *We're going **by** bus*

- **time**

  Wir fahren **um** neun ab   *We leave **at** nine*

- **reason**

  Sie konnte **wegen** des Schnees   *She couldn't travel **because of**
  nicht fahren   *the snow*

Prepositions and cases

The pronoun or noun phrase after the preposition is always in the accusative, genitive or dative – never the nominative. We say that the preposition 'governs' or 'takes' a particular case. The accusative and the dative are the most common cases.

> ## The most common prepositions

The commonest prepositions and their main English equivalents are:

Accusative	Dative	Accusative/Dative	Genitive
bis *by, until*	aus *from, out of*	an *at, on*	statt *instead of*
durch *through, by*	außer *apart from*	auf *on*	trotz *in spite of*
entlang *along*	bei *at, by (near)*	hinter *behind*	während *during*
für *for*	gegenüber *opposite*	in *in, into*	wegen *because of*
gegen *against, about*	mit *with, by (bus)*	neben *next to*	
ohne *without*	nach *to, after*	über *over, above*	
um *at, around*	seit *since, for (time)*	unter *under, among*	
wider *against*	von *from, of*	vor *before, in front of, outside*	
	zu *to*	zwischen *between*	

9.1 Prepositions followed by the accusative

bis	*till, by, as far as*	gegen	*against, towards*
durch	*through, by (means of)*		*about, approximately*
		ohne	*without*
entlang	*along*	um	*round, at (time), by*
für	*for*	wider	*against*

> **TIP** **How to remember the accusative prepositions**
> - One way of remembering the accusative prepositions is by their first letters:
>
>   **FUDGEBOW**
>
> - Another way of remembering them is to learn each preposition with an accusative pronoun, e.g. für mich, ohne mich, gegen mich.

▶ 9.1.1 bis

- **bis** is used alone only before names and adverbs; otherwise it is followed by another preposition, which determines the case of the following phrase.

a *as far as* **(referring to place)**

von oben **bis** unten	*from top to bottom*
Wir fahren **bis** **(nach)** Lübeck	*We're going as far as Lübeck*
bis zur Hauptstrasse	*as far as the main street*
bis ans Ende der Welt	*to the end of the world*

b *by, until* (time)

Bis dann!	*See you then!*
Bis wann bist du fertig?	*When will you be ready by?*
bis Montag/**bis** 5 Uhr/**bis zum** Wochenende	*by/until Monday/5 o'clock/the weekend*
vom 1. **bis zum** 20. Januar	*from 1st to 20th January*

▷ 9.1.2 durch

a *through*

Er ging **durch** die Tür	*He went through the door*
durch dick und dünn	*through thick and thin*
Sie reist **durch** viele Länder	*She's travelling through many countries*
durch den Winter	*through the winter*

b *By (means of)* (also with the passive – see 15.1.2a)

Sie hat es **durch** harte Arbeit geschafft	*She managed it by hard work*
Durch ihre Freundin hat sie ihren Mann kennengelernt	*Through her friend she got to know her husband*
Die Fabrik wurde **durch** Bomben zerstört	*The factory was destroyed by bombs*
‚Vorsprung **durch** Technik'	*'(Taking the) lead through technology'* (Audi advertising slogan)

▷ 9.1.3 entlang

✦ *along*; usually follows the noun

Sie läuft die Straße **entlang**	*She runs down the street*
Ich gehe den Fluß **entlang**	*I walk along the river*
Ich segle den Fluß **entlang**	*I sail along the river*

Note entlang is also sometimes used with an + dative:

Ich gehe **an** dem Fluß **entlang**	*I walk along(side) the river*

▷ 9.1.4 für

a *for*

Ich habe ein Geschenk **für** dich	*I have a present for you*
Er trainiert **für** die Olympiade	*He's training for the Olympics*
Für einen Ausländer spricht er ausgezeichnet Deutsch	*For a foreigner he speaks excellent German*

b *for* + time extending forward from the point of speaking

Wir fahren **für** drei Wochen nach Amerika	*We're going to America for three weeks*
Er fuhr **für** eine Woche nach Berlin	*He went to Berlin for a week*

Note If the time has already elapsed, use the accusative without a preposition:

Wir waren drei Wochen in Amerika	*We went to America for three weeks*

See Adverbs 6.1.4 for a fuller discussion of *for* + time in German.

c *by* in double-word idioms

Tag **für** Tag	*day by day*
Wort **für** Wort	*word for (by) word/verbatim*
Schritt **für** Schritt	*step by step*

▶ 9.1.5 gegen

a *against* (position)

Sie lehnte sich **gegen** die Wand	*She leaned against the wall*
Er fuhr **gegen** die Schranke	*He drove into the barrier*

b *against* (opposition to); *contrary to*

Heute spielt Schalke 04 **gegen** Bayern München	*Today Schalke 04 is playing against Bayern München*
Haben Sie etwas **gegen** Kopfschmerzen?	*Have you got anything for headaches?*
Gegen meine Erwartungen haben wir gewonnen	*Contrary to my expectations we won*

c *at about* (time)

Wir sind **gegen** halb eins da	*We'll be there at about half past twelve*
Erst **gegen** Morgen schlief sie ein	*She didn't fall asleep till towards morning*

▶ 9.1.6 ohne

✦ *without*

Sie fährt **ohne** ihn nach Amerika	*She's going to America without him*
Das habe ich **ohne** Absicht gemacht	*I did that without intending to*

▶ 9.1.7 um

a *round, around, about* (place)

Um die Ecke finden Sie sein Haus	*You'll find his house round the corner*

b *at* (with clock time); *at around* (with more general times; often with herum)

Wir sind **um** halb eins da	*We'll be there at half past twelve*
Um Weihnachten (herum) hat alles angefangen	*It was around Christmas when it all started*

c *about, concerning*

Sie streiten sich immer **um** nichts	*They're always arguing about nothing*
Er kämpft **um** sein Leben	*He's fighting for his life*

d *by* (a difference of)

Man hat den Preis **um** 10% reduziert	*They've reduced the price by 10%*
Dieses ist **um** 2 cm länger	*This one is longer by 2 cm*
Ich habe **um** ein Haar den Bus verpasst	*I missed the bus by a whisker*

▶ 9.1.8 wider *against*

- **wider** is uncommon except in a few set phrases and as part of compounds such as widersprechen *to contradict* (see 19.5.3b).

wider Erwarten	*contrary to expectations*
wider Willen	*against (his, my) will*

9.2 Prepositions followed by the dative

aus	*out of, made of*	nach	*to, after, according to*
außer	*besides, except*	seit	*since, for (time)*
bei	*at, near, in*	von	*from, of, by (someone)*
gegenüber	*opposite*	zu	*to, on, for*
mit	*with, by*		

> ▶ **TIP** **How to remember the dative prepositions**
> - One way of remembering the dative prepositions is by the nonsense phrase **MABZ VANS**, which is made up from the first letters of all of them, excluding gegenüber.
> - Another method is to learn each preposition with a pronoun which is clearly dative, e.g. bei mir, mit mir.

▶ 9.2.1 aus

a *out of, from* (direction, starting point, origin)

Sie kam **aus** ihrem Büro	*She came out of her office*
Er erwachte **aus** einem Traum	*He awoke from a dream*
Er kommt **aus** Köln	*He comes from Cologne*
ein Junge **aus** unserer Schule	*a boy from our school*
Musik **aus** dem 19. Jahrhundert	*Music from the nineteenth century*
Ich weiß **aus** Erfahrung, dass …	*I know from experience that …*
aus dem Englischen übersetzt	*translated from English*
Ich trinke Bier **aus** der Flasche	*I'm drinking beer from the bottle*

> ▶ **TIP** *from*: **aus** or **von**?
> - **aus** *from* (origin)
>
> | | |
> |---|---|
> | Er kommt **aus** Köln | *He comes from Cologne* |
> | Gewürze **aus** dem Osten | *spices from the East* |
>
> - **von** *from the direction of* – (its opposite is nach or zu)
>
> | | |
> |---|---|
> | der Zug **von** Köln nach Berlin | *the train from Cologne to Bonn* |

b *out of* (reason, cause)

aus diesem Grund	*for this reason; that's why*
aus Mangel an Zeit/Geld	*for lack of time/money*
aus Mitleid/Liebe	*out of sympathy/love*

c *made of* (materials)

eine Tasche **aus** Leder	*a bag made of leather*
Sie hat es **aus** einer alten Jacke gemacht	*She's made it from an old jacket*

9.2.2 außer

a *except (for), apart from*

Außer ihm war niemand da	*Apart from him there was no one there*
Man sah nichts **außer** dem Schnee	*You could see nothing apart from the snow*
Er hat alle gesehen **außer** mir	*He saw all of them except me*

b *out of, outside, no longer in...* (used in set phrases)

der Fahrstuhl ist **außer** Betrieb	*The lift is out of service*
Ich war **außer** mir vor Angst	*I was beside myself with fear*
außer Gefahr/Atem/Kontrolle	*out of danger/breath/control*

9.2.3 bei

a *at* (the house of), *for* (employer), *with* (person)

Er wohnt **bei** seinen Großeltern	*He lives with his grandparents*
Essen wir **bei** dir?	*Shall we eat at your house?*
Er ist **bei** der Armee	*He's in the Army*
Sie arbeitet **bei** Siemens	*She works for Siemens*
beim Arzt, **beim** Metzger	*at the doctor's, at the butcher's*
Das Buch erschien **bei** Suhrkamp	*The book was published by Suhrkamp*
Ich kaufe normalerweise **bei** Aldi ein	*I normally shop at Aldi*
Bei Shakespeare sind die Helden anders	*With Shakespeare the heroes are different*
Ich habe kein Geld **bei** mir	*I haven't got any money on me*
Er hatte kein Glück **bei** ihr	*He had no luck with her*
Das findet man nicht oft **bei** einem so kleinen Kind	*You don't find that often in such a young child*

Note bei never means *to* the house of; instead, **zu** must be used:

Gehen wir **zu** dir?	*Shall we go to your house?*

b *at, near* (place), equivalent to in der Nähe von

Bonn liegt **bei** Köln	*Bonn lies close to Cologne*
Ich bleibe **beim** Gepäck; du kannst Kaffee holen	*I'll stay with the luggage; you can get some coffee*
Sie saß **bei** uns	*She was sitting near us*
Sie wohnt **beim** Rathaus	*She lives near the town hall*

c *in view of, considering* (attendant circumstances)

bei schlechtem Wetter	*in bad weather*
Bei meinem Gehalt kann ich mir keinen Urlaub leisten	*On my salary I can't afford a holiday*

Das kann man **bei** 20 Grad unter null nicht machen	You can't do that at 20 degrees below
Dutzende Tote **bei** Bombenanschlag	Dozens killed in bomb attack (newspaper headline)

d *on ... -ing* on the occasion of, *while ...-ing* (time)

Ich habe sie **bei** der Hochzeit zum ersten Mal gesehen	The first time I saw her was at the wedding
Bei Ebbe ist das Wasser nicht tief genug	At low tide the water is not deep enough
Bei meiner Ankunft regnete es	It was raining when I arrived
Sie ist **bei** einem Eisenbahnunglück ums Leben gekommen	She was killed in a railway accident
Ich rufe dich **bei** der ersten Gelegenheit an	I'll phone you at the first opportunity
Man darf sein Handy **beim** Fahren nicht benutzen	It's illegal to use a mobile phone while driving
Wir sind **beim** Essen	We're just having a meal

9.2.4 gegenüber

♦ gegenüber follows a pronoun, but may stand before or after a noun.

a *opposite* (place)

gegenüber unserem Haus	opposite our house
meiner Frau **gegenüber**	opposite my wife
mir **gegenüber**	opposite me

Note gegenüber can also be used on its own:

Sie wohnen schräg **gegenüber**	They live diagonally opposite

b *in relation to, with regard to*

Er ist seinem Boss **gegenüber** immer sehr höflich	He's always very polite to his boss
Seine Blindheit **gegenüber** diesem Problem macht mir Sorgen	His blindness with regard to this problem is worrying

9.2.5 mit

a *with* in most senses of the English word

Kaffee **mit** Milch	coffee with milk
Ich gehe **mit** ihm ins Kino	I'm going to the cinema with him
mit freundlichen Grüßen	(with) best wishes/yours sincerely
Sie wohnt **mit** ihrem Freund in Bonn zusammen	She lives with her boyfriend in Bonn

b *by* (transport)

mit dem Bus/Auto/Rad	by bus/car/bike
mit der Bahn	by rail
But zu Fuß/**zu** Pferd	on foot/on horseback

c Idiomatic and colloquial phrases using mit

mit der Zeit	*in the course of time*
Er ging **mit** 40 in die Rente	*He retired at 40*
Das hast du **mit** Absicht getan!	*You did that on purpose!*
Er nickte **mit** dem Kopf	*He nodded his head*
Sie ist **mit** die beste in der Gruppe	*She's one of the best in the group*

(colloquial; the word anderen *others* would be the object of mit
and in the dative, but is omitted; see 8.3b for another example)

▶ 9.2.6 nach

a *to* a named place, neuter country,[1] compass direction, or adverb of place

nach Deutschland	*to Germany*
nach Wien	*to Vienna*
nach Norden	*northwards*
nach oben	*upstairs*
nach Hause	*home(wards)*

[1]**Note** feminine and plural countries use **in** – see 9.3.4.

b *in the direction of, towards* (often with hin)

Er griff **nach** seinem Revolver	*He reached for his gun*
Sie tastete im Dunkeln **nach** dem Lichtschalter	*In the darkness she felt for the light switch*
Das Wasser spritzte **nach** allen Seiten	*The water sprayed in all directions*

c *after* (time, sequence)

nach dem 1. Januar, **nach** dem Mittagessen, **nach** 5 Uhr, **nach** dem Krieg	
70 Jahre **nach** Christus (n.Chr.)	*70 AD*
einer **nach** dem anderen	*one after the other*
Bitte **nach** Ihnen!	*Please, after you!*

d *according to, judging by* (often follows the noun)

nach meiner Meinung ⎱	*in my opinion*
meiner Meinung **nach** ⎰	
Hähnchen **nach** französischer Art	*chicken cooked French style*
der Größe **nach**	*according to size*
der Reihe **nach**	*in turn*
das Evangelium **nach** Johannes	*the Gospel according to John*
der Karte **nach**	*according to the map*
nach dem Gesetz	*according to the law*

▶ 9.2.7 seit

a *since* or *for* (time up to now)

Ich **wohne** seit 1987 hier	*I've **been living** here since 1987*
Ich **kannte** sie seit sechs Wochen, als…	*I **had known** her for 6 weeks when…*

See Adverbs 6.1.4 for notes on *for* + time in German.

▶ 9.2.8 von

a *from* a place or person

eine Email **von** meinem Bruder	*an email from my brother*
der Zug **von** Hamburg nach Berlin	*the train from Hamburg to Berlin*
Mein Haus ist nur zehn Minuten **von** der Schule	*My house is only ten minutes from the school*

b *from* a time – often with an

von Montag/diesem Zeitpunkt **an**	*from Monday/this point onwards*
von Montag bis Freitag	*from Monday to Friday*

c *of*

der Vater **von** drei Kindern	*the father of three children*
einer **von** ihnen	*one of them*
eine Art **von** Tier	*a sort of animal*
ein Gedicht **von** Goethe	*a poem by Goethe/of Goethe's*
Das war sehr nett **von** dir	*That was very nice of you*

d von often replaces the genitive to express the possessive *of*, especially in spoken German (see also Cases 1.1.4)

das Auto **von** meinem Vater (= das Auto meines Vaters)	*my father's car*

e *by* with the passive – (see 15.1.2)

Die Stadt wurde **von** den Römern gegründet	*The city was founded by the Romans*

f Idiomatic phrases with von – a selection

von mir aus	*as far as I'm concerned/if you like*
Er ist Ingenieur **von** Beruf	*He's an engineer by profession*
Ich kenne ihn nur **vom** Sehen	*I only know him by sight*
Von der Form her finde ich es schön	*From the shape I think it's beautiful*
von wegen! (colloq.)	*no way!*

• Genitive prepositions are sometimes also used with von + dative (see 9.4.5).

▶ 9.2.9 zu

a *to* a place, person or event

Kommen Sie **zu** uns!	*Come to our house!*
Wie komme ich **zum** Bahnhof?	*How do I get to the station?*
Sie geht **zu** ihrem Vater	*She goes to her father*
von Tag zu Tag	*from day to day*
Komm **zu** meiner Party!	*Come to my party!*

b *at* + time (festival, or with Zeit or Mal)

zu Ostern, **zu** Weihnachten	*at/for Christmas, Easter*
zu dieser Zeit, **zur** Zeit	*at that time/at the moment*
zum ersten Mal	*for the first time*
zu Bismarcks Zeiten	*in Bismarck's day*

c *for* **a purpose, often used with an infinitive noun (compare with bei above)**

Zum Geburtstag hat sie mir ein Buch geschenkt	*For my birthday she gave me a book*
Hast du etwas **zum** Lesen?	*Have you got anything to read?*
Haben wir Zeit **zum** Einkaufen?	*Have we got time to go shopping?*

d Idiomatic uses of zu – a selection

Ich habe schon **zu** Mittag/**zu** Abend gegessen	*I've already had lunch/dinner*
zum Frühstück	*for breakfast*
Sie haben drei **zu** null gewonnen	*They won 3:0*
5 Briefmarken **zu** 90 Cent	*5 90-cent stamps*
zu Fuß	*on foot*
zu Hause	*at home*
zu Ende sein	*to finish, end*
zum Beispiel	*for example*
zum Sonderpreis	*at a special price*

▶ 9.2.10 Less common prepositions which take the dative

a ab *from ... onwards*

ab dem 1. Januar/**ab** neun Uhr	*from 1 January/from 9 o'clock onwards*

b dank *thanks to*

dank dem Computer	*thanks to the computer*

♦ dank is usually used with genitive if the following noun is plural:

dank seiner Computerkenntnisse	*thanks to his computer skills*

c entgegen *'contrary to'*

♦ entgegen occasionally follows the noun:

entgegen aller Wahrscheinlichkeit	*against the odds*
entgegen der akzeptierten Ansicht	*contrary to accepted opinion*
entgegen seinem Wunsch/ seinem Wunsch **entgegen**	*against his wishes*

d gemäß, laut, zufolge *according to*

♦ These prepositions are more or less interchangeable, though each has a slightly different emphasis, which may be deduced from the word itself:

gemäß	*'in accordance with'* instructions, the law, etc.; usually follows the noun
laut	*'according to what has been stated by'*; usually used without an article, but often followed by genitive if there is an article or adjective
zufolge	indicates a consequence; follows the noun

den Richtlinien **gemäß**	*in accordance with the guidelines*
laut Gesetz	*according to the law*
laut amtlicher Mitteilung	*according to the official report*
Einem Gerücht **zufolge** hat er das Land verlassen	*According to a rumour he's left the country*

e zuliebe *for the sake of*

+ zuliebe follows the noun:

Meinem Bruder zuliebe bin ich zu Hause geblieben	*I stayed at home for my brother's sake*

9.3 Prepositions followed by the accusative or dative

an	*at, to, by, on (up against)*	über	*above, via*
auf	*on (top of)*	unter	*under, among*
hinter	*behind*	vor	*in front of, before, ago*
in	*in, into*	zwischen	*between*
neben	*next to, near*		

+ *Accusative* indicates **movement forward, towards:**

Ich gehe in **die** Stadt	*I'm going into town*

+ *Dative* indicates **where something is or is happening:**

Ich arbeite in **der** Stadt	*I work in town*

Note The important thing is to decide how the motion of one noun relates to the movement of the other.

Accusative	*Dative*
Wir gehen in **den** Wald	*We're going into the forest*
Wir gehen **im** Wald spazieren	*We're going for a walk in the forest*
Der Hubschrauber flog über **die** Stadt	*The helicopter flew over the town* (...on its way to somewhere else)
Der Hubschrauber flog über **der** Stadt	*The helicopter was flying above the town* (... hovering or searching)

▶ 9.3.1 an

a *to, on* the side of/edge of	*on, at* the side of/by edge of
Er hängt das Poster **an** die Wand	Das Poster hängt **an** der Wand
He hangs the poster on the wall	*The poster is hanging on the wall*
Ich gehe **an** die Haltestelle	Ich warte **an** der Haltestelle
I go to the bus-stop	*I wait at the bus-stop*
Wir fahren **an** die Küste	das Licht **an** dem Auto
We're going to the sea-side	*the light on the car*
Sie setzte sich **an** den Kamin	Frankfurt **am** Main
She sat down by the fire	*Frankfurt on (the River) Main*
	am Stadtrand, **an** der Grenze
	on the edge of town, on the border

Accusative	Dative

Note The choice of case is usually, but not always, as obvious as one might think:

Sie klopfte **an** die Tür
She knocked at the door

b on, in days or part of days

am Montag	*on Monday*
am Abend	*in the evening*
am 1. Mai	*on 1 May*
am Wochenende	*at the weekend*
***But* in** der Nacht	*in the night*

c Idiomatic uses of an

Ich habe eine Bitte **an** Sie
I have a request to make of you
viele Grüße **an** deine Eltern
best wishes to your parents

Ich arbeite **am** Computer/**an** einem Projekt
I'm working at the computer/on a project
Du bist **an** dem Unfall schuld
The accident was your fault
das Interessante **an** dem Buch
The interesting thing about the book
an Krebs sterben
to die of cancer

Note an (+ dat.) ... vorbei *past:*

Er fuhr **an** mir vorbei
He drove past me

9.3.2 auf

a *on (-to, top of)* horizontal surface	*on (top of)*

Er stellt die Flasche **auf** den Tisch
He puts the bottle on the table

Die Flasche steht **auf** dem Tisch
The bottle is standing on the table

b Idiomatic uses of auf – a small selection

auf das Land
into the country
auf die Toilette gehen
to go to the toilet
mit Blick **auf** den Fluß
with a view of the river
auf den ersten Blick
at first sight
auf diese Weise
in this way, that's how
auf jeden Fall
in any case, anyhow
eine Antwort **auf** die Frage
an answer to the question
ich bin stolz **auf** ihn
I'm proud of him

auf dem Land
in the country
auf Deutsch
in German
auf dem Bild siehst du...
in the picture you can see...

Accusative	*Dative*

Note auf (+ acc.) ... zu *towards, up to*:
Er kam **auf** mich zu
  He came up to me

9.3.3 hinter

a *behind*	*behind*
Er lief **hinter** das Haus	Der Garten ist **hinter** dem Haus
He ran behind the house	*The garden is behind the house*
	Er lebt **hinter** dem Mond
	He's behind the times

9.3.4 in

a *in(-to)*	*in*
Er geht **ins** Haus	Er sitzt **im** Haus
'*He goes into the house*	*He's sitting in the house*
Tu das Geschirr **in** den Schrank!	Das Geschirr ist **im** Schrank
Put the crockery in(-to) the	*The crockery is in the cupboard*
cupboard	
Wir gehen **ins** Theater/Kino	**in** der Schule/Kirche, **im** Kino
We're going to the theatre,	*in school, in church, in the*
cinema	*cinema*
Ich muss **in** die Schule gehen	
I have to go to school	

b *to* **feminine or plural countries**	*in* **feminine or plural countries**
in die Schweiz, **in** die USA	**in** der Schweiz, **in** den USA

c **Idiomatic uses – a selection**

Wir fahren **ins** Ausland	Wir leben **im** Ausland
We're going abroad	*We live abroad*
Er verliebte sich **in** sie	**im** Fernsehen
He fell in love with her	*on television*
Was ist **in** dich gefahren?	Meine Wohnung ist **im** ersten Stock
What's got into you?	*My flat is on the first floor*
	in der Nähe
	near(-by), in the vicinity
	im Freien
	in the open air
	2000 Euro **im** Monat
	2000 Euros a month
	Er kommt um 8 Uhr **im** Büro an
	He arrives at the office at 8
	im Gegenteil
	on the contrary
	im Moment
	at the moment
	heute **in** drei Wochen
	three weeks today

Accusative	*Dative*

▶ 9.3.5 neben

a *next to*	*next to*
Ich setzte mich **neben** sie	Ich saß **neben** ihr
I sat down next to her	*I was sitting next to her*
	Er ging **neben** mir (her)
	He walked along next to me

b apart from, compared to

Neben Geld braucht man auch Zeit
Apart from money you also need time
Neben dir bin ich ganz intelligent
Compared to you I'm quite intelligent

▶ 9.3.6 über

a *over, above, across*	*over, above*
Ich hänge das Bild **über** das Bett	Das Bild hängt **über** dem Bett
I'm hanging the picture above the bed	*The picture is hanging above the bed*
Ich gehe **über** den Marktplatz	ein Gewitter **über** den Bergen
I'm going across the market place	*a storm over the mountains*

b about, concerning

ein Film **über** den Präsidenten
a film about the president

c over, more than

Kinder **über** 16 Jahre
children over the age of 16
Es kostet **über** 2000 Euro
It costs over 2000 Euros
Sie lebt **über** ihre Verhältnisse
She lives beyond her means

d by way of, via

Wir fahren **über** Leipzig nach Dresden
We're going to Dresden via Leipzig

▶ 9.3.7 unter

a *under, below*	*under(neath), below*
Er fährt **unter** die Brücke	Er steht **unter** der Brücke
He drives under the bridge	*He's standing under the bridge*
	unter dieser Regierung
	under this government
	unter britischer Flagge
	under the/a British flag

Accusative	*Dative*

	b *'among'*
	einer **unter** vielen Bewerbungen
	one among many applications
	unter anderem (often shortened to u.a.)
	among other things
	unter Freunden
	among friends

▷ 9.3.8 vor

a *in front of, outside*	*in front of, ahead of, outside*
Er trat **vor** die Tür	Sie wartete **vor** dem Kino
He stepped outside (the door)	*She waited outside the cinema*
Er stelite das Glas vor mich hin	**Vor** uns war ein Stau
He put the glass down in front	*Ahead of us there was a*
of me	*traffic jam*
	vor allem
	above all
	b *ago, before*
	vor zehn Jahren
	ten years ago
	vor den Ferien
	before the holidays
	vor Christus (v.Chr.)
	before Christ (BC)
	Es ist zehn **vor** eins
	It's ten to one (time)
	c *because of, due to*
	Er zitterte **vor** Kälte
	Ich habe Angst **vor** Hunden
Note **vor** sich (acc.) hin *'to oneself'*	
Ich singe oft **vor** mich **hin**	
I often sing to myself	
Er träumt **vor** sich **hin**	
He's day-dreaming	

▷ 9.3.9 zwischen

a *between*	*between*
Sie setzte sich **zwischen** ihre Freunde	Sie sitzt **zwischen** ihren Freunden
She sat down between her friends	*She's sitting between her friends*
	zwischen April und Oktober
	between April and October

9.4 Prepositions followed by the genitive

The many prepositions which take the genitive can conveniently be divided into three groups:

+ The four common prepositions (9.4.1).
+ Several others which denote position (9.4.2).
+ Others which are used only in formal language (9.4.3).

▶ 9.4.1 Four common prepositions followed by the genitive

statt/anstatt	*instead of*	wegen	*because of*
trotz	*in spite of*	während	*during*

+ The genitive is almost always used in written or formal German with these prepositions; in colloquial language they are often followed by the dative.

a statt *instead of* (anstatt is more formal)

Statt meines Bruders sah ich meinen Vater	*Instead of my brother I saw my father*
Er trägt eine Jacke **statt** eines Pullovers	*He's wearing a jacket instead of a jersey*

Note the adverb stattdessen *instead of that.*

+ If there is no determiner before a masculine or neuter noun after statt, the normal genitive –s ending is not added to the noun:

Wir trinken alle Bier **statt** Wein	*We're all drinking beer instead of wine*

+ statt is often used to join two noun phrases with the meaning 'and not...'. It is then <u>not</u> followed by the genitive; the second noun phrase is in the same case as the first:

Ich habe meinen Bruder **statt** meinen Vater besucht	*I visited my brother instead of my father*
Wir kaufen Fleisch beim Metzger **statt** im Supermarkt	*We buy meat at the butcher's instead of at the supermarket*

b trotz *in spite of, despite*

trotz des furchtbaren Wetters	*in spite of the terrible weather*
trotz aller Versuche	*despite all attempts*

Note trotz is often followed by the dative in southern Germany, Austria and Switzerland; elsewhere the dative is found in expressions such as

trotzdem	*nevertheless*
trotz allem/alledem	*in spite of everything*

c während *during*

während der Sommerferien	*during the summer holidays*
während des Krieges	*during the war*

d wegen *because of, due to*

wegen des schlechten Wetters	*because of the bad weather*

+ wegen is often followed by the dative if the noun stands alone, but if there is an accompanying article or adjective the genitive is considered better style:

wegen Umbau/Umbaus geschlossen	*closed for renovation*
wegen des kompletten Umbaus geschlossen	*closed for complete renovation*

- A pronoun after **wegen** is often in the dative, especially in spoken German, even though there is a genitive form

wegen dir/deinetwegen	*because of you, for your sake*
wegen mir/meinetwegen	*for my sake/as far as I'm concerned*
meinetwegen!	*If you like!*

Note The other forms of the genitive pronoun are:

seinetwegen	*because of him, for his sake, on his account*
ihretwegen	*because of her, etc.*
unseretwegen	*because of us, etc.*
euretwegen	*because of you, etc.*
ihretwegen	*because of them, etc.*
Ihretwegen	*because of you, etc.*

9.4.2 Prepositions denoting position followed by the genitive

außerhalb/innerhalb	*outside/inside*
oberhalb/unterhalb	*above/below*
diesseits/jenseits	*on this/the other side of*
beiderseits	*on both sides*
unweit	*not far from*

Ich wohne etwas **außerhalb** des Dorfes	*I live just outside the village*
Außerhalb der Saison ist es billiger	*Outside the holiday season it's cheaper*
jenseits des Flusses	*across/on the other side of the river*
beiderseits der Grenze	*on both sides of the border*
innerhalb der nächsten 10 Jahre	*within the next ten years*
unweit Münchens	*not far from Munich*

Note This group of prepositions is often used with **von** + dative.

unweit von München	*not far from Munich*
innerhalb von zwei Wochen	*within two weeks*
Jenseits von *Gut und Böse*	*Beyond Good and Evil* (title of book by Nietzsche)

9.4.3 Prepositions followed by the genitive which occur only in formal language

These are found only in official or formal (usually written) German. A selection of the most common is given here – there are many others.

angesichts	*in view of*	halber	*for the sake of*
anhand	*with the aid of*	hinsichtlich	*with regard to*
anlässlich	*on the occasion of*	seitens	*on the part of*
aufgrund	*on the basis of*	um … willen	*for the sake of*
dank	*thanks to*		

angesichts der aktuellen Situation	*in view of the current situation*
anhand eines Skizzes	*with the aid of a sketch*
anlässlich unseres Firmenjubiläums	*on the occasion of our company's anniversary*
aufgrund der zu hohen Kosten	*due to excessive costs*
dank seiner Computerkenntnisse	*thanks to his knowledge of computers*
der Fairness **halber**	*for the sake of fairness*
seine Entscheidung **hinsichtlich** dieser Sache	*his decision regarding this matter*
Beschwerden **seitens** des Kunden	*complaints on the part of the customer*
um der Klarheit **willen**	*for the sake of clarity*

9.5 The translation of *to* with places, countries and people

▶ **9.5.1** *to* + places, buildings, events

▶ **TIP**   **The prepositions for *to* with places**
  . The notes in 9.5.1a–d may be summarised as follows:
    + **in** if *into* is implied
    + **zu** general movement to or towards (sometimes auf)
    + **an** *up to*
  See also *to* countries and geographical regions in 9.5.2.

---

a in
The emphasis is on going ***into*** the place (not just *to* it):

Ich gehe **ins** Kino, **in** die Kirche	*I'm going to the cinema, to church*
in die, Schule, **in** die Stadt	*to school, to town*
in die Bäckerei	*to the baker's*
in ein Konzert	*to a concert*

Note After arrival, in + dative is used for *at/in*:

Wir waren **in** einem Konzert	*We were at a concert*
Das haben wir **in** der Schule gelernt	*We did that at school*

b zu
  . The emphasis is on **direction or going *to*** the place (not necessarily *into* it).
  . Note that zu is also sometimes used as a synonym of in + accusative:

Ich gehe **zur** Kirche	*I'm going to the church*
Fährt dieser Bus **zum** Rathaus?	*Does this bus go to the town hall?*
Ich gehe **zur** Bäckerei, **zu** einem Konzert, **zu** einer Party	*I'm going to the baker's, to a concert, to a party*

♦ **to** a person, or somebody's house or place:

Kommst du heute Abend **zu** uns? — *Would you like to come to our house this evening?*

Als ich bei meinem Bruder war, sind wir **zu** seiner Freundin gegangen — *While I was staying with my brother, we went to his girl-friend's house*

Note After arrival, bei + dative is used for 'at':

Er ist **bei** seiner Freundin — *He's at his girlfriend's house*

♦ **to** public buildings:

Ich gehe **zum** Bahnhof, **zum** Postamt — *I'm going to the station, to the post office*

Note After arrival, use auf + dative for *at*:

Ich begegnete ihm auf dem Bahnhof — *I met him at the station*

c auf

♦ **auf** is sometimes used instead of zu in more formal registers:

Ich gehe **auf** eine Party, **auf** die Post — *I'm going to a party, to the post office*

♦ **auf** is used in a small number of set phrases:

Wir fahren **aufs** Land, **auf** die Straße, **auf** die Jagd — *We're going into the country, on to the street, hunting*

Note After arrival, use auf + dative for '*in*', '*on*':

Wir wohnen **auf** dem Land — *We live in the country*

Sie spielen **auf** der Strasse — *They're playing in the street*

d an

♦ **up to**

Ich gehe **an** die Haltestelle, **an** das Fenster, **an** die Tür, **ans** Meer, **an** die Grenze — *I go to the bus-stop, to the window, to the door, to the sea, to the border*

Note After arrival, an + dative is used for *at*:

Ich warte **an** der Haltestelle — *I wait at the bus-stop*

ein Haus **am** Meer — *a house at (or by) the sea*

9.5.2 *to* + countries, geographical regions, etc.

a nach

♦ Continents, countries, towns, etc. are used **without an article**:

Wir fahren **nach** Afrika, **nach** Deutschland, **nach** Flensburg — *We're going to Africa, to Germany, to Flensburg*

nach Norden — *to the north /northwards*

b in

♦ Countries and regions are used **with an article**:

Wir fahren **in** die Schweiz, **in** die USA, **in** die Bretagne — *We're going to Switzerland, to the USA, to Brittany*

in den Schwarzwald, **in** die Alpen — *to the Black Forest, to the Alps*

Note 1 With other geographical names, other prepositions may be found:

an den Bodensee, **an** den Rhein   *to Lake Constance, to the Rhine*

Note 2 After arrival at or in the place, the preposition will be used with the dative:

in der Schweiz, **in** den USA   *in Switzerland, in the USA*

am Bodensee   *by Lake Constance*

9.5.3 *to* + people

a Dative case or an + accusative (indirect object)

Ich schicke **meinem** Vater eine Email }   *I'm sending an email to my father*
Ich schicke eine Email **an** meinen Vater }

b After geben, the dative must be used for *to*

Ich gebe **meinem** Vater ein Geschenk   *I give my father a present*

+ For 'to someone('s house)', see 9.5.1b above.

9.6 Contraction of prepositions with the definite article

Some prepositions may contract to a single word with certain forms of the definite article.

9.6.1 Prepositions which contract

a Prepositions which contract with certain forms of the definite article are

an das > **ans**	von dem > **vom**
an dem > **am**	zu dem > **zum**
bei dem > **beim**	zu der > **zur**
in das > **ins**	
in dem > **im**	

im Moment, **im** Büro, **ins** Haus, **zur** Schule, **am** Samstag, **zur** Zeit

b Where stress or emphasis is required, the preposition and article are not contracted

In dem Moment, als ich ihn   *Just at the moment when I saw*
  sah, …   *him…*

In dem Haus, wo wir jetzt   *In the house where we now live, …*
  wohnen, …

c Other contractions are possible, found mostly in spoken German

auf das > **aufs**		
durch das > **durchs**		
hinter den > **hintern**		hinter dem > **hinterm**
über den > **übern**	über das > **übers**	über dem > **überm**
um das > **ums**		
unter den > **untern**	unter das > **unters**	unter dem > **unterm**
außer dem > **außerm**		
vor dem > **vorm**		

Er kletterte **durchs** Fenster   *He climbed through the window*
Sie ist **ums** Leben gekommen   *She lost her life*
Du lebst ja **hinterm** Mond!   *You're really behind the times!*
Unterm Birnbaum   *Under the Pear-Tree* (title of a
        novel by Fontane)

10

Verbs: the indicative tenses – formation

OVERVIEW

What is a verb?

+ A verb is a word that expresses the 'action' of the sentence or clause; it may indicate a state or process:

  He **ate** dinner; then, because it **was getting** late and he **was** tired, he **fell** asleep

Infinitives and finite verbs

+ The **infinitive** is the basic, dictionary form of the verb.
+ In English, it is usually preceded by *to*; in German, it ends with -en or -n:

  kaufen *to buy*   sammeln *to collect*

+ A **finite verb** is one which is in a particular past, present or future tense:

  ich kaufe *I buy*   ich kaufte *I bought*   ich habe gekauft *I (have) bought*

Types of verb

The five categories of German verbs are almost identical to those found in English. This chapter deals with the first two.

+ **Weak verbs**: only the endings change. Most verbs fall into this category, e.g.

  er öffn**et** *he opens*   ich öffn**ete** *I opened*

+ **Strong verbs** change their endings, and frequently their stem vowels; as these changes happen in predictable patterns, they are not classed as irregular verbs, e.g.

  ich schwimm**e** *I swim*   ich schw**a**mm *I swam*
  ich sing**e** *I sing*   ich s**a**ng *I sang*

+ **Mixed verbs** (all with stems end in **-nn-** or **-nd-**): weak verb endings, but the stem vowel changes like strong verbs See 12.1 e.g.

  er kenn**t**   *he knows*   er k**a**nn**te** *he knew*

+ **Modal verbs** indicate something of the 'mood' or attitude of the speaker to the main verb. The main verb is always in the infinitive. There are six modal verbs: dürfen, können, mögen, müssen, sollen and wollen (see 12.2).

  Du **solltest** Deutsch lernen   *You should learn German*
  Du **kannst** Deutsch lernen   *You can learn German*

> • **Irregular verbs** are 'one-off' verbs: there are about fourteen of these, depending on how they are categorised. Apart from parts of sein, they all use weak or strong verb tense endings; many parts of these verbs are regular, e.g.
>
> | | | | |
> |---|---|---|---|
> | gehen *to go* | er geht | er ging | er ist gegangen |
> | werden *to become* | ich werde | du wirst | du bist geworden |
>
> ▸ **Tenses**
>
> This chapter deals with tenses of the **indicative** mood; these indicate an action that really happens or is likely to happen. See also Imperative (Chapter 16) and Subjunctive (Chapter 17).

▸ **TIP** **Transitive and intransitive verbs**
   • All verbs are either **transitive** (they take a direct object) or **intransitive** (they have no direct object). Often, verbs can be used in either way without any change in form, but sometimes a different form or verb is required (see 12.5).
   • **Transitive**

Ich **esse** Schokolade	*I eat chocolate*
Ich **wecke** meine Schwester	*I wake my sister up*

   • **Intransitive**

Ich **esse** in guten Restaurants	*I eat in good restaurants*
Ich **wache** um 7 Uhr **auf**	*I wake up at 7.00*

   • When using a dictionary, check which type of verb is required in your sentence – this can save time. Transitive verbs are marked VT, and intransitive VI. Verbs that can be used transitively or intransitively are marked VTI.

10.1 The present tense

▸ **10.1.1 Weak verbs**

a Formation of the present tense

> **Present tense – weak verbs**
>
> • Add these endings to the stem of the infinitive
>
> **sagen *to say***
>
> | | | | |
> |---|---|---|---|
> | ich | sag**e** | wir | sag**en** |
> | du | sag**st** | ihr | sag**t** |
> | er/sie es sag**t** | | sie/Sie sag**en** | |

b Irregularities
There are a few, slight irregularities in the formation of the present tense of weak verbs, mostly to enable the word to be pronounced clearly.

+ Stems which end in **-t, -d** (or **-m, -n** after a consonant) add an **-e** before the **-st** and **-t** endings, e.g. warten *to wait*:

ich	warte	wir	warten
du	wartest	ihr	wartet
er/sie/es	wartet	sie/Sie	warten

Compare this with the rule for strong verbs whose stems end similarly in 10.1.2b below.

Other verbs like warten include:

abtrocknen	*to dry up*	mieten	*to hire, rent*
arbeiten	*to work*	öffnen	*to open*
antworten	*to answer*	ordnen	*to put in order*
atmen	*to breathe*	rechnen	*to calculate*
baden	*to have a bath/to bathe*	reden	*to speak, talk*
bedeuten	*to mean*	retten	*to rescue*
bilden	*to form*	richten	*to judge*
dichten	*to write poetry*	schaden	*to harm, damage*
fürchten	*to fear*	töten	*to kill*
heiraten	*to get married*	trösten	*to comfort/console*
kosten	*to cost*	zeichnen	*to draw*

+ Stems which end in **-el** or **-er** (i.e. verbs whose infinitive ends with **-n**) have wir and sie/Sie forms ending in **-n** . This follows the pattern that the wir and sie forms are identical with the infinitive for all verbs. The ich form always loses the -e- of the stem with **-el** stem verbs, and sometimes with **-er** stem verbs, e.g. segeln *to sail:*

ich	segle	wir	segeln
du	segelst	ihr	segelt
er/sie/es	segelt	sie/Sie	segeln

Other verbs include:

bummeln	*to wander, stroll*	sammeln	*to collect*
handeln	*to act, bargain*	schütteln	*to shake*
klingeln	*to ring*	wechseln	*to change*
lächeln	*to smile*		

Note Verbs which end with **-ern** generally keep the -e- before the ending in the ich form. Ich wand**e**re (I like, go walking) is the normal form, rather than ich wandre.

Other verbs like wandern include:

ändern	*to change*	rudern	*to row (a boat)*	zittern	*to shiver*

+ Stems which end with **-s, -ss/ß, -x, -z,** drop the **-s-** from the **du -st** ending. This rule also applies to strong verbs (see 10.1.3b).

putzen *to clean* – du putzt (**not** du putzst)	lösen (*to solve*) – du löst
faxen (*to fax*) – du faxt	rasen (*to race*) – du rast
grüßen (*to greet*) – du grüßt	setzen (*to put*) – du setzt
küssen (*to kiss*) – du küsst	tanzen (*to dance*) – du tanzt

▶ 10.1.2 Strong verbs

a Formation of the present tense

+ Weak and strong verbs both take the same endings in the present tense. The only real differences between weak and strong verbs in the present tense concern strong verbs with -a- or -e- in the stem.
+ In the **du** and **er** forms only, strong verbs undergo the following changes:
  + Stem vowel -a- changes to -ä-
  + Stem vowel -e- changes to -ie- or -i-

Note Other vowels do not change.

Present tense – strong verbs singular		
a > ä: fahren *to go*	**e>i** geben *to give*	**e > ie** sehen *to see*
ich fahre	ich gebe	ich sehe
du fähr**st**	du gib**st**	du sieh**st**
er/sie/es fähr**t**	er/sie/es gib**t**	er/sie/es sieh**t**

a > ä

fallen (*to fall*) – er fällt	schlafen (*to sleep*) – er schläft
fangen (*to catch*) – er fängt	tragen (*to wear, carry*) – er trägt
laufen (*to run*) – er läuft	waschen (*to wash*) – er wäscht

e > i

helfen (*to help*) – er hilft	**e > ie**
nehmen (*to take*) – er nimmt	lesen (*to read*) – er liest
sprechen (*to speak*) – er spricht	stehlen (*to steal*) – er stiehlt
treffen (*to meet*) – er trifft	empfehlen (*to recommend*) – er empfiehlt
werfen (*to throw*) – er wirft	geschehen (*to happen*) – es geschieht

b Irregularities

+ Stems which end with **-t** or **-d** add an **-e-** before **-st** or **-t** endings, but *only* if the stem vowel does not change:

halten (*to hold*) – du hältst, er hält	**but** ihr haltet
laden (*to load*) – du lädst, er lädt	**but** ihr ladet
raten (*to advise*) – du rätst, er rät	**but** ihr ratet
treten (*to tread, kick*) – du trittst, er tritt	**but** ihr tretet

+ Stems which end with **-s, -ss/ß, -z** drop **-s** from the **du -st** ending. (The same rule applies to weak verbs; see 10.1.1b above.)

     lesen (*to read*) – du liest (**not** du liesst)

Similarly

beißen (*to bite*) – du beißt	lassen (*to let*) – du lässt
essen (*to eat*) – du isst	sitzen (*to be sitting*) – du sitzt
gießen (*to pour*) – du gießt	vergessen (*to forget*) – du vergisst
heißen (*to be called*) – du heißt	

> **TIP**   **Present tense endings common to all verbs**
> - These patterns for the present tense apply to all verbs except sein:
>   - The **wir** and **sie/Sie** forms of the verb are always the same as the infinitive.
>   - The **ich** form of the verb is always the infinitive less **-n** (except with modal verbs and verbs which end with **-eln** or **-ern**; see 10.1.2b).

- For modal verbs see 12.2.2a.
- For mixed verbs see 12.1.
- For irregular verbs see 12.4.

10.2 The simple past tense

▶ 10.2.1 Weak verbs

a Formation of the simple past tense

Simple past – weak verbs
• To the stem of the infinitive, add these endings

sagen   *to say*

ich sag**te**	wir sag**ten**
du sag**test**	ihr sag**tet**
er/sie/es sag**te**	sie/Sie sag**ten**

b Irregularities
- Stems which end in **-t, -d** or **-m, -n** after a consonant add **-e** before the simple past tense ending:

arbeiten	*to work*	ich arbeit**e**te, du arbeit**e**test, ihr arbeit**e**tet
öffnen	*to open*	ich öffn**e**te, er öffn**e**te, wir öffn**e**ten
reden	*to speak*	ich red**e**te, du red**e**test, sie red**e**ten

Note Stems which end in **-el** or **-er** (i.e. those with infinitives ending in -n) do not require an extra -e-:

| segeln | *to sail* | ich segel**te** |
| wandern | *to hike, go walking* | er wander**te** |

▶ 10.2.2 Strong verbs

a Formation of the simple past tense

Simple past – strong verbs
• The following endings are added to the stem of the infinitive.
• The stem vowel always changes from the infinitive, and does so in all persons.

fahren   *to go, travel*

ich fuhr	wir fuhr**en**
du fuhr**st**	ihr fuhr**t**
er/sie/es fuhr	sie/Sie fuhr**en**

. The patterns of stem vowel changes for the simple past tense and perfect tenses.

Infinitive	Present	Past	Perfect	Examples
a	ä	u	a	tragen: trägt – trug – hat getragen
	ä	i	a	fangen: fängt – fing – hat gefangen
	ä	ie	a	halten: hält – hielt – hat gehalten
e	i	a	e	geben: gibt – gab – hat gegeben
	ie	a	e	sehen: sieht – sah – hat gesehen
	i	a	o	helfen: hilft – half – hat geholfen
	ie	a	o	stehlen: stiehlt – stahl – hat gestohlen
ei	ei	ie	ie	steigen: steigt – stieg – ist gestiegen
	ei	i	i	beißen: beißt – biss – hat gebissen
i	i	a	u	singen: singt – sang – hat gesungen
	i	a	o	brechen: bricht – brach – hat gebrochen
ie	ie	o	o	bieten: bietet – bot – hat geboten

b Irregularities

. Strong verbs never add -e- before the simple past tense endings, even those which do so in the present tense; this follows the rule that -e- can be added only if the stem vowel does <u>not</u> change.

halten *to hold*	du hieltst, ihr hielt
laden *to load*	du ludst, ihr ludt
raten *to advise, guess*	du rietst, ihr riet
treten *to tread*	du tratst, ihr trat

. Stems ending in -s, -ss/ß or -z lose an -s- in the du form:

beißen *to bite*	du bisst (not du bissst)
lesen *to read*	du last
lassen *to leave*	du ließt
sitzen *to be sitting*	du saßt

. For modal verbs see 12.2.2b.
. For mixed verbs see 12.1.
. For irregular verbs see 12.4.

10.3 The perfect tense

▶ 10.3.1 Formation

. The perfect tense is formed from part of the present tense of haben or sein plus the past participle of the main verb.
. The past participle is formed as follows:

Weak verbs: **ge-** + stem of the infinitive + **-t**
Strong verbs: **ge-** + stem of the infinitive (vowel may change) + **-en**

. With separable verbs, the **ge-** is placed between the prefix and the verb:

an**ge**kommen
ein**ge**reist
vor**ge**lesen

haben *or* sein		Past participle	
		Weak **ge-** *(stem)* **-t**	**Strong** **ge-** *(stem*)* **-en** *(*vowel may change)*
ich habe du hast er/sie/es hat	wir haben ihr habt sie/Sie haben	ge**arbeit**et ge**sag**t ge**wohn**t	ge**les**en ge**trag**en ge**trunk**en
ich bin du bist er/sie/es ist	wir sind ihr seid sie/Sie sind	ge**eil**t ge**reis**t ge**segel**t	ab**gefahr**en an**gekomm**en ge**flog**en

▷ 10.3.2 Irregularities in the formation of the past participle

a Weak verbs whose stem ends with -d-, -t- (or with -m- or -n- after a consonant) add an -e- before the final -t

Ich habe gearbeit**e**t	*I worked*
Er hat sehr lange gered**e**t	*He spoke for a long time*
Sie hat tief geatm**e**t	*She breathed deeply*
Sie hat gezeichn**e**t	*She drew*

b ge- is not added to the past participles of certain verbs

Note A characteristic shared by all of these verbs is that their initial syllable is unstressed in pronunciation.

♦ Verbs whose infinitive ends with **-ieren** (these verbs are all weak). The stress in pronunciation falls on **-ier-**:

e.g.	gratulieren *to congratulate*	hat … gratuliert
	organisieren *to organise*	hat … organisiert
	probieren *to try out*	hat … probiert
	reparieren *to repair*	hat … repariert
	reservieren *to reserve*	hat … reserviert
	studieren *to study*	hat … studiert
	Ich habe Plätze für heute Abend **reserviert**	

♦ Verbs with an inseparable prefix (see 19.5.2, 19.5.3) such as **be-, ver-, zer-, ent-**. These verbs may be weak or strong

e.g.	besprechen *to discuss*	hat … besprochen
	entkommen *to escape*	ist … entkommen
	übersetzen *to translate*	hat … übersetzt
	verkaufen *to sell*	hat … verkauft
	zerbrechen *to smash*	hat … zerbrochen

Note Unlike separable verbs, the first syllable of inseparable verbs is always pronounced unstressed (see 19.5.2a).

♦ A few other verbs which are foreign in origin:

prophezeien *to prophesy*	hat … prophezeit
recykeln *to recycle*	hat … recykelt

c hören, lassen and sehen use the infinitive as past participle when combined with another verb in the infinitive

Wir **haben** ihn abfahren **hören**	*We heard him leave*
Hast du ihn spielen **sehen**?	*Did you see him play?*

Ich **habe** mir die Haare schneiden lassen	*I had my hair cut*
Weil er sein Auto nicht **hatte** reparieren lassen, …	*Because he hadn't had his car repaired, …*

* Notice the position of the auxiliary hatte in the last example, where it is used with two infinitives (see 18.1.4b).

10.3.3 haben or sein as auxiliary?

Although the majority of verbs form the perfect tense with **haben**, a number of very common verbs do so using **sein**.

a sein is used only with verbs which are _both_ intransitive (i.e. have no direct object) _and_ describe movement or a change of state
* Verbs which describe **movement** towards a place:

aufstehen	Ich **bin** um Mittag **aufgestanden**	*I got up at midday*
fahren	Er **ist** mit dem Zug **gefahren**	*He went by train*
laufen	Wir **sind** sehr schnell **gelaufen**	*We ran very fast*
reisen	Sie **ist** um die Welt **gereist**	*She travelled round the world*

* Verbs which show **a change of state**:

sterben	Der König **ist** gestern **gestorben**	*The king died yesterday*
auftauen	Das Eis **ist** in der Sonne **aufgetaut**	*The ice melted in the sun*
werden	Sie **ist** alt **geworden**	*She has become old*
einschlafen	Ich **bin** erst um 3 **eingeschlafen**	*I didn't get to sleep until three*
verschwinden	Sie **sind** im Dschungel **verschwunden**	*They've disappeared in the jungle*

Note Some of the verbs above may also be used **transitively** (i.e. with a direct object). They then form the perfect tense with **haben**. Compare these examples:

fahren	Sie **ist** mit dem Auto **gefahren**	*She went by car*
	Sie **hat** das Auto **gefahren**	*She drove the car*
fliegen	Wir **sind** nach Basel **geflogen**	*We flew to Basel*
	Der Pilot **hat** das Flugzeug **geflogen**	*The pilot flew the plane*

b Some other common verbs also take sein, many indicating
happen, succeed, fail

begegnen *to meet (by chance)*	bleiben *to stay*
gedeihen *to prosper*	gelingen/missglücken *to succeed/fail*
geschehen *to happen*	glücken/missglücken *to succeed/fail*
passieren *to happen*	sein *to be*
vorkommen *to happen*	zustoßen *to happen*

Er **ist** oft deprimiert **gewesen**	*He's often been depressed*
Ich **bin** gestern zu Hause **geblieben**	*I stayed at home yesterday*
Sie **ist** ihm zufällig in der Stadt **begegnet**	*She met him in town quite by chance*

Der Garten **ist** bei der vielen Sonne **gediehen**	The garden flourished in all the sunshine
Wann **ist** der Unfall **passiert**?	When did the accident happen?
Der neue Roman **ist** dem Schriftsteller **gelungen/ misslungen**	The author's new novel did (not) turn out well

c **Compounds of gehen and werden continue to be used with sein, even if they have a direct object**

| durchgehen *to go over* | Der Lehrer **ist** den Aufsatz mit dem Schüler **durchgegangen** |
| loswerden *to get rid of* | Ich **bin** mein altes Auto endlich **losgeworden** |

d **All other verbs, both transitive and intransitive, use haben to form the perfect tense. This includes reflexive verbs**

anrufen	Ich **habe** meine Eltern **angerufen**	I phoned my parents
glauben	Ich **habe** kein Wort **geglaubt**	I didn't believe a word
sich verlaufen	Er **hat** sich in der Altstadt **verlaufen**	He got lost in the old town
sich waschen	Sie **hat** sich **gewaschen**	She had a wash
wohnen	Wir **haben** in einem bequemen Hotel **gewohnt**	We stayed in a comfortable hotel

> **TIP** **Verbs which take sein**
>
> • The German equivalents of all the French verbs which form the perfect tense with **être** (except reflexive verbs) take **sein**, e.g. abfahren (*partir*), ankommen (*arriver*), bleiben (*rester*), sterben (*mourir*), werden (*devenir*).
> • Like their French equivalents, they are all intransitive verbs denoting movement or change of state.
> • There are, of course, other verbs which take **sein** in German; see 10.3.3b above.

10.4 The pluperfect tense

▶ 10.4.1 Formation

• The pluperfect tense is formed in the same way as the perfect tense, but using the simple past of haben or sein with the past participle of the main verb (see 10.3.1 above).

haben *or* sein		Past participle	
		Weak ge- (*stem*) **-t**	**Strong** ge- (*stem**) **-en** (**vowel may change*)
ich hatte	wir hatten	ge**wohn**t	ge**trunk**en
du hattest	ihr hattet	ge**sag**t	ge**les**en
er/sie/es hatte	sie/Sie hatten	ge**arbeit**et	ge**trag**en

haben *or* sein		Past participle	
ich war	wir waren	ge**segel**t	ab**gefahr**en
du warst	ihr wart	ge**reis**t	ge**flog**en
er/sie/es war	sie/Sie waren		an**gekomm**en

- The rules governing the use of **haben** or **sein** with the pluperfect tense are exactly the same as for verbs in the perfect tense. (see 10.3.3 above).

10.5 The future tense

▶ 10.5.1 Formation

- The future tense is formed using **werden** + the infinitive.

werden		+	Infinitive
ich werde	wir werden	...	kaufen
du wirst	ihr werdet		segeln
er/sie/es wird	sie/Sie werden		abfahren

10.6 The future perfect tense

▶ 10.6.1 Formation

- The future perfect is formed using **werden** + past participle + **haben** or **sein**.

| Bis Montag **werde** ich das Buch **gelesen haben** | By Monday I will have read the book |
| Trotz des Nebels **wird** sie schon zu Hause angekommen sein | Despite the fog she will probably have arrived home by now |

Verbs: the indicative tenses – uses

OVERVIEW – TENSES, MOODS AND VOICES

▶ What is a 'tense'?

'Tense' is grammar terminology for 'time'. The tense of the verb indicates the time when the action takes place – in the past, the present or the future.

▶ Tenses in German

The main tenses in German are very similar in use to those in English. Note that whereas English has both simple ('I work') and continuous or progressive ('I am working') forms for all tenses, German has just the one form for each tense:

Present	ich arbeite	*I work/I am working*
Perfect	ich habe gearbeitet	*I worked/I have worked*
Simple past/ imperfect	ich arbeitete	*I have been working/I was working*
Pluperfect	ich hatte gearbeitet	*I had worked/I had been working*
Future	ich werde arbeiten	*I will work/I will be working*
Future perfect	ich werde gearbeitet haben	*I will have worked/I will have been working*

▶ 'Indicative' and 'subjunctive' moods

- 'Mood' relates to the attitude of the speaker to what is being said (as do 'modal' verbs and 'modal' particles). The tenses above are said to be in the 'indicative mood', used for statements and questions where the action is certain or probable.
- Some actions are mere wishes, or they express something which is unreal or dependent on a condition being fulfilled, or polite requests. These forms of the verb are said to be in the 'subjunctive' mood, e.g.

Conditional	Ich würde arbeiten, wenn …	*I would work if …*
	Könntest du mir helfen?	*Could you help me?*
Conditional perfect	Ich hätte gearbeitet	*I would have worked*

> ### 'Imperative' mood

. The third mood in both English and German is the 'imperative' mood – the form of the verb used when giving commands:

> Bleiben Sie hier! *Stay here!*

> ### 'Active' and 'passive' voices

. All the verb forms at the top of this page are in the 'active' voice, i.e. the subject carries out the action of the verb. In the 'passive' voice the subject of the verb becomes the object of the action:

| **Active** | Maria verkauft ihr Auto | *Maria is selling her car* |
| **Passive** | Das Auto wird verkauft | *The car is being sold* |

The subjunctive, imperative and passive are dealt with in Chapters 17, 16 and 15 respectively.

11.1 The present tense

11.1.1 Example

> ich fahre
>
> *I travel/I am travelling*
> *I will travel/will be travelling*

11.1.2 Uses

a Repeated, habitual actions in the present

| Ich **fahre** jeden Tag in die Stadt | *I go into town every day* |
| Ich **lese** immer *Die Welt* | *I always read* Die Welt |

b Actions that are taking place at the moment of speaking

Ich **suche** meine Schuhe	*I'm looking for my shoes*
Im Moment **wohnt** sie in Berlin	*At the moment she's living in Berlin*
Der Mann, der da drüben **steht**, ist …	*The man who's standing over there is …*

c Future actions

. In German, the present tense is the normal means of referring to the future, as long as the context makes the idea of the future clear, often by an adverb of time:

Morgen **fahre** ich nach Dresden	*Tomorrow I'm driving to Dresden*
Er **kommt** um 7 Uhr an	*He'll be arriving at 7*
Vielleicht **besuche** ich sie	*Perhaps I'll visit them*
Sehen wir uns in Leipzig?	*Shall we see one another in Leipzig?*

. Using the future tense when the context makes it possible to use the present tense is perfectly permissible; its use then emphasises the intention or prediction:

Morgen **werde** ich nach China **fahren**	*Tomorrow I'll be going to China*
Meinst du, es **wird** heute Abend **schneien**?	*Do you think it'll snow this evening?*
Ich **werde** euch bald **besuchen**!	*I'll certainly visit you soon!*

. For examples of when the future tense *must* be used, see 11.4.2a below.

d Actions which began in the past and are continuing at the moment of speaking

The verb is usually used with seit – *since/for*, seitdem – *since*, schon – *up to now*:

Ich **wohne** seit 2001 hier	*I've been living here since 2001*
Er **wartet** schon lange auf sie	*He's been waiting for her for ages*
Seitdem er zu Hause **ist**, **sieht** er die ganze Zeit fern	*Since he's been at home, he's watched TV all the time*

See also 6.1.4 (*for* with time phrases).

e In fiction and in newspaper headlines (as in English) to lend immediacy to the narrative

Weißer Hai **spuckt** Opfer wieder aus!	*White shark spits out victim!*
Ein Aufschrei **zerreißt** die Luft	*A scream rends the air*

> **TIP** **Continuous action in German –** *I am reading, I was reading*
>
> . There are no continuous or progressive tenses in German; the context normally makes it clear whether the action is continuous. However, to emphasise continuous action, an adverb such as gerade may be added, or gleich may be added to verbs of motion:
>
> | | |
> |---|---|
> | Sie liest **gerade** ein Buch | *She's just reading a book* |
> | Ich komme **gleich** | *I'm just coming* |
>
> . Alternatively, (gerade) dabei sein + zu + infinitive may be used:
>
> | | |
> |---|---|
> | Er **war gerade dabei**, zu Hause anzurufen | *He was just (in the process of) phoning home* |
>
> . A noun, often based on an infinitive, may also be used with beim (see 14.1.3a):
>
> | | |
> |---|---|
> | Sie ist **beim Lesen** | *She's reading* |

11.2 The perfect and simple past tenses

. In English, the perfect tense is used for past events which are linked to the present time, while the simple past is used for events which are fully in the past:

> *He's **had** an accident* (...and is in hospital)
> *He **had** an accident* (...but is now back at work)

. In German, however, the distinction is much less clear-cut, and the two tenses are often interchangeable. In fact, the tense used depends more on region (in the south, the perfect is used almost exclusively, in the north less so), style and even just simplicity of expression than on difference in meaning. German-speakers move from perfect to simple past, even within a single sentence. This principle must be borne in mind when consulting the following 'rules', which are denoted by context rather than tense.

▶ 11.2.1 Examples

ich habe gesehen
ich sah

$\left\{\begin{array}{l}\textit{I saw} \\ \textit{I have seen} \\ \textit{I have been seeing} \\ \textit{I did see}\end{array}\right.$

▶ 11.2.2 Uses of the simple past and perfect tenses

a Spoken German, personal letters, etc.

. The **perfect tense** is the main past tense, for events completely in the past as well as those linked to the present:

Gestern **habe** ich den neuen Film **gesehen**	*I saw the new film yesterday*
Hast du den Film **gesehen**?	*Have you seen the film?*
Jeden Tag **bin** ich ins Büro **gegangen**	*I went/used to go to the office every day*
Ich **habe** dir oft **gesagt**, du kannst uns zu jeder Zeit besuchen	*I've often told you that you can visit us any time you like*

. The **simple past** is, however, more often used with the auxiliaries (haben, sein, werden, and the modals, e.g. können, müssen):

Ich **war** letzte Woche in London	*I went to/was in London last week*
Er **hatte** viel Arbeit und **konnte** uns bisher nicht besuchen	*He's had a lot of work and has been unable to visit us up to now*
Er **musste** ganz schnell in die Stadt	*He's had to nip into town*
Die Firma **wurde** letztes Jahr verkauft	*The company was sold last year*
Die Straßen **wurden** erst vor kurzem repariert	*The roads have only recently been repaired*

. The **simple past** is often used in spoken German in other instances:
  - To describe a **state or repeated action in the past**:

Sie **lag** wie tot auf dem Boden	*She lay on the floor as if dead*
Als ich jung **war**, **ging** ich oft in den Park	*When I was little, I often went to the park*
Es **gab** noch viele, die das **glaubten**	*There were still many who believed that*
Damals **fuhr** ich mit dem Rad dorthin	*I used to go there by bike*

  - With **some common verbs**, e.g. gehen, kommen, sagen, stehen as well as the perfect, especially in north Germany. In southern Germany, the perfect tense is almost always preferred:

Sie **stand** vor dem Kino und hat auf ihn gewartet	*She stood outside the cinema and waited for him*

Or Sie **hat** vor dem Kino
   gestanden …
      Er **sagte** nichts mehr   *He said no more*
Or Er **hat** nichts mehr **gesagt**

b Printed material, literature, news media

. The **simple past** is the main tense for all verbs in narrative in books and other printed media:

Vor dem Kaufhaus **lief** Vater   *Outside the department store*
   bereits unruhig auf und ab,   *father was already pacing*
   stürzte auf uns zu, als er uns   *impatiently up and down; he*
   kommen **sah**, und **fragte**: …   *rushed up to us when he saw*
                                             us coming and asked: …

. The **perfect tense** is used with all verbs except haben, sein and modals for:

– events continuing up to the present (but see also notes on seit in Adverbs 6.1.4):

Es **hat** so viel **geregnet**, dass wir   *It's been raining so hard that*
   jetzt Überschwemmungen   *we've now got floods*
   haben

Bisher **habe** ich es **geschafft**,   *Up to now, I've managed to do*
   alles Notwendige zu erledigen   *everything necessary*

– events taking place in the immediate past:

In den letzten paar Monaten **hat**   *In the last few months the*
   der Bundeskanzler Amerika   *Chancellor has visited America*
   dreimal **besucht**   *three times*

In letzter Zeit **sind** die Preise stark   *Recently prices have risen sharply*
   gestiegen

– past events that are felt to have an effect on the present:

Die Regierung **hat** um   *The government has asked for*
   internationale Hilfe **gebeten**   *international aid*

– Newspaper reports often begin with the perfect tense, then continue in the simple past:

Bei einem Selbstmordanschlag auf   *According to police statements, at*
   ein Luxushotel **sind** nach   *least 60 people have been*
   Polizeiangaben mindestens 60   *killed in a suicide attack on a*
   Menschen **getötet worden.**   *luxury hotel. The Marriott Hotel*
   Das in Flammen stehende   *was ablaze and in danger of*
   Marriott-Hotel **drohte**   *collapse…*
   einzustürzen …

c Other uses of the simple past tense

. The simple past is used with **seit** to indicate an action which had started before another past event took place. In English the pluperfect would be used.

Er **wohnte** schon seit 10 Jahren in   *He had been living in our road for*
   unserer Straße, als wir ihn   *10 years when we first met him*
   kennen gelernt haben

See 6.1.4 (*for* in adverbs of time).

d Other uses of the perfect tense

. To indicate a state which has been achieved by a particular course of action:

Wer keine Karten mehr hat, **hat gewonnen**	*The player who has no more cards is the winner*

. See also **future perfect** (11.5.2 below).

11.3 The pluperfect tense

▶ 11.3.1 Example

ich hatte gesehen	*I had seen*
	I had been seeing

▶ 11.3.2 Use

+ **The pluperfect is used to describe an event which took place before some other past occurrence**

Als er ankam, **hatten** wir schon **gegessen**	*When he arrived, we had already eaten*
Ich habe ihn angerufen, aber er **war** um 9 Uhr **abgefahren**	*I phoned him, but he had left at 9 o'clock*

11.4 The future tense

▶ 11.4.1 Example

ich werde fahren	*I will travel*
	I will be travelling
	I am going to travel

▶ 11.4.2 Use

a **The future tense is used to make it quite clear that an action will take place in the future. It must be used where the present tense would lead to ambiguity**

Das **werde** ich nie **vergessen**!	*That's something I'll never forget!*
Weißt du, dass sie in London **arbeiten wird**?	*Did you know she'll be working in London?*

b **The future tense is used to emphasise the intention or prediction of the speaker**

Meinst du, es **wird** heute abend **regnen**?	*Do you think it'll rain this evening?*
Ich **werde** euch bald **besuchen**!	*I'll certainly visit you soon!*
Wir **werden** uns bestimmt **wiedersehen!**	*We'll certainly meet again!*

c **The future tense is often replaced by the present tense as long as the context makes it clear that the future is being referred to (see present tense 11.1.2c above)**

11.5 The future perfect tense

▶ **11.5.1** Example

Er wird angekommen sein   *He will have arrived*

▶ **11.5.2** Use

a The future perfect is used for an event which will take place before another future event

Bis Montag **wird** sie den Brief **bekommen haben**	*By Monday she will have received the letter*

Note If the future action has already been completed, the perfect tense is used:

Wenn du morgen erst um 11 Uhr ankommst, **sind** wir schon **abgefahren**	*If you don't arrive till 11 o'clock tomorrow, we'll already have left*

b However, German-speakers rarely use the future perfect; the perfect tense is almost always preferred if the context makes it clear that the future is referred to

Bis Montag **habe** ich das Buch **gelesen**	*By Monday I will have read the book*
Trotz des Nebels **ist** sie wahrscheinlich schon zu Hause **angekommen**	*Despite the fog she will probably have arrived home by now*

c The use of the future perfect tense, rather than the perfect, emphasises the supposition or intention behind the statement, rather than the fact

Keine Ahnung, wo sie ist – sie **wird** den Termin **vergessen haben**	*No idea where she is – she'll have forgotten the appointment*
In ein paar Jahren **wird** der Eisbär **ausgestorben sein**	*In a few years' time the polar bear will be extinct*

12

Verbs: other types and forms

OVERVIEW

Chapter 11 described the forms of weak and strong verbs. This chapter first discusses the forms of the other three types:
- **mixed verbs** (e.g. brennen)
- **modal verbs** (e.g. müssen)
- **irregular verbs** (e.g. sein)

In addition, the chapter covers three other aspects of verbs:
- **transitive/intransitive forms** (e.g. liegen/legen)
- **impersonal verbs** (e.g. es regnet)
- **reflexive verbs** (e.g. sich waschen)

Transitive and intransitive verbs

Transitive verbs are those which have a direct object; intransitive verbs do not. Sometimes their forms are different, sometimes the same. See TIP box p. 115.

Transitive	Sie **beantwortete** meinen Brief	*She answered my letter*
Intransitive	Sie **antwortete** nicht	*She didn't answer*

Impersonal verbs

Impersonal verbs are used only (or almost always) in the third person, often with **es:**

Es regnet	*It is raining*
Das gefällt mir nicht	*I don't like that*

Reflexive verbs

Reflexive verbs are verbs in which the subject and the object refer to the same thing or person:

Ich wasche **mich**	*I have a wash*
Sie zieht **sich** an	*She's getting dressed*

12.1 Mixed verbs

- There are six mixed verbs, all with **-nn-** or **-nd-** in the stem. They are called 'mixed' verbs because they change their stem vowel in the past tenses (like strong verbs), but their endings are the same as those of weak verbs. The principal parts are:

Infinitive	Present	Imperfect	Perfect
brennen (*to burn*)	er brennt	er brannte	er hat … gebrannt
kennen (*to know*)	er kennt	er kannte	er hat … gekannt
nennen (*to name*)	er nennt	er nannte	er hat … genannt
rennen (*to race*)	er rennt	er rannte	er ist … gerannt
senden[1] (*to send*)	er sendet	er sandte	er hat … gesandt
wenden[2] (*to turn*)	er wendet	er wandte	er hat … gewandt

[1] senden may also be used to mean *to broadcast*, when it uses only the weak forms in the past tenses: sendete, hat gesendet.

[2] wenden may also be used to mean *to turn over* (e.g. pages) or *to turn round* (e.g. car), when it uses the weak forms in the past tenses: wendete, hat gewendet.

12.2 Modal verbs

- There are six modal verbs; they are so called because, rather like the modal particles in Chapter 7, they indicate something about the attitude of the speaker to the action ('*Can* I go?' – 'You *must* go!') rather than the occurrence of the action itself.
- wissen *to know* was once also a modal verb, and is still conjugated like one. It has been included in 12.4 (Irregular verbs).
- English modal verbs exist only in the present (e.g. *can, must, may*) and occasionally in the past/conditional (e.g. *could, should*); for other tenses other words have to be found (*had to, will be able to,* etc.). German modal verbs, however, have a full range of tenses.
- Note that only the main English equivalents of modal verbs are given in the table below; see 12.3 for further details of individual verbs.

12.2.1   Examples of the tenses (müssen)

Tense		
Present	Er **muss** das Buch kaufen	*He must buy the book*
Note also	Er **muss** das Buch gekauft haben	*He must have bought the book*
Simple past	Er **musste** das Buch kaufen	*He had to buy the book*
Perfect	Er **hat** das Buch kaufen **müssen**	*He has had to buy the book*
Pluperfect	Er **hatte** das Buch kaufen **müssen**	*He had had to buy the book*
Future	Er **wird** das Buch kaufen **müssen**	*He will have to buy the book*
Conditional (*Konjunktiv II*)	Er **müsste** das Buch kaufen	*He would have to buy the book*

Tense		
	Er **müsste** das Buch gekauft haben	He would have to have bought the book
Cond. perfect	Er **hätte** das Buch kaufen **müssen**	He should have bought the book
Reported speech (**Konjunktiv I**)	Er sagte, er **müsse** das Buch kaufen	He said he must buy the book

▶ 12.2.2 Formation of the tenses of modal verbs

a The present tense

	dürfen	können	mögen	müssen	sollen	wollen
	may, to be allowed to	*can, to be able to*	*to like*	*must, to have to*	*ought, should*	*to want*
ich	darf	kann	mag	muss	soll	will
du	darfst	kannst	magst	musst	sollst	willst
er, sie, es	darf	kann	mag	muss	soll	will
wir	dürfen	können	mögen	müssen	sollen	wollen
ihr	dürft	könnt	mögt	müsst	sollt	wollt
sie, Sie	dürfen	können	mögen	müssen	sollen	wollen

▶ **TIP** How to remember the present tense of modal verbs
  • Only the singular forms of modal verbs are irregular.
  • The **ich** and **er** forms are identical, as are the **wir** and **sie** plural forms.

b The simple past tense
  • Use the stem of the infinitive (without the umlaut); add weak verb endings.

> **e.g. können** *can, to be able to*
> ich   konn**te**   *I could, was able to*   wir   konn**ten**
> du   konn**test**   ihr   konn**tet**
> er, sie, es konn**te**   sie, Sie konn**ten**

  • The other modal verbs work similarly:

dürfen	ich durfte, du durftest, *etc.*	*I was allowed to*
mögen	ich mochte, du mochtest, *etc.*	*I liked*
müssen	ich musste, du musstest, *etc.*	*I had to*
sollen	ich sollte, du solltest, *etc.*	*I should, ought to*
wollen	ich wollte, du wolltest, *etc.*	*I wanted to*

c The perfect and pluperfect tenses
  • Germans usually prefer the simple past tense of a modal verb to its perfect tense form. However, the perfect tense is to be found quite frequently, especially in written forms and in southern Germany.
  • Modal verbs always form the perfect and pluperfect tenses with **haben**.

♦ Modal verbs are almost always used with another verb; the past participle of the modal verb is almost always identical to its infinitive (but see **12.2.2d** below).

Ich **habe** ihn seit langem nicht mehr sehen **wollen**	*I haven't wanted to see him for a long time*
Er **hat** leider nach Hause gehen **müssen**	*Unfortunately, he has had to go home*
Weil ich den Aufsatz nicht **habe** schreiben **können**[1], …	*Because I've been unable to write the essay…*
Nachdem sie nach Hause **hatte** gehen **müssen**[1], …	*After she had had to go home, …*

[1] Note the word order with the perfect and pluperfect tenses in a subordinate clause (see 18.1.4b).

d Perfect tense of modal verbs used without a following infinitive

♦ Occasionally, a modal verb will be used without another verb; in such cases, the past participle of modal verbs is as follows:

gedurft	gekonnt
gemocht	gemusst
gesollt	gewollt

Hast du diese Musik **gemocht**?	*Did you like that music?*
Meine Mutter **hat**'s **gewollt**	*It was my mother's wish* (Title of poem by Storm)
Weil er die Vokabeln nicht **gekonnt hatte** ….	*Because he hadn't known the vocabulary …*

e The future tense

♦ The future tense of modal verbs is formed, as with other verbs, by using **werden** + infinitive:

Wirst du mich besuchen **können**?	*Will you be able to visit me?*

♦ As with other verbs, the present tense may be used with an adverb of time which indicates the future (see 11.1.2c):

Ich **kann** morgen **kommen**	*I can come tomorrow*

f Conditional tense/*Konjunktiv II*

♦ Modal verbs form the conditional/*Konjunktiv II* in the normal way using *Konjunktiv II* form of the modal verb + infinitive.

Note that sollen and wollen do not add umlauts to the stem vowel:

Könntest du mir bitte **helfen**?	*Could you please help me?*
Solltest du sie **anrufen**?	*Should you phone them?*
Was **möchten** Sie?	*What would you like?*
Wenn er mir helfen **könnte**, …	*If he could help me, …*

g Conditional perfect

♦ The conditional perfect of modal verbs is formed in the usual way with the *Konjunktiv II* of haben: hätte + past participle:

Das **hätte** er nicht tun **dürfen**!	*He should not have been allowed to do that!*
Obwohl ich die Jacke nicht **hätte** kaufen **sollen**[1], …	*Although I shouldn't have bought the jacket …*

Weil ich sie sonst nie wieder **hätte** besuchen **können**[1], …	*Because I otherwise would never have been able to visit her again …*

[1] Note the word order in the subordinate clause (see 18.1.4b).

12.2.3   Modal constructions

+ **Note the difference between the meanings of these modal constructions, which English modal verbs do not distinguish**

'External view'	**'Internal motive'**
Sie **könnte** ihn angerufen haben	Sie **hätte** ihn anrufen **können**

She could have phoned him

(It's possible that she did phone him)	(She would have been capable of phoning)
Sie **müsste** ihn angerufen haben	Sie **hätte** ihn anrufen **müssen**

She must have phoned him

(It's likely that she phoned him)	(She should have, but didn't)
Sie **sollte** ihn angerufen **haben**	Sie **hätte** ihn anrufen **sollen**

She ought to have phoned him

(One would have expected her to phone him)	(She ought to have, but didn't)

12.2.4   Using two modals in the same clause

+ **Two modal verbs may be used in the same clause, following standard word order rules**

Das **sollte** er nicht tun **dürfen**	*He shouldn't be allowed to do that*
Ich **will** nicht nach Hause gehen **müssen**	*I don't want to have to go home*

Note In a subordinate clause, a simpler construction is often preferred:

Weil ich nicht nach Hause gehen **will**, …

12.2.5   Omitting the infinitive after a modal verb

+ **The infinitive may be omitted after a modal verb in several contexts**
a **If the infinitive is a verb of motion (usually gehen or fahren), and the sentence contains another indication of movement (an adverbial phrase or prefix)**

Ich **muss** in die Stadt	*I've got to go into town*
Wo **willst** du denn hin?	*Where are you going?*

b **When the verb is tun *to do***

Kannst du das?	*Can you do this?*
Was **kann** ich dafür?	*What do you want me to do about it?*

c **In some idiomatic phrases**

Was **soll** das?	*What's this all about?*
Ich **kann** nicht mehr	*I just can't do any more*

d **Where the main verb is understood from the context**

Ich **wollte** ihr helfen, aber ich **konnte** es nicht	*I wanted to help her, but I couldn't*

12.3 The uses of modal verbs

▷ 12.3.1 dürfen

a *may* (permission)*; to be allowed to*

Darf ich hier sitzen?	*May I sit here?*
Er **darf** heute abend ausgehen	*He's allowed to go out this evening*
Ich **durfte** erst mit sechzehn rauchen	*I wasn't allowed to smoke until I was sixteen*

b dürfen + nicht = *must not, may not* (see also müssen + nicht)

Hier **darf** man nicht rauchen	*You're not allowed to smoke here*

c *may (probability)* – stronger than können

Das **darf** nicht wahr sein!	*That just can't be true!*
Da **darf** er sich nicht wundern	*He shouldn't be surprised*

d Polite suggestions or requests

Dürfte ich ⎱ Ihren Ausweis sehen?	*May I see your ID?*
Darf ich ⎰	
Der Wein **dürfte** etwas kühler sein	*The wine could be a little cooler*

▷ 12.3.2 können

a *can, to be able*

Man **kann** alles, wenn man nur will	*Where there's a will there's a way*
Man **konnte** ihn retten	*They were able to rescue him*
Wenn du mir **hättest** helfen **können**[1], ...	*If you could have helped me ...*

[1] Note word order here; see 18.1.4b.

b *may, might* (possibility)

Das **könnte** stimmen	*That might be true*

Note German often prefers to use the adverb vielleicht instead of können in this sense:

Vielleicht hast du recht	*You might be right*

▶ **TIP** können or dürfen?

◆ Colloquial English tends to use *can* in preference to *may* except in polite requests; German is more likely than English to distinguish between können (ability) and dürfen (permission):

Darf Ralf auch mit?	*Can/may Ralph come too?*
Man **darf** schon mit achtzehn Auto fahren, aber ich **kann** es immer noch nicht	*You may/are allowed to drive a car at eighteen, but I still can't do it*

---

c **Polite requests**

Könntest du bitte hier warten?	*Could you please wait here?*

d *to know, to have learned*

Er **kann** sehr gut Deutsch	*He can speak German very well*
Ich **kann** dieses Lied	*I know (=how to play/sing) this song*
cf. ich kenne dieses Lied	*I know (=heard before) this song*

e **Note that *could* means both *was able to* (ich konnte) and *would be able to* (ich könnte)**

Ich **konnte** schon mit vier Jahren schwimmen	*I could swim when I was only four*
Ich **könnte** schwimmen, wenn ich meine Badesachen dabei hätte	*I could swim if I had my swimming things with me*

f **können is often <u>not</u> used with verbs of sensation (sehen, hören) where English uses *can***

Siehst du ihn noch?	*Can you still see him?*
Sch! Hörst du etwas?	*Shh! Can you hear something?*

g *I couldn't help ...* **is usually translated by ich musste ...**

Ich **musste** lachen	*I couldn't help laughing*

▶ 12.3.3   mögen

a *to like*

Ich **mag** keinen Wein	*I don't like wine*
Ich **habe** ihn nie **gemocht**	*I've never liked him*
Ich **möchte** lieber Kaffee	*I'd rather have coffee*
Möchtest du nach Hause?	*Would you like to go home?*

b *I would have liked* **is often expressed with hätte gern instead of mögen**

Ich **hätte** ihn **gern** besucht	*I would have liked to have visited him*

c *may* **(probability)**

Das **mag** er wohl gesagt haben	*He may well have said that*
Das **mag** wohl sein, aber ...	*That may well be true, but ...*
Sie **mochte** etwa zwanzig sein	*She was about twenty*
Es **mochte** vielleicht ein Jahr später sein, als ...	*It was probably a year later, when ...*

d **möchte: polite requests and enquiries**

Möchten Sie Bier oder Wein?	*Would you prefer beer or wine?*
Ich **möchte** bitte Franzi sprechen	*I'd like to speak to Franzi, please*

e **Concessive clauses**

Wie dem auch sein **mag**, ...	*However that may be, ...*
Was du auch sagen **magst**, ...	*Whatever you say, ...*

▷ 12.3.4 müssen

a *must, to have to, to have got to*

+ müssen implies an external obligation, while sollen has more to do with an internal sense of obligation, often a moral one

Wann **musst** du abfahren?	*When do you have to leave?*
Ich **muss** den Artikel bis heute Abend geschrieben haben	*I have to have written the article by this evening*
Ich **musste** einfach lachen	*I couldn't help laughing*
Wir **sollten** mehr für die Dritte Welt tun, aber ich **muss** leider ein neues Auto kaufen	*We ought to do more for the Third World, but I'm afraid I have to buy a new car*

b müssen + nicht = *don't have to, don't need to*

Du **musst nicht** alles essen!	*You don't have to eat everything!*

Note brauchen + nicht is more common: Du brauchst nicht alles essen.

+ Compare dürfen + nicht = *must not, may not*:

Du **darfst nicht** alles essen!	*You mustn't eat everything!*

c Likelihood or logical conclusion

Das **muss** ein Problem gewesen sein	*That must have been a problem*
So **musste** es ja kommen	*It was bound to turn out like that*
Es **muss** in der Nacht geregnet haben	*It must have been raining in the night*

d *Konjunktiv II* müsste = *should, ought*

+ müsste suggests likelihood, sollte suggests obligation:

So was **müsste** er schon wissen	*That's the sort of thing he's bound to know*
So was **sollte** er wissen	*He ought to know that*

+ müsste is also used for (unrealisable) wishes:

Geld **müsste** man haben!	*If only I had money!*

e English *have to* does not always suggest obligation

Compare:

Ich **muss** viel lernen	*I have to learn a lot*
Ich **habe** viel **zu** lernen	*I have a lot to learn*

▷ 12.3.5 sollen

a *should, ought* (obligation)

Soll ich dir helfen?	*Shall I help you?*
Ich weiß nicht, was ich tun **soll**	*I don't know what to do*
Das **sollte** man nicht tun	*People shouldn't do that*
Du **sollst** nicht töten	*Thou shalt not kill*
Das **hättest** du nicht tun **sollen**	*You shouldn't have done that*

b *is said to be, is supposed to be*

Er **soll** sehr reich sein	*He's supposed to be rich*
Sie **soll** es ihm gegeben haben	*She's said to have given it to him*

frisch und knackig, wie ein guter Salat sein **soll**	*fresh and crispy, just like a good salad is supposed to be*
Was **soll** denn das?	*What's this all about?*

c *to be to* (command)

Du **sollst** auf uns warten	*You're to wait for us*
Sag ihm, er **soll/solle** draußen warten	*Tell him, he's to wait outside*

d What was destined to happen (prediction)

Er **sollte** seine Familie nie wieder sehen	*He was never to see his family again*

e sollte is also a form of the conditional (see 17.2.3)

Falls er heute ankommen **sollte**, …	*If he should/were to arrive today …*
Sollte er schon heute ankommen, …	*Should he/If he were to arrive today …*

▶ 12.3.6   wollen

a *to want, wish, intend*

. Note that, unlike English *I will* + infinitive, German ich will + infinitive does not indicate future, except insofar as intentions have a future aspect to them.

Willst du dieses Buch lesen?	*Do you want to read this book?*
Ich **wollte** dich fragen, ob …	*I wanted to ask you whether …*
Was **will** man da schon machen?	*What are they intending to do about it?*
Was **willst** du damit sagen?	*What do you mean (by that)?*
Sie **will** nur dein Bestes	*She only wants the best for you*
Was **willst** du mit dem Hammer?	*What are you going to do with that hammer?*
Ich **wollte**, ich hätte es nie gekauft	*I wish I'd never bought it*
(wollte here is the *Konjunktiv II* form – see 17.2.3 note 2)	

b wollen + eben/gerade *to be about to, to be on the point of*

Wir **wollten eben** in die Stadt gehen	*We were about to go into town*

c *to claim, pretend*

Er **will** nichts gesehen haben	*He claims not to have seen anything*
Er **will** immer alles besser wissen	*He thinks he knows it all*
Keiner **will** es gewesen sein	*Nobody owns up to it*
Dies **wollen** Mediziner **nachgewiesen haben**	*Doctors claim to have proved this*

d wollen + nicht *to refuse, fail*

Der Motor **wollte nicht** anspringen	*The engine wouldn't start*

e Polite imperatives

Wollen wir jetzt gehen?	*Shall we go now?*
Wollen wir uns nicht setzen?	*Shall we take a seat?*

f As a synonym for müssen *must*

Tomaten **wollen** viel Sonne	*Tomatoes need a lot of sun*
Wein genießen **will** gelernt sein	*The enjoyment of wine has to be learned*

g *would* means both *would* (conditional) and *wanted* (past tense). German distinguishes between these two uses

Ich **würde** dieses Auto nicht verkaufen	*I wouldn't sell the car (if I were you)*
Ich **wollte** das Auto nicht verkaufen	*I wouldn't sell the car (I wanted to keep it)*

12.4 Irregular verbs

- There are only a very few verbs in German which fall into the category of irregular, or 'one-off', verbs.
- With the exception of sein *to be*, it is almost always obvious which verb an irregular form belongs to, as the stem consonants rarely change.
- No irregular verb (not even sein) is irregular in all forms.

In the list of the irregular verbs below, only the irregular forms are given; all other forms are regular (e.g. **haben:** ich habe, wir haben; **werden:** ich werde, wir werden; **wissen:** wir wissen, ihr wisst).

The irregular verbs			
Infinitive	**Present**	**Simple past**	**Past participle**
sein *to be*	ich bin wir sind du bist ihr seid er ist sie sind	ich war du warst, *etc.* *strong verb endings*	ist gewesen
haben *to have*	du hast er hat	ich hatte du hattest, *etc.* *weak verb endings*	hat gehabt
werden *to become*	du wirst er wird	ich wurde du wurdest, *etc.* *weak verb endings*	ist geworden
wissen[1] *to know*	ich weiß du weißt er weiß	ich wusste du wusstest, *etc.* *weak verb endings*	hat gewusst
• In addition, the following verbs have certain irregularities, mostly in their past tense forms			
bringen *to bring*		ich brachte du brachtest, *etc.* *weak verb endings*	hat gebracht
denken *to think*		ich dachte, du dachtest, *etc.* *weak verb endings*	hat gedacht

The irregular verbs			
Infinitive	**Present**	**Simple past**	**Past participle**
gehen *to go*		ich ging, du gingst, *etc.* *strong verb endings*	ist gegangen
leiden *to suffer*		ich litt du littst, *etc.* *strong verb endings*	hat gelitten
nehmen *to take*	du nimmst er nimmt	ich nahm du nahmst, *etc.* *strong verb endings*	hat genommen
schneiden *to cut*		ich schnitt du schnittst, *etc.* *strong verb endings*	hat geschnitten
sitzen *to sit*		ich saß, du saßt, *etc.* *strong verb endings*	hat gesessen
stehen *to stand*		ich stand, du standst, *etc.* *strong verb endings*	hat gestanden
tun *to do*	ich tue wir tun du tust ihr tut er tut sie tun	ich tat, du tatst, *etc.* *strong verb endings*	hat getan
ziehen *to pull, move*		ich zog, du zogst, *etc.* *strong verb endings*	hat/ist gezogen

[1] **wissen** works in the same way as a modal verb, which it in fact once was (and its French equivalent *savoir* still is).

12.5 Verbs with different transitive and intransitive forms

a **Most verbs can be used transitively (i.e. with a direct object) or intransitively (i.e. without a direct object) with no change of form**

Transitive:	Ich **lese** eine Zeitung	*I'm reading a paper*
Intransitive:	Ich **lese** im Wartezimmer	*I'm reading in the waiting room*

b **Some verbs, however, have different but related transitive and intransitive forms**

• All the verbs in the list below are weak unless stated (the strong vowel changes are given in brackets).

	Intransitive	**Transitive**
answer	antworten – *(give an) answer*	beantworten – *answer (letter, question)*
blind	erblinden – *go blind*	blenden – *blind, dazzle*
change	sich ändern	ändern

	Intransitive	Transitive
climb	steigen (ei-ie-ie) – *climb , rise*	besteigen (ei-ie-ie) – *climb (hill)*
continue	fortfahren (ä-u-a)	fortsetzen – *continue*
drop/fall	fallen (ä-ie-a)	fallen lassen (ä-ie-a) – *to drop something*
drown	ertrinken (i-a-u)	ertränken – *drown*
fall/fell	fallen (ä-ie-a) – *fall, drop*	fällen – *fell (tree)*
frighten	erschrecken (i-a-o) – *be frightened*	erschrecken – *frighten*
hang	hängen (ä-i-a)	hängen
lay/lie	liegen (ie-a-e) – *lie, be lying*	legen – *lay* / sich hinlegen – *to lie down*
open	sich öffnen – *open*	öffnen – *open*
remember/ remind	sich erinnern an – *remember*	erinnern – *to remind*
sell	sich verkaufen	verkaufen
sink/lower	sinken (i-a-u) – *sink, drop*	senken – *lower* / versenken – *to sink (ship)*
sit/set/seat	setzen – *place* / sich hinsetzen – *to sit down*	sitzen (irreg) – *sit, be sitting*
stand	stellen	stehen
wake	aufwachen – *wake up*	wecken – *to wake (s.o.)*

Examples

Intransitive:	„Ich weiß nicht", **antwortete** er	*'I don't know', he answered*
Transitive:	Sie hat meinen Brief nicht **beantwortet**	*She didn't answer my letter*
Intransitive:	Das Bild **hing** an der Wand	*The picture hung on the wall*
Transitive:	Sie **hängte** das Bild an die Wand	*She hung the picture on the wall*
Intransitive:	Ich bin um 7 **aufgewacht**	*I woke up at 7 o'clock*
Transitive:	Er **weckte** mich um 7 Uhr.	*He woke me up at 7 o'clock*
Intransitive:	Bücher **lagen** überall auf dem Boden	*Books were lying all over the floor*
Transitive:	Sie **legte** sich auf das Bett (hin)	*She lay down on the bed*
Intransitive:	Das Buch **verkauft sich** gut	*The book is selling well*
Transitive:	Ich **verkaufe** mein Fahrrad	*I'm selling my bicycle*

c **Note also the following pairs of verbs**

sich bewegen to *move (oneself)*	bewegen *move (sthg), induce*
schaffen (*weak*) to *manage to do*	schaffen (a-u-a) to *create*
springen (i-a-u) to *jump*	sprengen to *blow up*
weichen (ei-i-i) *yield, give way*	weichen to *soak*

12.6 Impersonal verbs

- Impersonal verbs are verbs which are typically used in the third person only – usually the singular, but sometimes the plural – rather than in the full range of forms. They often concern the weather (es regnet, es friert, der Schnee taut – *the snow is melting*), or health („Wie geht es Ihnen?" – „Es ist mir schlecht").

▶ 12.6.1 Impersonal **sein** and **werden** constructions

a Impersonal sein and werden phrases can be used in two ways

+ es + ist/wird + dative object + adjective
+ Dative object + ist/wird + adjective (es omitted)

This is because es is a 'placeholder', i.e. it occupies first position to ensure that the verb comes second; if the dative object is in first position, es is no longer required.

es ist mir übel	mir ist übel	*I feel ill*
es ist ihr warm/kalt	ihr ist warm/kalt	*she feels hot/cold*
es ist ihm schwindelig	ihm ist schwindelig	*he's dizzy*
es wurde mir kalt	mir wurde kalt	*I began to feel cold*

▶ 12.6.2 Other impersonal constructions

+ **Other impersonal constructions usually contain es or a subject in the nominative**

es **ekelt** mich vor +dat.	*I'm disgusted at …*
du ekelst mich	*you disgust me*
es **fällt** mir **ein**, dass … ⎫	*it occurs to me that …*
mir fällt ein, dass … ⎬	
es **fällt** mir **auf**, dass …	*it strikes me that …*
es **fehlt** mir an +dat.	*I'm short of*
es **gefällt** mir	*I like it*
diese Musik gefällt mir	*I like this music*
Bücher gefallen mir	*I like books*
es **geht**	*it's OK/not bad*
Geht das?	*How's it going?/Everything OK?*
es **geht** ihm gut/schlecht	*he's fine/not well*
es **geht** um +acc.	*it's about, it concerns*
es **gelingt** mir, … zu tun	*I succeed in doing sthg*
es ist mir gelungen	*I succeeded*
es **geschieht** dir recht	*it serves you right*
es **graut** mir vor + dat. ⎫	*I have a horror of …*
mir graut vor … ⎬	
es **handelt** von + dat.	*it's on the subject of*
es **heißt**, dass …	*it's said that …*
es **klingelte** an der Tür	*the doorbell rang*
es **klopfte** an der Tür	*there was a knock at the door*
es **kommt** auf +acc. an	*it depends on …*
es kommt darauf an, was …	*it all depends on what …*
es **liegt** daran, dass …	*It's due to the fact that …*
es **macht** nichts	*it doesn't matter*
es **schaudert** mich vor + dat. ⎫	*I shudder at …*
mich schaudert vor … ⎬	
es **schmeckt** mir	*it tastes good*
Schokolade schmeckt mir	*I like the taste of chocolate*
es **tut** mir **leid**	*I'm sorry*
sie tun mir leid	*I'm sorry for them*
es **wundert** mich, dass …	*I'm surprised that …*
es **zieht**	*it's draughty*

▶ 12.6.3   es gibt, es ist/es sind *there is/are*

♦ While there is in practice a certain amount of overlap in the use of **es gibt** and **es ist/es sind**, the following rules apply in almost all instances.

a es gibt indicates the *existence* of things or people in general

♦ It is always followed by the accusative:

Es gibt viele Leute, die das glauben	*There are many people who believe that*
In Köln **gibt es** zwölf romanische Kirchen	*In Cologne there are twelve Romanesque churches*
Es gab früher zwei Kinos in der Stadt	*There used to be two cinemas in the town*
Was **gibt es** in Berlin zu sehen?	*What is there to see in Berlin?*
Das **gibt's** doch nicht!	*I don't believe it!* (lit: *such things don't exist!*)

b es gibt is also used for events and occurrences

♦ This is especially the case when the speaker has in mind the unusual nature or the consequences of the event, or when referring to the future:

Plötzlich **gab es** einen lauten Knall	*Suddenly there was a loud crash*
Morgen **gibt es** noch mehr Schnee	*Tomorrow there will be more snow*
Wenn ich spät nach Hause komme, **gibt es** immer Streit mit meinen Eltern	*When I arrive home late, there is always an argument with my parents*

c es ist and es sind indicate the presence of things or people in a more limited place or for a temporary period

♦ These constructions are followed by the nominative:

Es ist ein Paket für dich da	*There's a parcel for you*
Es sind zwei Männer an der Tür	*There are two men at the door*
Es war niemand da, der mir helfen konnte	*There was no one there who could help me*

Note es is omitted with ist/sind if it is not in the initial position in the sentence:

Niemand **war** da, der mir helfen konnte
Zwei Männer **sind** an der Tür

▶ TIP   Avoiding es gibt and es ist/es sind

♦ German frequently prefers to use neither es gibt nor es ist/es sind, and it is easy for an English-speaker to overuse these constructions. Instead, a more specific verb is often used. Compare the following sentences with the forms above:

Zwei Männer **stehen** an der Tür

Die Stadt **hatte** früher zwei Kinos

Viele Leute **glauben** das

Plötzlich **hörte** man einen lauten Knall

Ich **bekomme** immer Streit mit meinen Eltern

12.7 Reflexive verbs

▶ 12.7.1 Reflexive verbs – an outline

a Reflexive verbs do not exist in the same way in English as they do in German
The closest equivalent is the use of e.g. *myself, yourself* in constructions such as

> *Let yourself in and make yourself at home!*
> *I'm going to buy myself a new car*

b Where German uses a reflexive verb English usually uses a normal intransitive verb

Die Tür öffnete **sich**	*The door opened*
Wo treffen wir **uns**?	*Where shall we meet?*
Ich will **mich** ausruhen	*I want to rest*
Ich frage **mich**, ob …	*I wonder if …*
Das hört **sich** aber schön an	*That sounds beautiful*

⁃ Occasionally, English uses a passive construction:

Das Buch verkauft **sich** gut	*The book is selling well*
Das Problem erklärt **sich** leicht	*The problem is easily explained*

c There are two forms of the reflexive in German
⁃ **The pronoun is in the accusative** as the direct object of the verb; see 12.7.2 below. (This is much the most common of the two):

Ich wasche **mich**	*I wash/have a wash*
Er zieht **sich** an	*He gets dressed/is getting dressed*

⁃ **The pronoun is in the dative** as the indirect object of the verb; see 12.7.3 below. (These pronouns differ from the accusative only in the ich and du forms):

Ich wasche **mir** die Hände	*I wash my hands*
Wann hast du **dir** das Bein gebrochen?	*When did you break your leg?*

▶ 12.7.2 The pronoun **sich**

⁃ With most pronouns there is no possibility of confusion; e.g. dich (or dir) refer back to du; uns refers back to wir. Only with the third person pronouns (singular er, sie, es, plural sie, Sie) is a special pronoun, sich, needed to show that the verb refers to *himself, herself, itself, themselves, yourself/yourselves.*

Wenn ein Kind sehr jung ist, müssen seine Eltern **es** anziehen, bis es **sich** selbst anziehen kann	*When a child is very young, it must be dressed by its parents until it can dress itself*

▶ 12.7.3 Accusative reflexive

⁃ **The verb parts of reflexive verbs are identical to normal weak and strong verbs in all forms and all tenses**
Only the fact that they have a reflexive pronoun (a pronoun which refers to the same person or thing as the subject) makes them any different.

Accusative reflexive verbs

ich wasche **mich**	wir waschen **uns**
du wäschst **dich**	ihr wascht **euch**
er/sie/es wäscht **sich**	sie/Sie waschen **sich**

Perfect tense: ich habe **mich** gewaschen
Simple past tense: ich wusch **mich**
Future tense: ich werde **mich** waschen

a Some verbs are always reflexive

Common examples:

sich auskennen	*to know one's way around*	sich bewerben um	*to apply for*
sich erholen	*to recover*	sich ereignen	*to occur, happen*
sich bedanken	*to thank*	sich erkälten	*to catch cold*
sich beeilen	*to hurry*	sich irren	*to be mistaken*
sich befinden	*to be situated*	sich verabschieden	*to say goodbye*
sich benehmen	*to behave*	sich verlieben in	*to fall in love*
sich beschweren	*to complain*	sich weigern	*to refuse*

Ich habe **mich** von ihm verabschiedet	*I said goodbye to him*
Sie haben **sich** ineinander verliebt	*They fell in love with one another*
Er weigerte **sich**, mir zu helfen	*He refused to help me*
Benimm **dich**!	*Behave yourself!*

b Many other verbs are used reflexively when the object and subject refer to the same thing or person, but are otherwise used as normal transitive verbs

Refl.:	**Er** wäscht **sich**	*He washes/has a wash*
Non-refl.:	Er wäscht das Auto	*He washes the car*
Refl.:	**Ich** interessiere **mich** für Musik	*I'm interested in music*
Non-refl.:	Diese Musik interessiert mich	*This music interests me*
Refl.:	Erinnerst **du dich** daran, wie wir ...?	*Do you remember how we ...?*
Non-refl.:	Er erinnert mich an meinen Bruder	*He reminds me of my brother*

• Examples of other verbs that work in the same way (note that the two forms may be expressed in slightly different ways in English):

Non-reflexive		Reflexive	
ärgern	*to annoy*	sich ärgern	*to get annoyed*
beherrschen	*to master (e.g. language)*	sich beherrschen	*to control oneself*
beruhigen	*to calm s.o.*	sich beruhigen	*to calm down*
beschäftigen	*to employ*	sich beschäftigen	*to deal with*
entschuldigen	*to excuse*	sich entschuldigen	*to apologise*
fürchten	*to fear sthg*	sich fürchten	*to be frightened*
hinlegen	*to lay down*	sich hinlegen	*to lie down*
langweilen	*to bore*	sich langweilen	*to be/get bored*
treffen	*to meet (unexpectedly)*	sich treffen mit	*to meet (arranged)*
verstehen	*to understand*	sich verstehen mit	*to get on with*

▶ 12.7.4   Dative reflexive

<table>
<tr><td colspan="2" align="center">Dative reflexive verbs</td></tr>
<tr><td>ich wasche mir die Hände</td><td>wir waschen uns die Hände</td></tr>
<tr><td>du wäschst dir die Hände</td><td>ihr wascht euch die Hände</td></tr>
<tr><td>er/sie/es wäscht sich die Hände</td><td>sie/Sie waschen sich die Hände</td></tr>
</table>

Perfect tense: ich habe **mir** die Hände gewaschen
Simple past tense: ich wusch **mir** die Hände
Future tense: ich werde **mir** die Hände waschen

Note Only the dative pronouns in the first and second person singular differ in form from the accusative pronouns.

There are three types of construction in which the reflexive pronoun may be found in the dative. All are considered to be reflexive because the object pronoun refers back to the subject:

a **Indirect object of the verb (and therefore automatically in the dative); this is often used when referring to parts of the body**

Ich wasche **mir** das Gesicht	*I wash my face*
Er hat **sich** den Arm gebrochen	*He's broken his arm*
Ich kann **mir** kein neues Auto leisten	*I can't afford a new car*
Hast du **dir** das Schloss angesehen?	*Have you had a look at the castle?*
Sie muss **sich** einen Wagen kaufen	*She's got to buy (herself) a new car*

b **Verbs that take a dative object (see 1.1.5), which here is a reflexive pronoun**

Das **lasse** ich **mir** nicht **gefallen**	*I won't stand for it*
Ich wusste **mir** nicht zu **helfen**	*I didn't know what to do*
Ich **erlaube mir** ein Glas Wein pro Tag	*I allow myself one glass of wine a day*
Ich **komme mir** dumm **vor**	*I feel stupid*

c **Verbs where the dative reflexive pronoun is a fixed part of the construction**

Das habe ich **mir** nur **eingebildet**.	*I only imagined it (i.e. wrongly)*
Stell dir vor, du gewinnst in der Lotterie!	*Just imagine you win the lottery!*
Ich **verbitte mir** dieses Benehmen!	*I won't tolerate this behaviour!*
Ich **habe mir vorgenommen**, das Rauchen aufzugeben	*I intend to give up smoking*

▶ 12.7.5   Other translations of the reflexive pronoun

a *to oneself* **is expressed in German by the construction vor sich hin**

Er murmelte **vor sich hin**	*He was mumbling to himself*
Singst du immer **vor dich hin**, wenn du arbeitest?	*Do you always sing to yourself when you're working?*

b one another may also be rendered by the reflexive pronoun (see 4.2.3)

Sie lieben **sich**	*They love one another*
Hasst ihr **euch**?	*Do you hate each other?*
Wir kennen **uns** seit Jahren	*We've known one another for years*
Damals hat man **sich** geholfen	*People used to help one another in those days*

▶ 12.7.6   Impersonal constructions with reflexive verbs

* Reflexive verbs may also be used in certain impersonal constructions. These may also be expressed with können

Mit einem Kuli **schreibt es sich** schnell	*It's fast writing with a ball-pen*
(**or** Mit einem Kuli kann man schnell schreiben)	
Hier **wohnt es sich** schön	*This is a good place to live*
Es fährt sich bequem in so einem Wagen	*Driving a car like this is comfortable*

Verbs with prepositional objects or unexpected cases

OVERVIEW

There are many differences between English and German from verb to verb – one language may have a preposition before the object, or the German verb may use a separable prefix instead. Here are a few examples:

Ich bezahle das Essen	*I'm paying **for** the meal*
Er trat **in** das Zimmer ein	*He entered the room*
Schrei mich nicht so **an**!	*Don't shout **at** me like that!*
Ich will seine Aussage nicht kommentieren	*I don't want to comment **on** his statement*

This chapter examines how German verbs relate to their objects.

▶ Verbs + prepositions

• Verbs are often connected to an object by a preposition:

> *He waited **for** me*
> *She is interested **in** science*

• In German, the preposition which goes with a particular verb is often different from what an English-speaker might expect; both it and the case it takes must be learned. The German for the sentences above would be

> Er wartete **auf** mich
> Sie interessiert sich **für** Naturwissenschaften

• As well as noun phrases or pronouns, the prepositional object may be, for instance, a subordinate or infinitive clause. The preposition becomes a **prepositional adverb**, made up from da(r)- + the preposition:

Es kommt **darauf** an, was sie dazu sagen wird	*It all depends on what she's going to say about it*
Sie hörte **damit** auf, ihn jeden Tag anzurufen	*She stopped phoning him every day*

> ### ▶ Verbs + cases other than the accusative
>
> The direct object of a transitive verb is usually in the accusative, and its indirect object is usually in the dative. However, a few verbs vary from this pattern:
> * verbs followed by the dative
> * verbs followed by the genitive
> * verbs where both objects are in the accusative

13.1 Verbs followed by prepositional objects

* The lists in sections 13.1.1 to 13.1.14 contain the commonest verbs used with particular prepositions.
* See also section 13.2 for what happens when the preposition is followed by something other than a noun phrase or pronoun.

▶ **TIP**   **Accusative or dative with 'double case' prepositions?**
* If in doubt as to whether prepositional objects such as an, auf, in should be followed by the accusative or the dative, remember that the majority govern the accusative.

▶ 13.1.1   an

a Followed by the accusative; many of these verbs relate to mental processes

denken an	to think of
erinnern an	to remind of
sich erinnern an	to remember
sich gewöhnen an	to get used to
glauben an	to believe in (sthg)
grenzen an	to border on
schreiben an	to write to
sich wenden an	to turn to

Erinnerst du dich **an** ihn?	*Do you remember him?*
Ich denke oft **an** meine Freundin	*I often think about my girlfriend*
Sie gewöhnt sich langsam **daran**, im Ausland zu leben	*She's gradually getting used to living abroad*

b Followed by the dative

arbeiten an	to work at
erkennen an	to recognise by
erkranken an	to fall ill with
sich freuen an[1]	to take pleasure in
hindern an	to prevent from
leiden an	to suffer from
sterben an	to die of (illness)
teilnehmen an	to take part in

vorbeigehen an	to go/walk past
zweifeln an	to doubt

[1] See also sich freuen auf and sich freuen über.

Sie ist **an** einem Herzinfarkt gestorben	She died of a heart attack
Er ging **an** mir vorbei	He walked past me

13.1.2   auf

a Followed by the accusative (i.e. almost all verbs with auf)

achten auf	to pay attention to
ankommen auf	to depend on
antworten auf	to answer
aufpassen auf	to look after
sich beziehen auf	to refer to
blicken auf	to look at
sich freuen auf[1]	to look forward to
hinweisen auf	to point sthg out to s.o.
hoffen auf	to hope for
kommen auf	to think of
sich konzentrieren auf	to concentrate on
reagieren auf	to react to
rechnen auf	to count on
schießen auf	to shoot at
sehen auf	to look at
sich spezialisieren auf	to specialise in
sich verlassen auf	to rely on
verzichten auf	to do without
warten auf	to wait for
zeigen auf	to point to/at
zukommen auf	to come up to (s.o.)
zurückkommen auf	to return to (a matter)

[1] See also ich freuen an and sich freuen über.

Ich warte **auf** den Bus	I'm waiting for the bus
Sie wies uns **auf** die Gefahr hin	She pointed out the danger to us
Wie kommst du **auf** diese Idee?	What made you think of that idea?
„Kommt er?" „ **Darauf** kannst du dich verlassen"	'Will he come?' 'You can depend on it'

b Followed by the dative

basieren auf	to be based on
beharren auf	to insist on
bestehen auf[1]	to insist on

[1] See also bestehen aus.

Sie beharrt **auf** ihrem Standpunkt	She insists on her point of view

▶ 13.1.3 aus

✦ Followed by the dative

bestehen aus[1]	*to consist of*
entstehen aus	*to arise from*
kommen aus	*to come from*
stammen aus	*to come/date/derive from*
übersetzen aus	*to translate from*
werden aus	*to become of*

[1]See also bestehen auf + dative.

Was ist **aus** ihm geworden?	*What became of him?*
Diese Münze stammt **aus** dem 18. Jahrhundert	*This coin dates from the eighteenth century*

▶ 13.1.4 bei

✦ Followed by the dative

sich bedanken bei	*to thank s.o.*
sich entschuldigen bei	*to apologise to*
helfen bei	*to help with*
nehmen bei	*to take by (e.g. the hand)*
wohnen bei	*to live with (i.e. at s.o.'s place)*

Er wohnt immer noch **bei** seinen Eltern	*He still lives with his parents*
Sie hilft mir **bei** meiner Arbeit	*She's helping me with my work*

▶ 13.1.5 für

✦ Followed by the accusative

sich begeistern für	*to be enthusiastic about*
danken für	*to thank for*
sich entscheiden für	*to decide on*
gelten für	*to apply to/be applicable to*
halten für	*to consider to be*
sich interessieren für	*to be interested in*
sich schämen für	*to be ashamed of*
sorgen für[1]	*to look after*

[1]See also sich sorgen um.

Das Gesetz gilt **für** alle	*The law applies to everyone*
Wir halten ihn **für** intelligent	*We think he's intelligent*
Jetzt schämt sie sich **dafür**, dass sie so etwas gesagt hat	*Now she's ashamed of having said that*

▶ 13.1.6 in

a Usually followed by the accusative

ausbrechen in	*to burst into*
einbrechen in	*to break into, burgle*
einsteigen in	*to get onto, in (e.g. bus, car)*
eintreten in	*to enter (e.g. room)*
sich ergeben in	*to resign o.s. to*

geraten in	to get into (difficulties)
sich mischen in	to get involved in
übersetzen in	to translate into
sich verlieben in	to fall in love with
sich vertiefen in	to become engrossed in
(sich) verwandeln in	to change, turn into

Sie stieg **in** den Bus ein	She got on the bus
Er veliebte sich **in** das Mädchen	He fell in love with the girl

b Followed by the dative

ankommen in	to arrive in, at
sich irren in	to be mistaken about
sich täuschen in	to be wrong about

Wir kamen **in** der nächsten Stadt an	We arrived in the next town
Er täuscht sich **in** seiner Erinnerung	His memory is at fault

▶ 13.1.7 mit

♦ Followed by the dative

sich abfinden mit	to be satisfied with
anfangen mit	to start sthg
aufhören mit	to stop doing sthg
sich beschäftigen mit	to occupy o.s. with
handeln mit	to deal, trade in
nicken mit	to nod
rechnen mit	to reckon on
sprechen mit	to speak, talk to
telefonieren mit	to phone
übereinstimmen mit	to agree with
sich unterhalten mit	to converse with
verbinden mit	to connect to, with
vergleichen mit	to compare with
sich verheiraten mit	to marry
versehen mit	to provide with

Hör **mit** dem Lärm auf!	Stop that noise!
Hör bitte **damit** auf!	Please stop doing that!
Sie nickte **mit** dem Kopf	She nodded (her head)

▶ 13.1.8 nach

♦ Followed by the dative; many of these verbs relate to perception

aussehen nach	to look like (e.g. rain)
sich erkundigen nach	to enquire about
fragen nach	to enquire about, ask after
graben nach	to dig for
greifen nach	to clutch at, grab at

riechen nach	to smell of
rufen nach	to call for s.o.
schicken nach	to send for
schmecken nach	to taste of
sich sehnen nach	to long for
stinken nach	to smell of
streben nach	to strive for
suchen nach	to look for
sich umsehen nach	to look around for
urteilen nach	to judge by
verlangen nach	to long for
Es sieht **nach** Regen aus	It looks like rain
Sie erkundigte sich **nach** dem Weg	She asked the way
Ich sehne mich **danach**, sie wiederzusehen	I'm longing to see her again

13.1.9   über

+ **With verbs, always followed by the accusative**

sich ärgern über	to get annoyed about
sich beklagen über	to complain about
erfahren über	to learn, find out about
sich freuen über[1]	to be pleased, happy about
herrschen über	to rule over
lachen über	to laugh about
nachdenken über	to think over
reden über	to talk about
schimpfen über	to grumble about
schreiben über	to write about
sprechen über	to speak about
streiten über	to argue about
sich streiten über	to quarrel about
sich täuschen über	to be mistaken about
sich unterhalten über	to converse about
verfügen über	to have at one's disposal
sich wundern über	to be surprised at

[1]See also sich freuen an, sich freuen auf.

Sie hat sich bei dem Manager **über** ihr Zimmer beklagt	She complained to the manager about her room
Er verfügt **über** viel Geld	He has a lot of money
Wir müssen **darüber** reden, wie wir das ohne sie schaffen	We must talk about how we're going to manage that without them

13.1.10 um

+ **Followed by the accusative**

sich bemühen um	to try to help
beneiden um	to envy s.o. sthg
sich bewerben um	to apply for
bitten um	to ask for, request
bringen um	to deprive, defraud of

es geht um	it's about, to do with
sich handeln um	to be a question/matter of
kommen um	to lose, be deprived of
sich kümmern um	to worry about
ringen um	to struggle for

Ich beneide ihn **um** sein Vermögen	I envy him his fortune
Sie hat sich **um** die Stelle beworben	She applied for the job
Es handelt sich **darum**, eine Lösung zu finden	It's a question of finding a solution

▶ 13.1.11 von

+ **Followed by the dative**

abhängen von	to rely on
abraten von	to advise against
denken von	to think, have an opinion about
erzählen von	to tell about
halten von	to think of, have an opinion about
leben von	to live on
sagen von	to say/tell about
sprechen von	to speak about
träumen von	to dream about
überzeugen von	to convince of
verstehen von	to understand about
weichen von	to budge from
wimmeln von	to be teeming with
wissen von	to know about

Was hältst du **von** ihm?	What do you think of him?
Was hältst du **davon**, dass wir sie einfach anrufen?	What do you think of the idea of just phoning them up?
Von seinem Gehalt kann er nicht leben	He can't live on his salary

▶ 13.1.12 vor

+ **Always followed by the dative when used with verbs. These verbs are often to do with (physical) reactions to, or protecting from, something**

Angst haben vor	to be frightened of
sich fürchten vor	to be frightened of
fliehen vor	to flee from
retten vor	to save from
sich schämen vor	to be ashamed of
schützen vor	to protect from
sterben vor	to die of
(sich) verbergen vor	to hide, conceal (o.s.) from
verstecken vor	to hide from
warnen vor	to warn of

weichen vor	*to give way to*
weinen vor	*to weep with/for*
zittern vor	*to shake, shiver with*

Sie schämt sich **vor** ihrer Familie	*She's ashamed of her family*
Er weinte **vor** Freude	*He was weeping with joy*
Der Tod? Ich habe keine Angst **davor**!	*Death? I'm not frightened of it!*

▶ 13.1.13   wegen

◆ Followed by the genitive

loben wegen	*to praise for*
tadeln wegen	*to criticise, rebuke for*
schelten wegen	*to scold for*
Man lobte sie **wegen** ihres Mutes	*She was praised for her courage*
Sie tadelte mich **wegen** meiner Faulheit	*She criticised me for my laziness*

▶ 13.1.14   zu

◆ Followed by the dative

beitragen zu	*to contribute to*
bestimmen zu	*to designate as, destine for*
brauchen zu	*to need for (a purpose)*
bringen zu	*to achieve sthg.*
dienen zu	*to serve/be used as*
einladen zu	*to invite to*
führen zu	*to lead to*
gehören zu	*to belong to, be part of*
gratulieren zu	*to congratulate on*
machen zu	*to make*
meinen zu	*to think of*
neigen zu	*to tend to*
passen zu	*to match, go with*
provozieren zu	*to provoke to*
raten zu	*to advise*
treiben zu	*to drive/force to*
überreden zu	*to persuade to*
verführen zu	*to seduce to*
wählen zu	*to elect as*
sich wenden zu	*to turn round to*
zwingen zu	*to force to*

Sie hat es bis **zum** Chef gebracht	*She got to be boss*
Kann ich dich **zu** einem Kaffee überreden?	*Can I persuade you to have a cup of coffee?*
Ich fühle mich **dazu** gezwungen, ihn finanziell zu unterstützen	*I feel obliged to support him financially*
Was meinst du **dazu**?	*What do you think about it?*

13.2 Prepositional adverbs

▶ 13.2.1 Prepositional adverb: da(r)- + preposition

- Normally, prepositions are followed by noun phrases or pronouns. When they are followed by an infinitive clause or subordinate clause instead, the preposition changes from e.g. an, auf, zu to daran, darauf, dazu by the addition of the prefix **da(r)-**. This form is called a **prepositional adverb**.
- The clause which follows the main clause containing daran, darauf, etc. may be:
  - **zu** + an **infinitive clause** – if the subject applies to both clauses
  - a **subordinate clause** beginning with e.g. **dass** – if the subject of each clause is different, or if the writer repeats the subject.

The second example in each pair below uses dass as it has a different subject in each clause, except in the last example:

Ich freue mich **darauf**, Köln **zu besuchen**	*I'm looking forward to visiting Cologne*
But …, dass du uns besuchst	*…to you visiting us*
Sie hat sich **daran** gewöhnt, ihn nur ab und zu **zu sehen**	*She got used to seeing him only occasionally*
But …, dass er sie nie besuchte	*… that he never visited her*
Er entschuldigte sich **dafür**, so spät angekommen **zu sein**	*He apologised for having arrived so late*
Or …, dass er so spät angekommen war	*… that he had arrived so late*

Note As an alternative to the subordinate clause beginning with e.g. dass, a simple object may often be used:

Ich freue mich auf deinen Besuch.
Er entschuldigte sich für seine späte Ankunft

The prepositional adverb is also used in place of a preposition + pronoun (see 4.1.4).

▶ 13.2.2 Omission of the prepositional adverb

- **In colloquial German, the prepositional adverb may often be omitted; this is most common with verbs used with zu**

  Er riet mir (**dazu**), ihn anzurufen   *He advised me to phone him up*

13.3 Verbs used with unexpected cases

Most transitive verbs take an object in the accusative case. There are a few, however, which take a dative or even a genitive object, or which are followed by two objects in the accusative, instead of a direct (accusative) and an indirect (dative) object.

▶ 13.3.1 Verbs which take a dative object

a These verbs govern the dative in German
Common examples:

antworten	*to answer*
begegnen	*to meet (by chance)*
beistehen[1]	*to support*

beitreten[1]	*to join*
danken	*to thank*
drohen	*to threaten*
einfallen	*to occur (idea)*
entkommen[1]	*to escape*
entgegenkommen[1]	*to accommodate (requests)*
folgen	*to follow*
gehorchen	*to obey*
gehören	*to belong to*
geschehen	*to happen*
glauben	*to believe*
gratulieren	*to congratulate*
helfen	*to help*
imponieren	*to impress*
nachlaufen[1]	*to run after*
sich nähern	*to approach*
nutzen	*to be of use*
passen	*to suit*
schaden	*to harm*
trauen	*to trust*
vertrauen	*to trust*
wehtun	*to hurt*
widersprechen[1]	*to contradict*
widerstehen[1]	*to resist*
zuhören[1]	*to listen*
zusehen[1]	*to watch*
zustimmen[1]	*to agree*

[1]Verbs with the prefixes **bei-, entgegen-, nach-, wider-** and **zu-** always take the dative, as do some with the prefix **ent-** when the verb signifies escape.

Ich glaube **dir** kein Wort	*I don't believe a word you say*
Diese Musik gefällt **meinem** Vater gut, aber nicht **mir**	*My father really likes this music but I don't*
Er antwortete **mir** kurz	*He answered me briefly*
Ich bin **ihm** in der Stadt begegnet	*I met him in town*
Gehört **dir** dieser Wagen?	*Does this car belong to you?*
Kann ich **Ihnen** helfen?	*Can I help you?*
Du sollst **mir** endlich zuhören!	*Now you listen to me!*

b Note also these verbs, several impersonal, where the dative object in German is the subject in English

fehlen	*to be short of*	leidtun	*to feel sorry (for)*
gefallen	*to please (= to like)*	schmecken	*to taste*
gelingen	*to succeed*		

Du fehlst **mir**!	*I'm missing you!*
Mir fehlt das Geld für ein Auto	*I haven't got enough money for a car*
Diese Schuhe gefallen **mir**	*I like these shoes*
Es ist **ihm** gelungen, sie zu finden	*He succeeded in finding her*
Er tut **mir** Leid	*I'm sorry for him*
Der Wein schmeckt **mir**	*I like this wine*
Lass es **dir** schmecken!	*Enjoy it!*

See also 12.6 (impersonal verbs) and 12.7.3 (dative reflexive pronouns).

▶ 13.3.2 Verbs which take a dative and an accusative object

Many verbs take not only a direct object in the accusative but also an indirect object in the dative. For obvious reasons, many of the verbs relate to giving and taking, or to communicating something to someone.

Note The difference between direct and indirect objects is explained in TIP, p. 8.

The following list contains a few examples:

anbieten	*to offer*
beibringen	*to teach*
bringen	*to bring*
empfehlen	*to recommend*
erklären	*to explain*
erlauben	*to allow, permit*
erzählen	*to tell, relate*
geben	*to give*
leihen	*to lend*
mitteilen	*to inform of*
nehmen	*to take (away)*
raten	*to advise*
reichen	*to pass*
sagen	*to say*
schicken	*to send*
schreiben	*to write*
stehlen	*to steal, rob*
verkaufen	*to sell*
versprechen	*to promise*
vorlesen	*to read aloud*
vorstellen	*to introduce*
wünschen	*to wish*
zeigen	*to show*

Er erklärte **mir das Problem**	*He explained the problem to me*
Sie hat **ihrem Kind Schwimmen** beigebracht	*She taught her child to swim*
Ich gab **ihr ein tolles Geschenk**	*I gave her a lovely present*
Ich schreibe **ihnen einen Brief**	*I'm writing them a letter*
Das hat **mir den ganzen Spaß** genommen	*That's taken all my fun*
Er las **seinen Kindern eine Geschichte** vor	*He read his children a story*

▶ 13.3.3 Verbs with two accusative objects

+ With a small number of verbs, both objects are in the accusative, where they might reasonably be expected to have one dative and one accusative object

The most common are:

fragen *to ask*	Er fragte mich, wo ich wohne	*He asked me where I live*
	Ich fragte ihn etwas	*I asked him something*
kosten *to cost*	Das hat mich eine Menge Geld gekostet	*That cost me a lot of money*
lehren *to teach*	Er hat mich Mathe gelehrt	*He taught me maths*
nennen *to call*	Man nennt ihn einen Idioten	*They call him an idiot*

▷ 13.3.4 Verbs which take a genitive object

a **A small number of verbs (some of them reflexive) take an object in the genitive**

Most of these are now regarded as formal or are used in legal language. In everyday German, the more common equivalents given in brackets (where given) are preferred:

sich annehmen	*to take care of, attend to*	(more usual: sich kümmern um)
berauben	*to rob s.o. of*	(more usual: jm etw rauben)
bedürfen	*to need, require*	(more usual: brauchen)
sich bemächtigen	*to seize hold of*	(more usual: ergreifen, nehmen)
sich enthalten	*to abstain from*	(more usual: verzichten auf)
sich erwehren	*to escape, avoid*	
sich freuen	*to enjoy*	(more usual: geniessen)
gedenken	*to remember (the dead)*	(more usual: denken an)
sich schämen	*to be ashamed of*	(more usual: sich schämen für)

Sie bedürfen **unserer Hilfe**	*They need our help*
Sie konnte sich **der Tränen** nicht enthalten	*She couldn't keep back her tears*
Man kann sich **des Eindrucks** nicht erwehren, dass …	*You can't help feeling that …*
Sie freuen sich **des Lebens**	*They enjoy life*
Sie gedachten **ihrer toten Freunden**	*They remembered their dead friends*

b **A few other verbs govern an accusative and a genitive object**

anklagen	*to accuse of*
beschuldigen	*to charge with (crime)*
entheben	*to relieve of*
verdächtigen	*to suspect of*

Die Polizei verdächtigt sie **des Verbrechens**	*The police suspected her of the crime*
Man enthob ihn **seiner Stellung**	*He was relieved of his job*
Er wird **des Mordes** beschuldigt	*He's charged with murder*

The infinitive and participles

The **infinitive** and the **participles** are parts of the verb which do not change their endings to agree with the subject.

The infinitive

- The **infinitive** is the basic, dictionary form of the verb.

In English, it is usually preceded by *to (to eat, to run)*; in German, it usually ends with -en (essen, laufen). A few infinitives end with –n, mostly verbs whose stems end in -el- and -er-:

sein *to be*	klingeln *to ring*
tun *to do*	wandern *to go walking*
ausgehen *to go out*	

- An **infinitive clause** is the infinitive together with zu, and objects or adverbs, if any:

Ich hoffe, nach London **zu fahren**   *I'm hoping to go to London*

The past and present participles

- There are two participles, present and past.

Present:	English:	infinitive + -ing	*eating, dancing*
	German:	infinitive + -d	essend, tanzend
Past:	English:	past participle	*eaten, danced*
	German:	past participle	gegessen, getanzt

- There are some similarities between the ways the participles are used in English and German, notably as adjectives. However, German does not have the 'continuous' tenses found in English, and the English -ing form is only rarely translated by the German present participle:

das **schlafende** Kind	*the sleeping child*
das **gestohlene** Auto	*the stolen car*
But	
Ich **warte** auf dich; ich könnte	*I'm waiting for you; I could be*
schon zu Hause **sitzen**	*sitting at home*

14.1 The infinitive

 ◆ **The infinitive is almost always used with a finite verb**
Normally, the infinitive is preceded by zu, although there are exceptions – see
14.1.2 below.

▶ **TIP** **Finite verb + zu + infinitive, or omit zu?**
 ◆ As a general guide, **zu** is omitted in the same instances as **to** in English:
  ◆ after modal verbs:

Kannst du mir helfen?	*Can you help me?*
Ich sollte früher aufstehen	*I should get up earlier*

  ◆ after some common verbs such as gehen, lassen and sehen:

Er ging einkaufen	*He went shopping*
Ich lasse mir das Auto reparieren	*I'm having the car repaired*
Sie lässt alles herumliegen	*She leaves everything lying around*
Hast du sie ankommen gesehen?	*Did you see her arrive?*

 ◆ Otherwise, the infinitive is usually preceded by **zu**:

Ich hoffe in die Stadt **zu** gehen	*I'm hoping to go into town*
Er vergisst oft mich an**zu**rufen	*He often forgets to phone me*

▶ ### 14.1.1 The infinitive with **zu**

 a zu always stands directly in front of the infinitive
 ◆ If the infinitive is a separable verb, **zu** stands between the prefix and the verb, and
the whole is written as one word:

Ich habe viel **zu** tun	*I have lots to do*
Das ist kaum **zu** glauben!	*I can hardly believe it!*
Wir hoffen um 7 Uhr ab**zu**fahren	*We're hoping to leave at 7 o'clock*
Medikamente sind kühl auf**zu**bewahren	*Medicines are to be stored in a cool place*

 ◆ The infinitive may be the auxiliary of a compound verb form such as the perfect
or passive:

Ich hasse es, so angeschrien **zu werden**	*I hate being shouted at like that*
Es freut mich, ihn kennengelernt **zu haben**	*I'm really pleased to have met him*

 b Verbs commonly linked to an infinitive by using zu

anfangen	*to begin*
anbieten	*to offer*
aufhören	*to stop*
beabsichtigen	*to intend*
beginnen	*to begin*
beschließen	*to decide*
bitten	*to ask*
bleiben	*to remain*

brauchen[1]	*to need*
entscheiden	*to decide*
erlauben	*to allow*
haben	*to have*
hoffen	*to hope*
raten	*to advise*
scheinen	*to seem*
verbieten	*to forbid*
vergessen	*to forget*
versprechen	*to promise*
versuchen	*to try*
vorhaben	*to intend*
vorschlagen	*to suggest*
wissen	*to know how to*

Er bat mich, ihm **zu** helfen	*He asked me to help him.*
Sie hat beschlossen, nichts **zu** sagen	*She decided to say nothing*
Es bleibt ab**zu**warten, ob …	*It remains to be seen whether …*
Ich rate dir, sie sofort an**zu**rufen	*I advise you to phone her immediately*
Er weiß das Leben **zu** genießen	*He knows how to enjoy life*

[1] In formal and written German, brauchen requires zu. In colloquial German, it is often used without zu. Note also that in colloquial usage braucht nicht is more common than muss nicht.

Du brauchst nicht allein hier (**zu**) bleiben	*You don't need to stay here on your own*

c Verbs + daran, darauf, etc. + zu + infinitive clause

• For verbs which are always used with a prepositional object, the preposition becomes a prepositional adverb (da(r)- + preposition) before zu + an infinitive clause:

Ich freue mich **darauf**, dich **zu** besuchen	*I'm looking forward to visiting you*
Sie hat Angst **davor**, ihn anzurufen	*She's frightened of phoning him*

See 13.2 for further details.

d Conjunctions with zu + infinitive

(an)statt … zu *instead of*
außer … zu *without, apart from*
ohne … zu *without, except*
um … zu *in order to*
$\left.\right\}$ **+ infinitive clause**

• If the two clauses linked by one of these conjunctions have the **same subject**, these conjunctions may be used with **zu** + infinitive clause. **dass** + a finite verb may be used instead, though this is not regarded as such good style.

• If the clauses have **different subjects**, **dass** + a finite verb is used with all except um … zu … (see 13.2.1).

• **(an)statt … zu…**

Er sah fern, **(an)statt zu** arbeiten	*He watched TV instead of working*

Or ..., **anstatt dass** er arbeitete

But Du könntest mit dem Bus | *You could go by bus, instead of*
fahren, **anstatt dass ich** dich | *me taking you to the station*
zum Bahnhof bringe

◆ **außer ... zu ...**

Außer sie an**zu**rufen, können wir | *Apart from phoning her, we can*
nur warten | *only wait*

Or Außer dass wir sie anrufen, ...

But Ich habe von dem Dieb nichts | *I didn't see anything of the thief*
gesehen, **außer dass er** eine | *except that he was wearing a*
Mütze trug | *cap*

◆ **ohne ... zu ...**

Sie hat die Tür geschlossen, **ohne** | *She closed the door without*
ein einziges Wort **zu** sagen | *saying a single word*

Or ..., **ohne dass** sie ein einziges
Wort sagte

But Sie hat die Tür geschlossen,
ohne dass er sie hörte

◆ **um ... zu ...**

Ich ging in die Stadt, **um** ein Lineal | *I went into town (in order) to buy a*
zu kaufen | *ruler*

Ich habe ihm eine E-mail | *I sent him an e-mail (in order) to*
geschickt, **um** ihm **zu** sagen, | *tell him that ...*
dass ...

◆ - um ... zu ... is also used after an adjective with zu or genug, as long as the subject
of both clauses remains the same:

Ich verdiene zu wenig Geld, **um** | *I earn too little money to be able to*
mir ein Auto leisten **zu** können | *afford a car*

Er ist nicht stark genug, **um** dieses | *He isn't strong enough to lift*
Gewicht heben **zu** können | *that weight*

But If the two clauses have different subjects, another construction must be
used in place of um ... zu ....

Ich habe eine E-mail bekommen, | *I received an e-mail to tell me*
in der man mir sagte, dass ... | *that ...*

Ich verdiene zu wenig Geld, **als** | *I earn too little money for her to go*
dass sie mit mir ausgehen | *out with me*
würde

◆ Colloquially, simpler constructions would be preferred:

... also würde sie nicht mit mir ausgehen

▷ 14.1.2 The infinitive without **zu**

◆ **The infinitive is used without zu in the same categories of verb as in English
constructions without *to***

a   After modal verbs (e.g. können + infinitive)

◆ dürfen, können, mögen, müssen, sollen and wollen are used without zu before a
following infinitive:

Ich **kann** meine Schlüssel nicht | *I can't find my keys*
finden

| Sie **wollte** uns nicht **besuchen** | *She didn't want to visit us* |
| Man **kann** sich auf ihn **verlassen** | *You can't rely on him* |

+ The infinitive may be the auxiliary of a compound verb form such as the perfect or a passive:

Das **muss** man mal **gesehen haben**!	*It's something you just have to see!*
Er **soll** gestern **abgefahren sein**	*Apparently he left yesterday*
Das **könnte** gestohlen **werden**	*That might be stolen*

b After lassen

Sie **lässt** mich nie ruhig **arbeiten**	*She never lets me work in peace*
Diese Vokabeln **lassen** sich leicht **lernen**	*This vocabulary is easy to learn*
Ich **lasse** mir den Rasenmäher **reparieren**	*I'm having the lawnmower repaired*
Sie **lässt** alles **herumliegen**	*She leaves everything lying around*

c After bleiben with a verb denoting position (see also 14.1.1b)

Wer nicht fleißig arbeitet, **bleibt sitzen**	*Anyone who doesn't work hard has to repeat the year*
Meine Uhr ist schon wieder **stehengeblieben**	*My watch has stopped again*
Er **blieb** wie angewurzelt **stehen**	*He stopped as if rooted to the spot*

d After verbs of perception – sehen, hören, fühlen, spüren (see also 14.1.3b)

| Wir **hörten** sie **abfahren** | *We heard them leave* |
| Er **sah** sie **ankommen** | *He saw her arrive* |

+ A common alternative to the above is wie + a subordinate clause:

| Wir hörten, **wie** er das Haus verließ | *We heard him leave the house* |

e After some verbs of motion – gehen, fahren, kommen

| Er **ging einkaufen** | *He went shopping* |
| **Kommst** du mit **radfahren**? | *Are you coming for a cycle ride with me?* |

f After the verbs helfen, lehren, lernen, zu is optional, though preferred if the clause is long

| Schon mit drei Jahren **lernte** sie **schreiben** | *At three she was already learning to write* |
| Er **hilft** mir die Hausaufgaben **machen** | *He helps me to do my homework* |

But Er hilft mir, die Hausaufgaben besser und schneller **zu** machen

14.1.3 Other uses of the infinitive

a The infinitive can be used as a noun; it is always neuter

+ Nouns formed in such a way often equate to an English noun ending in -*ing*:

ein einziges Kommen und Gehen	*a constant coming and going*
das Hinundherfahren	*driving around aimlessly*
das Autofahren	*driving, motoring*
das Fürsichleben	*living for oneself*

+ Infinitive nouns are often used with beim (*while -ing, on -ing*), or zum (*for, to*):

Ich trinke Kaffee **beim Fernsehen**   *I drink coffee while watching television*

Das ist ja **zum Totlachen**!   *That's so funny!*

b The infinitive is also used instead of a past participle

+ For modal verbs used with another infinitive (which is the norm):

Sie hat es nicht finden **können**   *She's been unable to find it*

Du hättest ihn besuchen **sollen**!   *You should have visited him!*

+ After lassen:

Ich habe das Auto **reparieren** lassen   *I've had the car repaired*

Menschen, die bereits sehr viel Geld besaßen, haben sich **bestechen lassen**   *People who already had a lot of money have accepted bribes*

+ For verbs of perception, e.g. sehen, hören, used with another infinitive:

Wir haben sie abfahren **hören**   *We heard them leave*

Er hat sie ankommen **sehen**   *He saw her arrive*

c The infinitive is also used in some forms of the imperative (see 16.2)

+ See also 18.5 (Word order with infinitive clauses).

14.2 The past participle

▶ 14.2.1 Formation of the past participle

+ See notes on the perfect tense 10.3.1–2.

▶ 14.2.2 Uses

a The main use of the past participle is in the formation of the perfect and pluperfect tenses (see 10.3 and 10.4), as well as the passive voice (see 15.1.1)

b It is also used as an adjective, and, like any other adjective, takes case endings

das **gestohlene** Auto   *the stolen car*

ein **gestohlenes** Auto   *a stolen car*

gestohlene Autos   *stolen cars*

+ The single participle-adjective can be extended into an adjectival phrase before the noun; in English, this would often be expressed by a relative clause. Adjectival phrases are much loved by journalists, but are not used in everyday German:

das **gestern gestohlene** Auto   *the car (which was) stolen yesterday*

das **von Jugendlichen gestohlene** Auto   *the car (which was) stolen by youths*

+ If the verb has a reflexive pronoun, this is omitted in an adjectival phrase based on the past participle:

sich anstrengen   *to make a real effort*

angestrengte Schüler   *pupils who have made a real effort*

sich vorstellen	*to imagine*
das oft **vorgestellte** Problem	*the problem which is often envisaged*

14.3 The present participle

▶ 14.3.1 Formation

+ **The present participle is formed by adding -d to the infinitive**

fahren	fahren**d**
werden	werden**d**

▶ 14.3.2 Uses

a **The present participle is *never* used in the formation of tenses**

+ Its main use is as an **attributive adjective** (i.e. an adjective placed before the noun), and, like any other adjective, it takes case endings:

ein **führender** Politiker	*a leading politician*
mangelnde Sicherheit	*lack of safety precautions*

+ The single participle-adjective can be extended into an adjectival phrase before the noun; in English, this would often be expressed by a relative clause:

das **marktführende** Auto	*the car which leads the field*
ein **nicht zu unterschätzendes** Problem	*a problem which should not be underestimated*
mit einem **immer lauter werdenden** Lärm	*with a noise (which was) growing louder and louder*

+ If the verb has a reflexive pronoun, this is retained in an adjectival phrase based on the present participle (compare this with the past participle used as an adjective, 14.2.2b).

die **sich anstrengenden** Schüler	*the pupils who are making a real effort*
der **sich** viele Probleme **vorstellende** Lehrer	*the teacher envisaging many problems*

b **The adjectival form of the present participle can be used as a noun**

+ It can be any gender, and continues to take adjective endings:

der/die Auszubildende	*trainee*
der/die Vorsitzende	*chairman*
das Spannende	*the exciting thing*
das Interessante daran ist …	*the interesting thing about it is …*

c **The present participle can be used as an adverb**

Er sah mich **lächelnd** an	*He looked at me, smiling*
Sie spricht **verwirrend** schnell	*She speaks confusingly fast*

14.4 The translation of English *-ing* forms

With the exception of the few present participle uses given above, German has no direct equivalent of English *-ing* constructions. The examples given below simply show the main possibilities. You will notice that almost all of these constructions are mentioned elsewhere in the book, and the student is advised to concentrate on the German modes of expression rather than trying to learn exact equivalents for each one; in any case, there are almost always several ways to express the same idea.

14.4.1 Present participle

+ **The present participle may be used as an adjective, adverb or noun (see 14.3.2.b above)**

ein spannender Film	*an exciting film*
eine gutaussehende Frau	*a good-looking woman*
das Hervorragende	*the outstanding thing*

14.4.2 Infinitive

a **The infinitive may be used as a verbal noun (= gerund). Such nouns are always neuter**

Meine Hobbys sind **Lesen** und **Kanufahren**	*My hobbies are reading and canoeing*
Das **Rauchen** ist verboten	*Smoking is forbidden*
Beim **Lesen** bin ich eingeschlafen	*While reading I fell asleep*
Beim **Autofahren** bekomme ich immer Kopfschmerzen	*I always get a headache when driving*
Durch **Schwimmen** bleibe ich fit	*I keep fit by swimming*

TIP *-ing* **words: gerund (=verbal noun) or present participle?**

+ If the word ending in -ing can be replaced by the question 'What?', the word in question is a gerund.

What is your hobby?	*My hobby is **cycling***

+ If, however, the question must be formed using more than one word, or with the verb *to do*, it is a present participle.

What is he doing?	*He is cycling*
What is the film like?	*It's exciting*

---

b **The infinitive is used after verbs of perception (e.g. sehen, hören) (see 14.1.2d above)**

Er fühlte sein Herz **schlagen**	*he felt his heart beating*

c **An infinitive clause may be used with zu when there is no change of subject (see 14.1.1d above)**

Es ist schön, dich **zu sehen**	*It's lovely seeing you*
Ohne **zu fragen**, hat er das Haus verlassen	*He left the house without asking*
Er versuchte, mir **zu helfen**	*He tried helping me*

14.4.3 Subordinate clause

a **A subordinate clause beginning with one of the following conjunctions often indicates *while... -ing, by ...-ing***

während	= two actions occurring simultaneously

wobei	*as (he) did so*; (=at the same time as the action just mentioned)
indem or **dadurch, dass**	*by... -ing* (= the means by which)
Während er zu Abend isst, sieht er fern	*He watches TV while eating his dinner*
Sie bediente den Kunden, **wobei** sie mit ihrer Kollegin plauderte	*She served the customer, chatting to her colleague as she did so*
Er lernt Deutsch, **indem** er jedes Jahr nach Kiel fährt	
Er lernt Deutsch **dadurch, dass** er jedes Jahr nach Kiel fährt	*He learns German by going to Kiel every year*

b Many other subordinating conjunctions may also give rise to English *-ing* constructions

Es ist toll hier, **wenn** wir alle miteinander plaudern	*It's great here, with us all chatting away to each other*
Als ich das Haus betrat, sah ich den Einbrecher	*On entering the house, I saw the burglar*
Bevor ich ins Bett ging, sah ich fern	*Before going to bed, I watched TV*
Nachdem sie das Haus verlassen hatte, ...	*After leaving the house, she ...*

+ **wie after verbs of perception:**

Er fühlte, **wie** sein Herz schlug	*He felt his heart beating*
Ich sah, **wie** sie aus dem Haus ging	*I watched her leaving the house*

c A relative clause may also sometimes be translated by an *-ing* construction

ein Wort, **das** mit *s* beginnt	*a word beginning with s*
ein Mann, **der** eine Krawatte trägt	*a man wearing a tie*

▶ 14.4.4 Other forms

a Main clauses joined by und

Ich betrat das Haus **und** sah den Einbrecher	*On entering the house, I saw the burglar*
Sie öffnete die Tür **und** verließ das Haus	*Opening the door, she left the house*

b Past participle after kommen

Er kam die Straße entlang **gelaufen**	*He came running down the street*

c weiter + verb – *to keep on ...-ing*

Er schlief ruhig **weiter**	*He carried on sleeping peacefully*
Wir müssen **weiter**fahren	*We'll have to keep on driving*

15

The passive voice

OVERVIEW

+ In the **active voice**, the subject 'acts' or performs an action on the object. This is the normal way of speaking and writing about actions:

    Shakespeare **schrieb** *Hamlet*   *Shakespeare wrote* Hamlet
    Meine Eltern **kaufen** dieses Haus   *My parents are buying that house*

+ In the **passive voice**, the subject is the receiver of the action. In the examples above, the direct object of the active sentence (*'Hamlet'*, or *'that house'*) becomes the subject. The original subject (*'Shakespeare'*, or *'my parents'*), called the '**agent**' of the action, is now introduced by the word *by*, or in German by *von*:

    Hamlet **wurde** von Shakespeare   Hamlet *was written by*
        geschrieben   *Shakespeare*
    Dieses Haus **wird** von meinen   *That house is being bought by my*
        Eltern **gekauft**   *parents*

+ The passive is useful because it emphasises the action rather than the thing or person who is doing it. In fact, the 'doer' of the action may not even be mentioned:

    Die Straße **wird** endlich **repariert**   *At last the road is being repaired*

+ German passive forms can distinguish between the process and the resulting state of affairs, which English cannot:

    Die Brücke **wurde** zerstört   *The bridge was destroyed (… by a bomb)*

    Die Brücke **war** zerstört   *The bridge was destroyed (… and could not be used)*

+ German makes less use of the passive than English:
    Endlich **repariert man** die Straße   *At last the road is being repaired*

15.1 The passive voice: formation and use

▶ 15.1.1 Formation of the passive

a The passive is formed using werden + past participle

The 'agent' (when included) is often introduced by von + dative (but see below).

Present	Er **wird** von seinem Vater **abgeholt**	*He's being picked up by ...*
Simple past	Er **wurde** von seinem Vater **abgeholt**	*He was picked up by ...*
Perfect	Er **ist** von seinem Vater **abgeholt worden**[1]	*He has been picked up by ...*
Pluperfect	Er **war** von seinem Vater **abgeholt worden**[1]	*He had been picked up by ...*
Future	Er **wird** von seinem Vater **abgeholt werden**[2]	*He will be picked up by ...*

[1] The past participle **geworden** loses its prefix **ge-**.

[2] The future passive is rarely used; just as in many active sentences German prefers to use the present tense together with an adverb of time:

Dieser Brief **wird** morgen **geschickt**	*This letter will be sent tomorrow*
Er **wird** später von seinem Vater **abgeholt**	*He will be picked up later by his father*

b The passive may also be formed with a modal verb + past participle + werden (used as an infinitive)

Tenses other than present and past are extremely rare.

+ **Present:**

Er **will** von seinem Vater **abgeholt werden**	*He wants to be picked up by his father*

+ **Simple past:**

Er **wollte** von seinem Vater **abgeholt werden**	*He wanted to be picked up by his father*
Der Wiederaufbau nach dem Krieg **konnte** in beschleunigtem Tempo **fortgesetzt werden**	*Post-war rebuilding could be continued at a faster rate*

+ **Perfect:**

Er **muss** von seinem Vater **abgeholt worden sein**	*He must have been picked up by his father*

Note Germans normally prefer a less formal construction than the one above:

Sein Vater hat ihn bestimmt abgeholt

+ wollen in an active sentence often becomes sollen in the passive:

Man **will** hier eine neue Straße bauen	*They're intending to build a new road here*
Hier **soll** eine neue Straße **gebaut werden**	*A new road is intended here*

▷ 15.1.2 The agent *by*

a The agent of the action (i.e. what would be the subject of the sentence in the active voice) is introduced by von, durch, or mit

von	usually persons, or an inanimate force
durch	'the means by which' – usually things, or person as intermediary
mit	the instrument: 'by using'

In other words, von and durch are to some extent interchangeable.

* Agent: person, inanimate force:

Das Auto wird **von** dem Mechaniker repariert	*The car was repaired by the mechanic*
Koblenz wurde **von** dem (*or* **durch** den) Rhein überschwemmt	*Koblenz was flooded by the Rhine*

* Agent: means:

Das Haus ist **durch** eine Bombe zerstört worden	*The house has been destroyed by a bomb*
Die Flugkarte wurde **von** Herrn Braun **durch** seine Sekretärin reserviert	*The air-ticket was booked by Mr Braun through his secretary*

* Instrument: 'by using':

Dieses Buch wurde **mit** einem Computer geschrieben	*This book was written with a computer*

Note The instrument ('by using') keeps this role in both active and passive sentences:

Ich habe das Buch **mit dem Computer** geschrieben

b The agent is often omitted completely

This may be because the perpetrator of an action is not known or is considered unimportant in that particular statement.

Dieses Haus wurde im 16. Jahrhundert gebaut	*This house was built in the sixteenth century*
Ein neues Kaufhaus wird heute eröffnet	*A new store is being opened today*

Note The active subject **man** one, 'they', 'people', never becomes the agent in a passive sentence.

▷ 15.1.3 The subject of the passive sentence

a Only the direct object of an active sentence can be used as the subject (i.e. in the nominative case) of a passive sentence

* The **indirect object** of an active sentence remains in the **dative**. It cannot be used as the subject – note how what appears to be the subject does not agree with the verb in the second example below.

This is different from English, where the direct or indirect object may often be used as the subject of the passive sentence.

Active:	Man gab **meinem Freund** ein Auto	
Passive:	**Meinem Freund** wurde ein Auto gegeben	*My friend was given a car* (lit: 'To my friend was given...')
Not Mein Freund wurde ...		
Active:	Man sagte **ihnen**, sie müssten ...	
Passive:	**Ihnen** wurde gesagt, sie müssten ...	*They were told they would have to ...*
Not Sie wurden ...		

- Similarly, prepositional phrases and dative noun phrases remain unchanged in a passive clause:

Mir wurde nicht erlaubt, mit ihm zu sprechen	*I was not allowed to speak to him*
Uns wird nicht geglaubt	*We are not believed*
Über mich wurde viel gelacht	*I was laughed at a lot*
Darüber wird in dieser Zeitung nicht geschrieben	*Nothing is written about that in this newspaper*

▶ 15.1.4 'Subjectless' or 'impersonal' passive

a The passive is frequently used without a subject

If there is no other introductory idea, such as an adverb, **es** is inserted (to ensure that the verb stands in second position), but it is better style to avoid this.

Den ganzen Abend **wurde gefeiert**	*There were celebrations all evening*
Or **Es wurde** den ganzen Abend **gefeiert**	
Nachmittags **wird** immer Kaffee **getrunken**	*In the afternoons people always drink coffee*
Hier **wird** nicht **geraucht!**	*There's to be no smoking here!*
Jetzt **wird** bitte **gegessen** und nicht **gealbert!**	*Stop messing around and eat your meal!* (instruction to child)

b In subordinate clauses containing a passive, es is never used, as the conjunction (weil, dass, etc.) occupies the first position

Wir waren froh, dass den ganzen Abend **gefeiert wurde**

▶ 15.1.5 The passive using **sein**

a By using sein instead of werden, German can distinguish between a state and the action which led to it

The **werden** passive is more common, but the choice depends on the emphasis the speaker wishes to place on the statement.

Das Auto **wird repariert**	*The car is being repaired*
(=Someone is repairing the car)	
Das Auto **ist repariert**	*The car is repaired*
(=The repairs are complete)	
Als wir es fanden, **war** mein Auto schwer **beschädigt**, aber ich weiß immer noch nicht, wie es **beschädigt wurde**	*When we found it, my car was badly damaged, but I still don't know how it was damaged*

(The sein passive emphasises the damaged state, the werden passive emphasises the event.)

b   The sein passive may indicate an existing or permanent state of affairs
This state is not necessarily the result of an action.

Das Geschäft **ist** durchgehend **geöffnet**	*The shop is open all hours*
Der Staatsvertrag **wurde** erst zustande **gebracht** als der Krieg bereits seit zehn Jahren **beendet war**	*The international treaty only came into being when the war had already been over for ten years*
Deutschland **wäre** viel Zerstörung erspart **geblieben**	*Germany would have been spared much destruction*

c   Note the use of sein and werden passives with geboren

Ich **bin** in Köln **geboren**	*I was born in Cologne*

(place of birth only)

Ich **wurde** 1983 in Köln **geboren**	*I was born in 1983 in Cologne*

(date or other details mentioned)

Bach **wurde/war** 1685 in Eisenach **geboren**	*Bach was born in 1685 in Eisenach*

(For people now dead, either form may be used)

▶ 15.1.6   Verbs which cannot be used in the passive

a   A number of transitive verbs may form a passive in English but not in German
The active voice must be used, or a different verb chosen:
♦ Verbs of perception when used with an infinitive
   e.g. hören *to hear*, sehen *to see*
♦ A few other verbs:

haben	*to have*	enthalten *to contain*
besitzen	*to own*	kennen, wissen *to know*
bekommen		
erhalten	} *to receive*	
kriegen		

Dieser Schauspieler ist nicht sehr bekannt	*This actor is not well known*
Not …wird nicht gekannt	
Das Gemälde gehört meiner Familie seit jeher	*The painting has been owned by my family for years*
Not wird … besessen	
Er wurde vor kurzem in London gesehen	*He was seen recently in London*
But	
Der Polizist hat gesehen, wie er bei Rot über die Kreuzung gefahren ist	*He was seen by the policeman crossing the junction on red*
Not Er wurde … fahren gesehen	

Ihre Mail ist gestern eingetroffen	*Your e-mail was received yesterday*
Not wurde … bekommen	

15.1.7 The passive in infinitive constructions

a The passive may also be used in infinitive clauses, as long as the main and subordinate clause share the same subject

Er hofft, um 9 Uhr **abgeholt zu werden**.	*He's hoping to be picked up at 9 o'clock*
Er hoffte, um 9 Uhr **abgeholt zu werden**.	*He was hoping to be picked up at 9 o'clock*

+ The two sentences above could also be expressed as passives in normal subordinate clauses:

Er hofft, dass er um 9 Uhr **abgeholt wird**	*He is hoping that he'll be picked up at 9 o'clock*
Er hoffte, dass er um 9 Uhr **abgeholt wurde**	*He was hoping that he'd be picked up at 9 o'clock*

Note the use of the **past participle + worden zu sein**

Er behauptete, um 9 Uhr **abgeholt worden zu sein**	*He claimed to have been picked up at 9 o'clock*

Or

Er behauptete, dass er um 9 Uhr **abgeholt worden war**	*He claimed that he had been picked up at 9 o'clock*

15.2 Alternatives to the passive

+ The passive is often used in English in order to rearrange a sentence so that it can begin with an idea other than the subject, or to avoid using a pronoun such as 'one':

> *This computer program can be learned easily*

+ In German, however, it is easy to place the object of the sentence before the verb, and the pronoun **man** is frequently used. These, together with a number of other common constructions, mean that the passive tends to be used less frequently than in English, though it is not at all uncommon, especially in formal writing.
+ Here is a passive sentence followed by several common ways of expressing the same idea without using the passive:

Das Computerprogramm **kann** leicht **gelernt werden**	*The computer program can be learned easily*
or Das Computerprogramm **lässt sich** leicht **lernen**	
or Das Computerprogramm **ist** leicht **lernbar**	
or Das Computerprogramm **ist** leicht **zu lernen**	
or **Man kann** das Computerprogramm leicht **lernen**	

a The passive can be avoided by using man as the subject

This is very much more common than *one* in English.

Da hat **man** die Straße schon wieder gesperrt	*The road's been closed off yet again*

b The subject and the object can be inverted

Diese Landschaft beschreibt der Schriftsteller in seinen Romanen	*This landscape is described by the writer in his novels*

c A reflexive verb can sometimes be used

Das Buch **verkauft sich** sehr gut	*The book is selling very well*
Dieser Wein **trinkt sich** gut	*This wine slips down easily*
Eine Lösung wird **sich finden**	*A solution will be found*

d sein + zu + infinitive is often used to indicate possibility or obligation

Ist diese Idee **zu rechtfertigen**?	*Can this idea be justified?*
Es **ist zu befürchten**, dass viele Leute gestorben sind	*It is to be feared that many people have died*

e In formal German, an adjectival phrase based on a participle may be used (see 14.2.2. and 14.3.2)

ein nicht zu unterschätzendes Problem	*a problem which should not be underestimated*

f sich lassen + infinitive is often used to indicate possibility

Das Fenster **ließ sich** nur schwer **öffnen**	*The window could only be opened with difficulty*
Es **lässt sich** nicht **leugnen**, dass …	*It cannot be denied that …*

g bekommen or kriegen + past participle is sometimes used

Sie **bekam** das Auto **geschenkt**	*She was given the car*
Er will das **übersetzt kriegen**	*He wants to get this translated*

16

The imperative mood

OVERVIEW

▶ **The imperative mood**

The imperative is one of three 'moods', or forms of the verb which express the **attitude** of the speaker to the action.

- The **indicative mood** indicates real events and is for that reason the most common:

  Ich arbeite fleißig   *I'm working hard*

- The **subjunctive mood** is used, for instance, for wishes and hypothetical events:

  Wenn er nur fleißig wäre!   *If only he were hard-working!*

- The **imperative mood** is used for commands:

  Setz dich! ⎫
  Setzt euch! ⎬   *Sit down!*
  Setzen Sie sich! ⎭
  Setzen wir uns!   *Let's sit down*

▶ **Types of imperative**

There are two main types of imperative, just as there are in English, depending on who is being given the command:

- The **you** imperative. There are three forms in German, corresponding to the **du**, **ihr** and **Sie** forms of the pronoun. See examples above.
- The **we** imperative, expressed in English by *Let's ...* and in German by the **wir** form of the verb. See example above.
- Other forms of the verb, notably the infinitive, are also used to give instructions or commands:

  Stehenbleiben!   *Halt!*
  Die Eiweiße steif schlagen   *Beat the egg whites until stiff*

16.1 The imperative: formation and use

16.1.1 Example

(du)	Hör auf!	*Stop doing that!*
(ihr)	Wartet auf mich!	*Wait for me!*
(Sie)	Warten Sie bitte einen Augenblick!	*Please wait a moment!*
(wir)	Gehen wir nach Hause!	*Let's go home!*

♦ See also section 16.2 below.

16.1.2 Formation

du:	weak verbs:	du form of present tense less –st
	strong verbs:	as above, retaining vowel change (**But** ä becomes a)
ihr:	all verbs:	ihr form without ihr
Sie:	all verbs:	Sie form, inverted (i.e. Sie after the verb)
wir:	all verbs:	wir form of verb, inverted (i.e. wir after the verb)

	Infinitive	du	ihr	Sie	wir
Weak	*machen*	mach!	macht!	machen Sie!	machen wir!
	aufhören	hör auf!	hört auf!	hören Sie auf!	hören wir auf!
	sich setzen	setz dich!	setzt euch!	setzen Sie sich!	setzen wir uns!
Strong	*geben*	gib!	gebt!	geben Sie!	geben wir!
	lesen	lies!	lest!	lesen Sie!	lesen wir!
	fahren	fahr!	fahrt!	fahren Sie!	fahren wir!
Irregular	*sein*	sei!	seid!	seien Sie!	seien wir!
	haben	habe!	habt!	haben Sie!	haben wir!
	werden	werde!	werdet!	werden Sie!	werden wir!

16.1.3 The **du** form

a Most verbs form the imperative simply by dropping the -st from the du form

Bring einen Freund mit!	*Bring a friend with you!*
Spiel das bitte noch einmal vor!	*Please play that again!*
Gib ihm noch eine Chance!	*Give him another chance!*

b The du forms of some verbs *always* add an -e in the imperative

♦ verbs with stems ending in -d, -t, or -m, -n after another consonant (i.e. verbs which have an -e- before the ending in the standard du form):

Warte!	*Wait!*	Öffne die Tür!	*Open the door!*
		Arbeite fleißiger!	*Work harder!*

♦ verbs whose infinitives end in -eln or -igen:

Entschuldige!	*Excuse me!*

c Other verbs *may* add -e in the du form of the imperative

♦ In written German, the du form of the imperative (**except** for verbs whose stem vowel changes from -e- to -i- or -ie-) sometimes appears with the ending -e. This addition is not obligatory, even in formal German.

Schick**e** mir dein Foto!	*Send me your photo!*
Or Schick mir …	
Fahr**e** mit mir in die Schweiz!	*Come with me to Switzerland!*
Or Fahr mit mir …	

d Strong verbs with a stem vowel which changes to i or ie in the du and er/sie/es forms *never* add -e in the du form of the imperative

Nimm dieses Buch!	*Take this book!*
Gib mir das Buch!	*Give me the book!*
Lies diesen Artikel!	*Read this article!*

▶ 16.1.4 Polite commands and requests

• The imperative used alone can sound blunt or imperious. Where English often prefers a different form ('*Could you …?*') German almost always makes a command or request more polite in one or more of the following ways:

a Adding a particle such as mal or doch

Ruf mich **mal** an!	*Just give me a call!*
Hör **doch** damit auf!	*Do stop doing that!*
Bringt mir **mal** eure Bücher!	*Just bring me your books!*

b Making a request instead of using the imperative, often with bitte *please*

• It is the intonation which gives the request its politeness:

Gibst du mir bitte das Salz?	*Could you pass the salt, please?*
Sagst du es bitte mal lauter?	*Could you just say it louder, please?*

• Among friends or family, bitte may be omitted without loss of politeness:

Gibst du mir mal die Mayo, Mama?	*Could you pass the mayonnaise please, Mum?*

c Very polite requests can be expressed in the form of a suggestion by using können in the present tense or in its *Konjunktiv II* form, or würden Sie …

Können Sie mir bitte mal helfen?	*Can you help me please?*
Könnten Sie mich bitte morgen anrufen?	*Could you please phone me tomorrow?*
Würden Sie bitte einen Moment warten?	*Would you wait just one moment, please?*

Note In business communications German does not use its counterparts of *could* or *would* to the extent required in polite formal English:

Bitte schicken Sie mir Ihren neuen Katalog	*I should be grateful if you would send me a copy of your latest catalogue*

▶ 16.1.5 Adding emphasis to a command or request

a Although normally omitted, du or ihr are sometimes included for emphasis

Sprich **du** doch mit ihm!	*You go and talk to him yourself!*
Ruft **ihr** sie selber an!	*You phone her yourselves!*

b A request uttered with the intonation of a command makes it sound more definite than a simple imperative

Compare these two examples:

Hör endlich damit auf!	*Just stop that!*
Hörst du jetzt endlich damit auf?!	*STOP that this instant!*

16.1.6 **wir** forms of the imperative

♦ ***Let's …* is usually expressed by the inverted wir form**

OK, gehen wir!	*OK, let's go!*
Machen wir uns auf die Socken!	*Let's get going!*
Seien wir froh, dass ihm nichts Schlimmeres passiert ist!	*Let's be glad that nothing worse happened to him*

See also 16.3g below.

16.2 The infinitive in general and official instructions

a The infinitive is often used for general and official commands and instructions

♦ It is also used in instructions for, for instance, equipment and cooking recipes. It is used because it does not focus on a particular person or group.

Nicht **rauchen**!	*No smoking*
Bitte **lächeln**!	*Smile, please!*
Bitte **einsteigen** und Türen **schließen**! (at a railway station)	*Please get in and close the doors*
Nur Siemens-Originalfilter **verwenden**	*Use only original Siemens filters*
Die Äpfel in kleine Würfel **schneiden** …	*Cut the apples into small cubes…*

b Reflexive verbs used in this way lose the reflexive pronoun

Nicht hinauslehnen! (on windows of railway trains)	*Do not lean out!*
Bitte anschnallen!	*Fasten your seatbelts!*

c The Sie form is sometimes used instead of the infinitive in instruction manuals

Erneuern Sie den Bürstenkopf alle sechs Monate	*Renew the brush head every six months*

16.3 Other ways of expressing commands

a Nouns, adjectives, and particles can be used in short commands

Vorsicht!	*Look out!*
Herein!	*Come in!*
Entschuldigung!	*Excuse me!*

b In cafés and restaurants, the ich form is often used when placing an order

Ich bekomme ein Schnitzel mit Salat, bitte	*I'll have a schnitzel with salad, please*

c Sollen (also with reported speech)

Du **sollst** mir zuhören!	*You're to listen to me!*
Die Chefin sagte ihm, er **sollte/** **soll** eine neue Stelle suchen	*The boss told him to look for a new job*

d Statements

Sie sind so nett und bleiben hier!	*Please be so kind as to wait here!*

e The use of haben or sein + zu + infinitive

Diese Aufgabe **ist** sofort **zu** **erledigen**, verstanden?	*This task is to be carried out immediately – understood?*
Du **hast** mir **zuzuhören**!	*You're to listen to me!*

f The verb is omitted (because the meaning is quite clear without it)

Bitte nicht!	*Please don't!*
Herein!	*Come in!*

g An impersonal passive

Jetzt **wird** hier **gearbeitet**!	*Let's have some work done here!*
Jetzt **wird** bitte nicht mehr **gealbert**!	*No more messing around, please!*

17

The subjunctive mood

OVERVIEW

▶ **The subjunctive mood**

There are three **moods** (or modes of expression): the **indicative mood** (e.g. present, perfect, simple past and future tenses), which is the most common, and describes actual, real or likely events, the **imperative mood**, used for commands, and the **subjunctive**.

The **subjunctive** (in German, *Konjunktiv*) is the forms of the verb used, in essence, to take a step back from the actual or likely events described by the indicative. It is used to describe, for example,
+ events which *would* happen *if …*
+ events which *might* happen
+ events which we *wish* would happen
+ or events or statements which we are merely reporting from someone else.

▶ **Subjunctive 1/*Konjunktiv I***

+ **Reported speech**
  The main use of **Subjunctive 1** is for reported speech; the subjunctive is required, as what is reported may or may not be true:

Er sagte, er **sei** nach Amerika **gefahren**	*He said he's been to America*
Sie sagt, sie **habe** keine Zeit	*She says she has no time*

  (…but I'm just reporting that – it may or may not be true)

▶ **Subjunctive 2/*Konjunktiv II***

+ *If* **statements**
  The main use of **Subjunctive 2** is for unlikely or hypothetical events:

Wenn ich genug Geld **hätte**, **würde** ich nach Amerika **fahren**	*If I had enough money, I would go to America*

  (…but I don't have enough, so it's unlikely or hypothetical)

+ **Wishes**

Ich wünschte, ich **könnte** nach Amerika fahren	*I wish I could go to America*

  (… but I can't, so it's hypothetical)

+ **Polite requests**

Könnten Sie mir bitte helfen?	*Could you help me, please?*

17.1 Subjunctive 1/*Konjunktiv I*: formation and summary

▷ **17.1.1** Example

Sie sagte, sie **sei** krank und **bleibe** zu Hause	*She said she was ill and was staying at home*

▷ **17.1.2** Main use

* Reported speech in formal and written language. See 17.3.

▷ **17.1.3** Formation

* **Stem of the infinitive + subjunctive endings (see table below), also called 'present subjunctive'**
* The only irregular verb is sein.

	Weak	Strong	Modal	Auxiliaries		
	machen	**halten**	**können**	**werden**	**haben**	**sein**
ich	mache	halte	könne	werde	habe	sei
du	machest	haltest	könnest	werdest	habest	seist
er/sie/es	mache	halte	könne	werde	habe	sei
wir	machen	halten	können	werden	haben	seien
ihr	machet	haltet	könnet	werdet	habet	seiet
sie/Sie	machen	halten	können	werden	haben	seien

Note Only the er/sie/es forms of Subjunctive 1 are still in common use for most verbs, except for sein and the modals, where all forms are used.

▷ **17.1.4** Reporting present, past and future statements

* For statements in the **present tense** (whatever the tense of the introductory verb), use **Subjunctive 1** of the finite verb.

Er sagt, er **kaufe** …	*He says he's buying …*
Er hat gesagt, er **kaufe** …	*He said he bought …*

* For statements in any of the **past tenses** (past, perfect or pluperfect), there is only one form: use **Subjunctive 1** of **haben** or **sein + past participle.**

Er sagt, er **habe** … **gekauft**	*He says he bought …*
Sie sagt, sie **habe** … **müssen**	*She says she had to …*
Sie sagt, er **sei** … **gefahren**	*She says he went …*

* For statements in the **future**, use the **Subjunctive 1** of werden + **infinitive.**

Er sagt, er **werde** … **kaufen**	*He says he'll buy …*

17.2 Subjunctive 2/*Konjunktiv II*: formation and summary

▶ 17.2.1 Example

> Wenn ich krank **wäre**, **würde** ich   *If I were ill, I would stay at home*
> zu Hause **bleiben**

▶ 17.2.2 Main uses

- Unreal, hypothetical or possible events and wishes (17.4.2)
- Polite requests (17.4.4)
- After als ob (*as if*) (17.4.6)

▶ 17.2.3 Formation

a Stem of the simple past + subjunctive endings
- Strong, irregular and modal verbs add an umlaut if possible (except wollen and sollen: er wollte, er sollte).
- Weak verbs do not add an umlaut and are identical with the indicative simple past forms.

	Weak	Strong[1]	Modal[2]	Auxiliaries[2]		
	machen	**halten**	**können**	**werden**	**haben**	**sein**
ich	machte	hielte	könnte	würde	hätte	wäre
du	macht**est**	hiel**test**	könn**test**	würd**est**	hätt**est**	wär**est**
er/sie/es	machte	hielte	könnte	würde	hätte	wäre
wir	macht**en**	hiel**ten**	könn**ten**	würd**en**	hätt**en**	wär**en**
ihr	macht**et**	hiel**tet**	könn**tet**	würd**et**	hätt**et**	wär**et**
sie/Sie	macht**en**	hiel**ten**	könn**ten**	würd**en**	hätt**en**	wär**en**

[1] In practice, only a few strong and irregular verbs are still relatively common in this simple (one-word) past form. Apart from halten, they are:

finden	ich fände	heißen	ich hieße	nehmen	ich nähme
geben	ich gäbe	kommen	ich käme	tun	ich täte
gehen	ich ginge	lassen	ich ließe	wissen	ich wüsste

[2] The auxiliaries are always used in the simple (one-word) form:
- haben, sein, werden (listed above)
- the modal verbs; apart from können (listed above), these are:

dürfen: ich dürfte   mögen: ich möchte   müssen: ich müsste   sollen: ich sollte   wollen: ich wollte

b würde + infinitive (sometimes called the conditional)
- These forms are identical in use and meaning to the one-word forms.
  > er ginge/er würde gehen   *he would go*
- The würde + infinitive forms of the modals are also used in colloquial German.
  > Er wusste, dass er bis 3 Uhr das Buch   *He knew that he would have finished*
  > zu Ende gelesen **haben würde**   *reading the book by 3 o'clock*
  > Ich **würde** dorthin fahren **können**,   *I'd be able to go there if …*
  > wenn …

▶ 17.2.4 Conditional in the past (or pluperfect subjunctive)

- To refer to past hypothetical events; hätte or wäre + past participle. See 17.5.

Sie hätte ... gemacht	*She would have done ...*
Er wäre ... gefahren	*He would have gone ...*

17.3 Subjunctive 1/*Konjunktiv I*: use

> **TIP** **Remembering the Subjunctive 1/*Konjunktiv I* forms for reported speech**
> - Mostly, one reports what one other person has said. For the **er/sie/es** form, simply take the infinitive, and remove the **-n**. This works with all verbs, including strong verbs, modals, irregulars, and **sein**.
> - Verbs which end in **-eln** or **-ern** lose the -e from the stem.
>
> Er sagt, er **segle** nach Island   *He says he's sailing to Iceland*

▶ 17.3.1 Statements in reported or indirect speech

a **The tense of the reported statement remains in the tense of the original direct statement, and Subjunctive 1 of the reported finite verb is used (but see 17.3.1b below)**

- In English, by contrast, the tense of the reported statement changes according to the tense of the introductory verb. Compare the German and English in these pairs of statements:

Direct: Sie hat gesagt: „Ich fahre morgen in die USA"	*She said, 'I'm going to the USA tomorrow'*
Reported: Sie sagt, sie **fahre** morgen in die USA	*She says she **is going** to the USA tomorrow*
Sie hat gesagt, sie **fahre** morgen in die USA	*She said she **was going** to the USA tomorrow*
Direct: Er meint: „ich habe kein Geld mehr"	*He says, 'I've got no more money'*
Reported: Er meint, er **habe** kein Geld mehr	*He says he **has** no more money*
Er meinte, er **habe** kein Geld mehr	*He said he **had** no more money*
Direct: Ihre Mutter sagte: „sie sind krank"	*Their mother said, 'they're ill'*
Reported: Sie sagt, sie **seien** krank	*She says they**'re** ill*
Sie hat gesagt, sie **seien** krank	*She said they **were** ill*
Direct: „Die Ausgangssperre **ist** eine Vorsichtsmaßnahme und **gilt** bis 18.00 Uhr", meldete die Nachrichtenagentur	*The news agency reported, 'The curfew **is** a security measure and **is in force** until 6 p.m.'*
Reported: Die Ausgangssperre **sei** eine Vorsichtsmaßnahme und **gelte** bis 18.00 Uhr, meldete die Nachrichtenagentur	*The curfew **was** a security measure and **was in force** until 6 p.m., the news agency reported*

b However, if the Subjunctive 1 form is the same as the indicative, German uses the Subjunctive 2 form

♦ The **würde + infinitive** form is common here, as the one-word Subjunctive 2 form is now limited to a very few verbs (see 17.2.3a above). Care must be taken not to confuse this with English *would.*

Sie sagen, sie **hätten** (*not* haben) keine Zeit	*They say they have no time*
Er sagt, sie **könnten** es sich nicht leisten (*not* können)	*He says they can't afford it*
Sie sagten, sie **würden** nach Hause **gehen**	*They said they were going home*
Or ...sie **gingen** (*but not* gehen) nach Hause	
Er sagte, ich **würde** zu viel Geld **ausgeben** (*not* ich gebe)	*He said I was spending too much money*

c Pronouns and possessives must be changed to the sense of the reported statement

Direct: Sie sagte: „Ich habe meiner Mutter mein Auto geliehen"	*She said: 'I lent my mother my car'*
Reported: Sie sagte, sie habe **ihrer** Mutter **ihr** Auto geliehen	*She says she lent her mother her car*

> ▶ **TIP**   **German makes clear when speech is being reported**
>
> ♦ It is not necessary to repeat phrases such as sie sagte in every sentence to remind the reader that the speech is reported, as the verb form itself makes this clear, even in longer passages found in news coverage in the press or on television. Note also the use of soll – *is said to.*
>
> | | |
> |---|---|
> | Der Ministerpräsident **soll** gewusst haben, dass der Geheimdienst auch Flughäfen in Spanien benutzt hat. Die USA **hätten** die Regierung um Erlaubnis **gebeten**, den spanischen Luftraum zu durchfliegen | *The prime minister is said to have known that the secret service had also used airports in Spain. The USA had, it is said, requested permission from the government to use Spanish air-space* |

d To report statements in any of the past tenses, German uses Subjunctive 1 of haben or sein with the past participle

♦ If the form of **haben** is the same as the indicative (a problem which cannot arise with **sein**), Subjunctive 2 is used.

♦ There is only one form for reporting any of the past tenses, whether perfect, imperfect (simple past), or pluperfect:

Direct:	**Reported:**
Er schrieb: „Ich **bin** nach Berlin **gefahren**"	
Er schrieb: „Ich **fuhr** nach London" }	Er schrieb, er **sei** nach London **gefahren**
Er schrieb: „Ich **war** nach London **gefahren**"	

Direct:	Reported:
Sie sagten: „Wir **haben** den Film **gesehen**" ⎫	Sie sagten, sie **hätten**
Sie sagten: „Wir **sahen** den Film" ⎬	den Film **gesehen**
Sie sagten: „Wir **hatten** den Film **gesehen**" ⎭	(**not**:…, sie haben den Film gesehen)

e To report statements in the future tense, German uses Subjunctive 1 of werden plus the infinitive

✦ If this is identical to the indicative, the Subjunctive 2 of werden is used:

Direct: Sie sagte: „Ich werde auf die Uni gehen"

Reported: Sie sagte, sie **werde** auf die Uni **gehen**   *She said she would go to university*

Direct: Sie sagten: „Wir werden bestimmt dorthin fahren"

Reported: Sie sagten, sie **würden** bestimmt dorthin **fahren** (**not:** sie werden)   *They said they would definitely go there*

▶ 17.3.2 Commands in reported speech

✦ **Commands are usually expressed in reported speech by using sollen**

As in other forms of reported speech, the Subjunctive 2 form is used if necessary to avoid ambiguity.

Direct: Er sagte ihm: „Warten Sie einen Augenblick"

Reported: Er sagte ihm, er **solle** einen Augenblick warten   *He told him to wait for a moment*

Direct: Er sagte uns: „Warten Sie einen Augenblick"

Reported: Er sagte uns, wir **sollten** einen Augenblick warten   *He told us to wait for a moment*

▶ 17.3.3 Questions and requests in reported speech

a Reported questions become subordinate clauses introduced by the interrogative

Direct: „Wann fährt der Zug?", fragte er

Reported: Er fragte, **wann** der Zug **abfahre**   *He asked when the train left*

b If there is no interrogative, the reported question is introduced with ob *if*

Direct: „Ist der Zug schon abgefahren?", fragte er

Reported: Er fragte, **ob** der Zug schon **abgefahren sei**   *He asked if the train had already left*

▶ 17.3.4 Avoiding the use of reported speech

a While formal usage usually requires the Subjunctive 1, dass plus a subordinate clause in the indicative is acceptable, even in formal German, and will often be found alongside the subjunctive

Sie wies darauf hin, **dass** die Ausländer einen bedeutenden Faktor **darstellen**	She pointed out that foreigners were a significant factor
Sie kommt zu dem Schluss, **dass** Arbeitsplätze nicht beliebig getauscht werden **können**	She concludes that jobs cannot simply be exchanged at will

♦ If dass is omitted, the subjunctive must be used:

Sie wies darauf hin, die Ausländer **stellten** einen bedeutenden Faktor **dar**	She pointed out that foreigners were a significant factor

b Colloquial German mostly avoids the Subjunctive 1 completely

Er sagt, er **hat** einfach keine Zeit	He says he just doesn't have the time
Sie sagt, sie **wird** uns bald besuchen	She says she'll visit us soon

♦ Used in colloquial language, the choice of Subjunctive 1 implies considerable doubt on the part of the speaker:

Sie sagt, sie **sei** krank	She says she's ill (…but I think she's probably pretending)

▶ 17.3.5 Subjunctive 1 in wishes and commands

♦ **This use is mostly restricted to the third person**

Es **lebe** die Freiheit!	Long live freedom!
Gott **sei** Dank!	Thank goodness!
Seien[1] wir froh, dass…	Let's be happy that …

[1] The normal **wir** form of the imperative is in fact a Subjunctive 1. However, **sein** is the only verb where this is clear.

17.4 Subjunctive 2/*Konjunktiv II*: use

♦ **Note** The English use of *would* for repeated actions in the past (*Every day, he would go to the park*) is not a subjunctive, but a past tense.

▶ 17.4.1 One-word and two-word forms and register

a German today uses the würde + infinitive almost exclusively, apart from the auxiliaries, the modals, and a few strong and irregular verbs listed in 17.2.3a above, though even here würde + infinitive is now used colloquially

♦ This is acceptable even if würde is used twice, separated only by a comma:

Wenn ich dort **arbeiten würde**, **würde** ich **versuchen**, eine neue Stelle zu finden	If I worked there, I would try to find a new job

◆ würde may be used in wenn clauses, unlike English, where *would* cannot usually appear in the same clause as *if*:

Wenn er morgen **ankommen** **würde, würde** ich mich **freuen**	*If he arrived tomorrow, I'd be really pleased*

▶ **TIP** Simple (one-word) Subjunctive 2 or würde + infinitive?
An easy to remember rule is:
◆ One word forms: auxiliaries, modal verbs and geben
    hätte, wäre, würde, könnte, müsste, dürfte, möchte, es gäbe
◆ Two-word forms: all other verbs
    er würde … kaufen, sie würde … gehen

---

b In formal language, the one-word forms of weak verbs are occasionally found

Wenn er nicht **rauchte**, wäre er viel gesünder	*If he didn't smoke, he would be much healthier*
Wenn ich dort **arbeitete**, müsste ich versuchen, eine neue Stelle zu finden	*If I worked there, I would have to try to find a new job*

Note If the one-word form of the verb is used, it is important that the statement is *clearly* subjunctive, if that is what is required. Compare these two sentences; the weak verb in the first clause could be either indicative or conditional; the verb in the following clause makes it clear:

Wenn ich ihn **besuchte**, **versuchte** ich ihm zu helfen	*Whenever I visited him, I tried to help him*
Wenn ich ihn **besuchte**, **würde** ich **versuchen**, ihm zu helfen	*If I visited him, I would try to help him*

▶ 17.4.2 'Real' and 'unlikely' conditions and events

◆ Conditions are usually introduced by **wenn**; alternatively, **falls** may be used, as it is completely unambiguous in meaning *if, in case*. For other possibilities see 17.4.2e below.

a 'Real' conditions and events. For events and conditions which are quite possible, the indicative is used

Wenn ich Zeit **habe**, **gehe** ich ins Kino	*If I have the time, I'll go to the cinema*
Falls du in den Supermarkt **gehst**, **kannst** du bitte Milch holen?	*If you happen to go to the supermarket, can you get some milk?*
Nimm den Regenschirm mit, falls es **regnet**	*Take the umbrella with you in case it rains*

b 'Unlikely' conditions and events. For events which are felt to be less likely, or are less certain, the Subjunctive 2 is used

Wenn ich Zeit **hätte**, **würde** ich öfter ins Kino gehen	*If I had the time, I'd go to the cinema more often*
An deiner Stelle **würde** ich nein sagen	*If I were you, I'd say no*

Es **wäre** toll, wenn du uns
besuchen **könntest**

*It would be great if you could
visit us*

Wenn ich in Berlin leben **würde,**
würde ich oft in die Oper
gehen

*If I lived in Berlin, I would go to the
opera often*

+ This also includes tentative statements:

Das **dürfte** wohl die beste Lösung
sein

*That might well be the best
solution*

Er **dürfte** sechzehn sein

He is perhaps sixteen

c even if ...

+ Auch wenn…/ selbst wenn … / sogar wenn …/wenn…auch… all mean 'even if…'

Auch wenn ich das **wüsste,**
würde ich es dir nicht **sagen**

*Even if I knew that, I wouldn't tell
you*

▶ **TIP** **Conditional in both wenn clause and main clause**

+ While English uses the simple past tense in the *if* clause (apart from *to be* as in:
If I were …) and the conditional in the main clause, **German uses Subjunctive 2
in both clauses.**

Wenn ich ihn **besuchte/besuchen**
würde, könnte ich ihm helfen

If I visited him, I could help him

---

d wenn is sometimes omitted, though not normally in everyday speech

+ The condition is stated first, with the verb at the start. The second clause quite
often starts with so or dann:

Hätte ich genug Geld, (so) **würde**
ich nach Amerika **fahren**

*If I had enough money, I would go
to America*

Hätte ich das gewusst, (so) **wäre**
ich zu Hause geblieben

*Had I known that, I'd have stayed
at home*

Wäre ich so reich wie du, …

If I were as rich as you, …

e Other phrases may introduce unreal or unlikely conditions

An deiner Stelle würde ich sie
sofort anrufen

*If I were you, I would phone her
immediately*

In so einem Fall könnte ich dir
vielleicht helfen

*In such a case I might be able to
help you*

▷ 17.4.3 Wishes

+ **Wishes are also hypothetical conditions, so Subjunctive 2 may be used**

Ich **würde** so gerne hier **bleiben**!   *I'd really love to stay here!*

Wenn es doch nicht so kalt **wäre**!   *If only it weren't so cold!*

Wenn ich doch mehr Geld
verdiente!

If only I earned more money!

(*Or* … **verdienen würde**)

▶ 17.4.4 Polite requests and statements

+ **As in English, Subjunctive 2 is used to make requests, statements, etc. sound more polite**

Könntest du mir helfen?	*Could you help me?*
Ich **möchte** ein Pfund Butter	*I'd like a pound of butter*
„**Hätten** Sie noch einen Wunsch?"	*'Is there anything else?'*
„Nein, danke. Das **wär's**"	*'No thanks. That's all'*
Ich **hätte** noch eine Frage	*I'd like to ask another question*
Ich **würde sagen**, dass …	*I'd say that …*

Note With friends and family, **bitte** gives quite enough politeness to a request made with a rising, querying tone; Subjunctive 2 is not necessary.

Gibst du mir **bitte** das Salz?	*Could you pass the salt, please?*
Kannst du mir **bitte** mal helfen?	*Could you just help me, please?*

▶ 17.4.5 Future in the past

+ **The conditional is often used for a future event from the point of view of the past**

Ich wusste schon mit sechzehn, ich **würde** Politiker **werden**	*Even at sixteen, I knew that I would become a politician*
Niemand glaubte, dass wir ihn nie **wiedersehen würden**	*Nobody believed that we would never see him again*

▶ 17.4.6 als ob + Subjunctive 2

a **als ob (*as if*) must be followed by the subjunctive – usually Subjunctive 2. See 17.4.6b below**

Er sieht aus, als ob er **weinen würde**	*He looks as if he's crying (or: about to cry)*
Er sah aus, als ob er krank **wäre**	*He looked as if he were (or: was) ill*
Er tat, als ob er nichts **hörte**	*He pretended not to hear anything*

+ Occasionally, for the sake of clarity, the indicative may be used:

Es scheint, als ob fast alles, was der Bursche anfasst, zu Gold **wird**	*It seems as if everything the youngster touches turns to gold*

b **ob can be omitted; als is then followed by the verb**

+ This usually occurs only in written German:

Er tat, als **wüsste** er nichts davon	*He pretended he knew nothing about it*
Sie vermitteln keineswegs den Eindruck, als **stünde** der Niedergang bevor	*They do not give the least impression that they are facing defeat*
Man behandelt sie, als **seien** sie Untermenschen	*They're treated as if they were subhuman*

c In spoken German, the indicative is often used after als ob, instead of Subjunctive 2

Er sieht aus, als ob er **schläft**	*He looks as if he's asleep*
Er sah aus, als ob er krank **war**	*He looked as if he were ill*

d The Subjunctive 2 is also sometimes used after als dass, nicht dass and ohne dass, for events which were possible, but which did not take place

+ It is not obligatory, however, and the indicative is also acceptable:

Das Haus ist zu teuer, als dass wir es kaufen **könnten** (*or*: können)	*The house is too expensive for us to buy it*
Nicht dass ich geizig **wäre**, aber ... (*or*: bin)	*Not that I'm stingy, but ...*
Er hat mir geholfen, ohne dass ich ihn darum **gebeten hätte** (*or*: gebeten hatte)	*He helped me without me asking him*

17.5 'Conditional in the past': uses

+ The 'conditional in the past' is sometimes called the 'pluperfect subjunctive'.
+ The conditional in the past is used for events which might have been possible but did not in the end happen.
+ Where there is a condition (often introduced by wenn), German uses the Subjunctive 2 of haben or sein + past participle in both clauses:

Wenn ich Zeit **gehabt hätte**, **wäre** ich öfter ins Kino **gegangen**	*If I had had time, I would have gone to the cinema more often*
Ich **hätte** viel Geld sparen **können**, wenn ich einen Diesel **gekauft hätte**	*I could have saved a lot of money if I had bought a diesel*
Was wäre geschehen, **hätte** Hitler im November 1939 den Bürgerbräukeller eine halbe Stunde später **verlassen** und **wäre** von der Bombe **getroffen worden**?	*What would have happened if Hitler had left the Bürgerbräukeller half an hour later and had been hit by the bomb?*
Deutschland **wäre** viel Zerstörung erspart **geblieben**	*Germany would have been spared much of the destruction*
Viele der Opfer **wären** zu retten **gewesen**	*Many of the victims could have been saved*
Deutschland **hätte** das Spiel fast **verloren**	*Germany nearly lost the match (but didn't)*

Word order

▶ Clauses

• A **clause** is a group of words with a subject and a verb. There may also be an **object** or an **adverbial phrase**. The following are clauses:

> Richard schläft   Ich fahre mit dem Bus   Wenn es kalt ist, …

• A **main clause** is a clause which in a longer sentence would make sense standing alone; a sentence may consist of just one such clause, as in the first two examples above. The following example contains two main clauses joined by und:

> Ich fahre in die Stadt **und** sie geht in die Uni

• A **subordinate clause** is one which will not make sense standing alone, because it starts with a subordinating conjunction, e.g. weil *because*, wenn *if, when*:

> **Wenn** ich in die Stadt fahre, …
> …, **weil** sie auf die Uni geht

• A **conjunction** is a word used to join two clauses, e.g. *wenn, weil, und, oder*

▶ Sentences

• A **simple sentence** consists of one clause with a finite verb:

> Ich bleibe zu Hause   Sie muss arbeiten   Er hat ein Auto gekauft

• A **compound sentence** consists of two clauses joined by a co-ordinating conjunction:

> Ich bleibe zu Hause, **aber** sie muss arbeiten

• A **complex sentence** consists of a main clause and one or more subordinate clauses, joined by a **subordinating conjunction**:

> Ich bleibe zu Hause, **weil** ich arbeiten muss

▶ Word order

• In German, it is case endings which indicate the subject and the object of the verb, not always, as in English, the relative position of subject – verb – object. These two sentences have the same meaning, because of the sense and the accusative ending on **den**:

> Mein Bruder will den Wagen kaufen
> Den Wagen will mein Bruder kaufen

+ Most issues of word order concern the position of the finite verb.
  + **Main clause**: verb second
  + **Subordinate clause**: verb at the end
  + **Questions**: subject and verb inverted
  + **Commands**: verb first

18.1 The position of the verb

+ In **statements** (i.e. any sentence that is not a question or command), there are only two positions for the verb: as the **second idea** in a main clause, or **at the end** of a subordinate clause.
+ For word order in **questions** and **commands** see 18.1.3 below.

18.1.1   Main clauses

a **Word order Rule 1. In a main clause, the finite verb[1] is the second idea**
+ The **first idea** may be the **subject**, an **adverbial**, the **object** of the verb, or a **subordinate clause** (see section 18.1.4 below).
+ **Any other part of the verb** (which may be a separable prefix, a past participle or an infinitive) stands **at the end of the clause**. This characteristically German pattern is called the **verbal bracket**, and the position after the verb is often referred to as the *Mittelfeld* (central position).

[1]The **finite verb** is the conjugated verb with its tense and personal endings added, i.e. not the infinitive or a participle.

First idea (*Vorfeld*)	Finite verb (second idea)	Central section (*Mittelfeld*)	Prefix, infinitive, past participle
Am liebsten	**esse**	ich Fisch	
Ich	**habe**	diesen Film noch nicht	**gesehen**
Diesen Film	**müssen**	wir unbedingt	**sehen!**
Mein Freund	**ruft**	mich jeden Abend	**an**
Auch gestern	**bin**	ich viel zu spät	**abgefahren**
Weil es spät war,	**musste**	er bei uns	**übernachten**

b **Interjections – ja, nein, ach, nun, etc. – and names as forms of address have no effect on the word order**

Nein, ich kann dir nicht helfen	*No, I can't help you!*
Peter, da bist du ja!	*Peter, there you are!*
Du meine Güte, es schneit!	*My goodness, it's snowing!*
Aua, das tut weh!	*Ouch! That hurts!*

18.1.2   The first position in a main clause (*Vorfeld*)

+ German word order is highly flexible. As long as the verb stands in the second position, almost any element of a statement can stand in the first position. No verb forms or other grammar need be changed.

So habe ich es nicht gemeint	*That's not how I meant it*
Erst mit sechzehn durfte ich …	*It was only when I reached sixteen that I was allowed to …*
Das habe ich auch gesagt!	*That's what I said too!*

a There can be only one idea in the *Vorfeld*

• In English, by contrast, several elements may appear before the verb:

Dann hat er die Tür langsam aufgemacht	*Then, slowly, he opened the door*
Or **Langsam** hat er dann die Tür aufgemacht	

b The first element is usually the link to what is already known to the listener/reader

• It usually refers to something already mentioned, and about which the writer/speaker wishes now to say something new, such as about Peter in the examples below. It is not 'for emphasis', as is often assumed; that is achieved in a different way (see 18.3.4c).

Kennst du **Peter**? …

(subject)	**Er** ist gestern abgefahren	*He left yesterday*
(adverb)	**Mit ihm** gehe ich ins Kino	*I'm going to the cinema with him*
(object)	**Ihn** will ich nie wieder sehen!	*I never want to see him again!*
(subordinate clause)	**Wenn er Zeit hat,** treffen wir uns	*If he has the time, we'll meet*

Ich esse **gern** Fleisch, aber **am liebsten** esse ich Fisch	*I like eating meat, but I like fish best*
Hier ist das **Kino**programm. **Diesen Film** müssen wir unbedingt sehen!	*Here's the cinema programme. We just have to see this film!*
Deine Freundin lässt dich manchmal in Ruhe. **Mein Freund** ruft mich jeden Abend an	*Your girlfriend leaves you in peace sometimes. My boyfriend phones me every evening*

▶18.1.3   Questions and commands

a In questions, the verb comes before the subject; it may be preceded by an interrogative

Hat sie Geschwister?	*Does she have brothers or sisters?*
Kennst du Peter?	*Do you know Peter?*
Wo **wohnen Sie**?	*Where do you live?*
In welcher Stadt **hat er** früher gearbeitet?	*In which town did he used to work?*

b In commands, the verb stands in first position

Bleib hier!	*Stay here!*
Warte auf mich!	*Wait for me!*
Bedient euch!	*Help yourselves!*
Rufen Sie mich an!	*Give me a call!*
Kommen Sie herein!	*Come in!*
Gehen wir!	*Let's go!*

- The only exception to this rule is with the infinitive used as imperative in formal instructions, when it must come last.

  Nicht **rauchen!**   *No smoking!*

18.1.4   Subordinate clauses

- Any clause which starts with a subordinating conjunction (wenn, weil, etc.) would not make sense as a sentence on its own; it is therefore *subordinate* to a main clause. For the same reason it is sometimes called a *dependent clause*.
- a **Word order Rule 2. In a subordinate clause, the finite verb stands at the end of the clause.**
- All other elements remain the same as for a main clause; it is normal, however, for the subject of the clause to follow immediately after the conjunction.

Main clause	Conjunction	Subject		Infinitive or past participle	Finite verb
...	obwohl	ich	am liebsten Fisch		**esse**
	weil	ich	diesen Film nicht	gesehen	**habe**
	da	wir	diesen Film unbedingt	sehen	**müssen**
	dass	mein Freund	mich jeden Abend		an**ruft**
	so dass	ich	gestern viel zu spät	abgefahren	**bin**

- b **But in a subordinate clause which contains two infinitives, the finite verb stands before the infinitives**
- One of the two infinitives is always that of a **modal verb**; or, more rarely, the infinitive of **lassen** or a **verb of perception** (e.g. sehen) used as a past participle. The finite verb in the clause is always an auxiliary (haben, sein, werden or another modal verb):

  Weil er mir nicht **hätte** helfen können, …   *Because he couldn't have helped me,…*

  Der Teller, den ich **habe** fallen lassen, …   *The plate which I've dropped, …*

  Obwohl er diesen Aufsatz **sollte** schreiben können, …   *Although he ought to be able to write this essay, …*

  Da er das Buch **wird** kaufen müssen, …   *As he'll have to buy the book …*

  Da ich sie nicht **hatte** abfahren sehen, …   *As I hadn't seen them leave,…*

  Es gibt genug Beispiele, dass Menschen sich **haben** bestechen lassen   *There are plenty of examples of people who have accepted bribes*

18.1.5   Verb position in compound or complex sentences

- A sentence always contains a main clause; it may also contain another main clause and/or a subordinate clause or two. Beyond three clauses in length, it becomes unwieldy. In all instances, however, the rules outlined above still apply.

a Main clause + subordinate clause (= Rule 1 + Rule 2)

Ich **kaufe** manchmal Steak, obwohl ich am liebsten Fisch **esse**	*I sometimes buy steak, although I like eating fish most of all*
Wir **sind** ins Kino gegangen, weil wir den neuen Film sehen **wollten**	*We went to the cinema because we wanted to see the new film*

b Subordinate clause + main clause (= Rule 2 + Rule 1)

+ The subordinate clause counts as the first idea, and is therefore followed by the verb of the main clause. Note the characteristic **verb – comma – verb** pattern in the middle of the sentence:

Obwohl ich am liebsten Fisch **esse**, **kaufe** ich manchmal Steak	*Although I like eating fish most of all, I sometimes buy steak*
Weil wir den Film sehen **wollten**, **sind** wir ins Kino gegangen	*Because we wanted to see the new film we went to the cinema*

c Two main or two subordinate clauses

+ Conjunctions such as **und**, **aber**, **oder**, and **denn** join two main (usually) or (occasionally) two subordinate clauses. (See also co-ordinating conjunctions 18.2.1.) They retain their usual main or subordinate clause word order:

Ich **bleibe** zu Hause, **und** er **geht** einkaufen	*I'm staying at home and he's going shopping*
Ich habe Hunger, **weil** ich zu Mittag nichts **aß und** den ganzen Nachmittag Fussball **spielte**	*I'm hungry because I had no lunch and played football all afternoon*

► **TIP** **Keep clauses separate**

+ Always complete one clause before introducing the next:

Ich stehe **auf**, wenn der Wecker klingelt
   Not Ich stehe wenn der Wecker klingelt auf
Er verlässt das Haus, weil er vor **hat**, in die Stadt zu fahren
   Not Er verlässt das Haus, weil er in die Stadt zu fahren vor hat
Ich hoffe, dass ich es **kaufen kann**, wenn ich genug Geld habe
   Not Ich hoffe, dass wenn ich genug Geld habe ich es kaufen kann

+ For the two small exceptions to this rule, see 18.5b below.

18.2 Conjunctions

▶ 18.2.1 Co-ordinating conjunctions

a Co-ordinating conjunctions, as their name implies, join two main or two subordinate clauses

They are in 'zero position' – i.e. they have no effect on word order; when joining main clauses they are followed by the subject of the clause (not an adverb) and then the verb.

◆ The common co-ordinating conjunctions used to join clauses are:

aber[1]	*but*	oder	*or*
denn[2]	*because*	sondern[3]	*but* (after a negative)
doch	*but*	und	*and*
jedoch	*but*		

See also Correlative conjunctions, 18.2.3 below.

[1] **aber** does not have to stay as the first idea:

> Sie darf am Samstag ausgehen, **aber** sie muss am Freitag zu Hause bleiben
> Sie darf am Samstag ausgehen, sie muss **aber** am Freitag zu Hause bleiben
> Sie darf am Samstag ausgehen, am Freitag **aber** muss sie zu Hause bleiben

[2] **denn** is not used as the first word in a sentence.
[3] **sondern** is used after a clause with a negative (nicht, kein):

> Er fährt nicht nach Paris, **sondern** (er) bleibt in Berlin

b Co-ordinating conjunctions may join two main clauses (see 18.1.5c)

Wir **fahren** nicht ins Ausland, **sondern** wir **verbringen** zwei Wochen an der Nordsee	*We're not going abroad, but spending two weeks by the North Sea*

c Co-ordinating conjunctions may join two subordinate clauses (see 18.1.5c)

This is much less common than joining two main clauses.

Obwohl ich kein Geld **habe und** mein Freund zuviel Arbeit **hat**, gehen wir ins Kino	*Although I have no money and my friend has too much work, we're going to the cinema*

TIP   Verb position in clauses joined by co-ordinating conjunctions

When two clauses are joined with a co-ordinating conjunction, the verb in the second clause will be in exactly the same position as the verb in the first clause, either second (if the first clause is a main clause), or at the end (if the first clause is a subordinate clause). Compare the sentences in 18.2.1b and 18.2.1c above.

◆ Two main clauses joined by a co-ordinating conjunction:

> Ich **habe** kein Geld und mein Freund **hat** zuviel Arbeit
> Ich **habe** kein Geld und (ich) **kann** nicht ausgehen

Two subordinate clauses joined by und:

> Obwohl ich kein Geld **habe** und mein Freund zuviel Arbeit **hat**, …
> Weil ich kein Geld **habe** und nicht ausgehen **kann**, …

◆ This correspondence is also true of other items joined by coordinating conjunctions, e.g. noun phrases:

> mit **meinem** Bruder und **meiner** Mutter

▷ 18.2.2   Subordinating conjunctions

◆ **As their name implies, subordinating conjunctions make the following clause subordinate to, or dependent on, a main clause to complete their meaning**

. The main subordinating conjunctions are:

Time		Manner and degree	
als	*when, than*	als	*than*
bevor, ehe	*before*	als ob	*as if*
bis	*until, till, by the time*	(an)statt dass	*instead of*
erst als/wenn	*not until*	außer wenn	*except when, unless*
seit, seitdem	*since (time)*	dadurch, dass	*by ...-ing*
indem	*while, as, by -ing*	indem	*by ...-ing*
indes, indessen	*while*	je ... desto[1] ...	*the more, the more*
nachdem	*after*	nur dass	*only that*
während	*while, whereas*	ohne dass	*without ... -ing*
wenn	*when, whenever*	sofern	*provided that*
sobald	*as soon as*	soweit	*as far as*
sowie	*as well as*	wie	*as, like*
solange	*as long as*		
sooft	*as often as*	**Condition**	
kaum dass	*hardly, scarcely*	wenn	*if*
		falls	*if, in case*
Cause, reason			
da	*as, since, because*	**Other**	
um so mehr, als/da/ weil	*all the more because*	als ob	*as if*
weil	*because*	anstatt dass	*instead of*
zumal	*especially as*	außer dass	*except that*
		außer wenn	*except when*
		dass	*that*
Purpose, result		ob	*if, whether*
damit	*so that (purpose)*	ohne dass	*without ...-ing*
so dass	*so that (result)*	vorausgesetzt, dass	*provided that*
		was ... auch	*whatever*
Concession		wie	*when, as*
obwohl	*although*	wenn ... nicht	*unless*
obgleich	*although*	wer ... auch	*whoever*
obschon	*although*	wo ... auch	*wherever*
		wohingegen	*whereas (contrast) (formal)*

[1]See correlative conjunctions, section 18.2.3 below

a als, wie

Er ist nicht so intelligent, **wie** ich gedacht hatte	*He is not as intelligent **as** I had thought*
Er ist noch intelligenter, **als** ich gedacht hatte	*He is even more intelligent **than** I had thought*

See also 18.2.2e *when* below.

b als ob is the one conjunction which always requires the use of the Subjunctive 2 (see 17.4.6)

Er fährt das Auto immer, **als ob** er Rennfahrer wäre	*He always drives the car as if he were a racing driver*

c dass may sometimes be omitted; the word order then reverts to normal Rule 1 (main clause)

+ …colloquially after verbs of perception, thinking, etc.:

Ich meine, du hast recht	*I think you're right*

+ …in reported speech:

Sie sagte, sie habe eine Erkältung	*She said she had a cold*

+ dass should not be followed immediately by another conjunction:

Er sagte, **dass** er mir helfen würde, **wenn** er Zeit hätte	*He said he would help me if he had the time*
Not Er sagte, dass, wenn er Zeit hätte, er mir helfen würde	

d anstatt dass/ohne dass are usually replaced by anstatt … zu + inf or ohne … zu + inf (see 14.1.1d)

e *when* may be expressed by one of three conjunctions

+ als: once in the past:

Als ich um 7 Uhr aufgestanden bin, …	*When I got up at 7 o'clock …*
Als ich ein kleiner Junge war, …	*When I was a young boy …*

+ wann: questions (direct or indirect):

Ich weiß nicht, **wann** ich sie zum letzten Mal sah	*I don't know when I last saw her*

+ wenn: all other uses (i.e. present, future, repeated actions in any tense):

Jeden Tag, **wenn** ich mit dem Bus fuhr, ….	*Every day when I went on the bus…*
Wenn ich früh aufstehe, …	*When(ever) I get up early…*
Wenn du uns im Sommer besuchst,…	*When you visit us next summer…*

f Interrogatives are also used as subordinating conjunctions

inwiefern	*in what way*	wie	*how*
inwieweit	*to what extent*	wie viel	*how much*
wann	*when*	wie viele	*how many*
warum	*why*	wo	*where*
was	*what*	woher	*where … from*
wer, wen, wem	*who, whom*	wohin	*where … to*
weshalb	*why*	womit, wozu	*what … with/for*, etc.
wessen	*whose*		

Ich weiß nicht, **wo** er jetzt wohnt | *I don't know where he's living now*

Sie hat mir nicht gesagt, mit **wem** sie ins Kino geht | *She didn't tell me who she's going to the cinema with*

g Relative pronouns also introduce subordinate clauses (see 4.7)

Kennst du den Mann, **der** in der Ecke **sitzt**? | *Do you know the man who's sitting in the corner?*

Das ist der Freund, mit **dem** ich gestern gesprochen **habe** | *That's the friend I was talking to yesterday*

18.2.3 Correlative (two-part) conjunctions

+ **Note the word order in the following two-part constructions**

a je ... desto/um so ... *the more ... the more...*

je introduces a subordinate clause, and desto/um so ... a main clause:

Je länger er arbeiten muss, **desto** schlechter gelaunt ist er | *The longer he has to work, the worse his mood becomes*

Je öfter ich diese Musik höre, **um so** besser gefällt sie mir | *The more I listen to this music, the more I like it*

b entweder ... oder *either ... or...*

Entweder bleibst du bei uns, **oder** du gehst nach Hause | *Either you stay with us or you go back home*

Du bleibst **entweder** bei uns oder **bei** seinen Eltern | *You can stay either with us or with his parents*

c weder ... noch *neither ... nor*

Er hatte **weder** Geld, **noch** konnte er Arbeit finden | *He had no money, nor could he find any work*

Er hatte **weder** Geld **noch** Arbeit | *He had neither money nor work*

Weder hat sie uns besucht, **noch** hat sie von sich hören lassen | *She has neither visited us nor been in touch*

d nicht nur ... , sondern ... auch *not only ..., but also*

Er war **nicht nur** deprimiert, **sondern** er hatte **auch** finanzielle Probleme | *He was not only depressed, but also had financial problems*

e bald ... bald *now ... now*

Bald lachte sie, **bald** weinte sie | *Now she was laughing, now crying*

f mal ... mal *sometimes ... sometimes*

Mal arbeite ich im Haus, **mal** im Garten | *Sometimes I work in the house, sometimes in the garden*

▷ 18.2.4   Variations from the verb-position rules for main clauses (18.1.1) and subordinate clauses (18.1.4)

a   Certain two-part conjunctions + main clause

was… auch…	whatever
welche … auch…	whichever
so/wie … auch…	however
ob … oder…	whether or not

◆ Note that the subject and verb in the main clause are not inverted:

In welche Richtung man auch sehen mag, **man kann** …	In whatever direction you look, … you can…
Ob es kalt ist oder nicht, **ich gehe** …	Whether it's cold or not, I go …

b   Parenthetical clauses

◆ Subject and verb invert only in very short parenthetical clauses:

Sie sei, **heißt es**, sehr intelligent	She is, it's said, very intelligent
Er ist, **glaube ich**, sehr reich	He is, I believe, very rich

◆ With longer constructions, there is no inversion:

Er ist – **ich habe es oft gehört** – sehr reich	He is – I've often heard – very rich

▷ 18.2.5   Adverbs used to link main clauses

a   In colloquial German, as in English, a conjunction is not always needed, and an adverb will suffice to link main clauses

◆ Common adverbs used to link main clauses:

also	⎫	danach	⎫ then
daher		dann	⎭
darum	⎬ and so,	dennoch	yet, nevertheless
deshalb	therefore	kaum	hardly
deswegen	⎭	sonst	otherwise
auch	also	trotzdem	in spite of that
außerdem	besides	übrigens	moreover, besides
da	so, then (cf.: da – conjunction)	zwar	it's true

b   The adverb is always followed by the verb

Ich muss mich beeilen, **sonst verpasse** ich den Bus	I must hurry, otherwise I'll miss the bus
Wir verbringen zwei Wochen an der Küste, **danach fahren** wir in die Schweiz	We're spending two weeks at the coast, then we're going to Switzerland
Zwar war ich da, aber ich habe fast nichts gesehen	It's true I was there, but I saw almost nothing

c   also, daher, darum, deshalb, deswegen have almost identical meanings, and usually answer the question 'Why?'

Morgen habe ich eine Prüfung, **also** muss ich heute viel lernen	I have an exam tomorrow so I'll have to work hard today

d In more formal German, a conjunction and a subordinate clause can be used

Ich muss heute viel lernen, **weil** ich morgen eine Prüfung habe	*I have to work hard today, because I have an exam tomorrow*
Wenn ich mich nicht beeile, verpasse ich den Bus	*If I don't hurry, I'll miss the bus*
Obwohl ich da war, habe ich fast nichts gesehen	*Although I was there, I saw almost nothing*

18.3 The position of elements within the clause

▶ 18.3.1 Predicative adjectives

+ **Predicative adjectives usually stand at the end of the main clause, except with compound verbs; in subordinate clauses the verb stands last**

Das Wetter ist heute **schlecht**	*The weather is bad today*
Das Museum ist auch für Kinder **interessant**	*The museum is interesting even for children*
Das Wetter ist heute **schlecht** gewesen	*The weather has been bad today*
Weil das Wetter heute **schlecht** gewesen ist, …	*As the weather has been bad today…*

▶ 18.3.2 Pronouns and nouns

a Two or more pronouns (including reflexive pronouns): object pronouns usually stand straight after the finite verb, accusative then dative

+ The subject pronoun (nominative), if it is not in first position, precedes them:

„Diesen Film müssen **wir** unbedingt sehen!"	*'We really just have to see this film!'*
„Morgen sehen **wir ihn** im Kino"	*'Tomorrow we're going to see it at the cinema'*
Dann setzte **er sich**	*Then he sat down*
Heute schickt **er ihn** seinem Freund	*Today he's sending it to his friend*
Er schickt **ihn ihm**	*He's sending it to him*
Wenn **er ihn ihm** schickt, …	*If he's sending it to him, …*
Setzen **Sie sich**, bitte!	*Please sit down!*
Hoffentlich erholst **du dich** schnell	*I hope you'll feel better soon*

+ In infinitive clauses, pronouns precede the infinitive, obeying the rule that infinitives stand at the end:

Sie ging in ihr Zimmer, um **sich** umzuziehen	*She went to her room to get changed*

b A pronoun and a noun phrase: pronouns (including reflexive pronouns) come first, immediately after the verb of the main clause

Heute schickt der Junge seinem Freund den Brief	*Today the boy is sending his friend the letter*
– Heute schickt **ihm** der Junge den Brief	*– Today the boy is sending him the letter*

– Heute schickt **ihn** der Junge seinem Freund	– *Today the boy is sending it to his friend*
– Er schickt **ihm** den Brief	– *He's sending him the letter*
– Er schickt **ihn** seinem Freund	– *He's sending it to his friend*
Gestern sahen **ihn** meine Freunde im Kino	*Yesterday my friends saw him at the cinema*
Mein Sohn wäscht **sich** die Hände	*My son is washing his hands*
Jetzt wäscht **sich** mein Sohn die Hände	*Now my son is washing his hands*

◆ In a subordinate clause, the verb of course stands at the end, and the subject follows the conjunction; otherwise the word order is as above:

> ..., dass der Junge ihm (heute) den Brief schickt
> ..., dass mein Sohn sich (jetzt) die Hände wäscht

c Demonstrative or indefinite pronouns come after personal pronouns, even if they are the subject

Hat dir das **niemand** erklärt?	*Did no one explain it to you?*
Sofort hat ihm **dieser** gefallen	*He liked this one immediately*
Gestern habe ich ihm **so einen** gekauft	*Yesterday I bought him one like that*

◆ This word order (personal pronoun + demonstrative/indefinite pronoun) is retained in subordinate clauses:

Wenn dir das **niemand** erklärt hat, ...	*If no one's explained it to you, ...*
..., weil ihm **dieser** sofort gefallen hat	*..., because he liked this one immediately*

d Two or more nouns: nominative before dative before accusative

◆ This pattern is as in English if the word *to* is not used:

Heute schickt **der Junge** seinem Freund einen Brief	*Today the boy is sending his friend a letter*
Er schickt **seinem Freund** einen Brief	*He's sending his friend a letter*
Als **der Junge** seinem Freund einen Brief schickte, ...	*When the boy sent his friend a letter, ...*

e Prepositional phrases usually follow other objects

Er schickt den Brief **an seinen Freund**	*He's sending the letter to his friend*
Sie wäscht sich die Hände **mit Seife**	*She's washing her hands with soap*

◆ This includes the prepositional objects of verbs such as *warten auf* *to wait for* (see Chapter 13). These prepositional objects stand as close as possible to the end of the main clause – either at the very end, or directly in front of the infinitive, past participle or infinitive clause:

Man kann sich immer **auf ihn** verlassen	*You can always rely on him*
Man muss manchmal stundenlang **auf den Bus** warten	*Sometimes you have to wait hours for the bus*

Natürlich freue ich mich immer **darauf**, dich wiederzusehen	*Of course I always look forward to seeing you again*

▷ 18.3.3 The order of adverbs

a Adverbs used together: as a rule of thumb, adverbs usually stand in the order Time – Manner – Place

Ich bin <u>letzte Woche</u> *mit dem Bus* <u>nach Frankfurt</u> gefahren
Last week I went by bus to Frankfurt

* However, it is common practice to place one of these adverbs (often that of time) before the verb:

  <u>Letzte Woche</u> bin ich <u>mit dem Bus</u> <u>nach Frankfurt</u> gefahren

* The English pattern of placing an adverb of time between the article and the verb is not found in German, as the verb must come second:

  Ich stehe **immer** früh auf   *I **always** get up early*

b When two adverbs of time occur together, the more general adverb stands before the specific

Ich stehe <u>jeden Tag</u> <u>um sieben Uhr</u> auf   *I get up every day at 7 o'clock*

c The Time – Manner – Place rule is, however, rather more flexible in practice than the above might suggest

* Time adverbs are usually preceded by comment adverbs and followed by reason adverbs:

Er muss <u>leider</u>	<u>heute</u>	<u>wegen des Wetters</u>	<u>zu Hause</u>	bleiben
comment	time	reason	place (complement)	

Unfortunately he has to stay at home today because of the weather

d The complement of the verb (i.e. elements which complete the meaning of the verb) stands next to the verb, even if this means ignoring the Time – Manner – Place rule:

Man kann <u>in unserer Stadt</u> <u>gut</u> einkaufen
Place (adverb) manner
There's good shopping in our town

* See also section 18.3.4c below.

▷ 18.3.4 Adverbs in relation to the objects of the verb

a Adverbs stand after subject/object pronouns

Seine Freundin hat ihm **letzte Woche** ein Geschenk gegeben	*His girlfriend gave him a present last week*
Nach dem Essen hat er mir **schnell** einen Kaffee gekocht	*After the meal he quickly made me a coffee*

b Adverbs often stand between noun objects

Anna hat ihrem Freund **letzte Woche** ein Geschenk gegeben	*Anna gave her boyfriend a present last week*

c **The order of adverbs and objects may be changed to emphasise different elements**

+ The order of the elements after the verb can be changed, with the emphasis falling on the one which comes later:

Sie hat ihm das Geschenk **letzte Woche** gegeben	Emphasis on **when**
Sie hat ihm letzte Woche **das Geschenk** gegeben	Emphasis on **the gift**
Sie hat das Geschenk letzte Woche **ihrem Mann** gegeben	Emphasis on **recipient**

18.4 The position of nicht

a **nicht goes *before***

+ a predicative adjective:

Deutsch zu lernen ist **nicht** schwierig	*Learning German isn't hard*

+ an adverb of manner or place:

Sie ist heute **nicht** im Büro	*She's not in the office today*
Ich interessiere mich **nicht** für diese Musik	*I'm not interested in this music*

+ parts of the verb which are not the finite verb (infinitive, past participle, prefix):

Wir haben den Film **nicht** gesehen	*We haven't seen the film*
Fährst du **nicht** mit?	*Aren't you coming with us?*
Man darf hier **nicht** rauchen	*You're not allowed to smoke here*

b **If these are not present, nicht goes to the end**

Sie kommt heute **nicht**	*She's not coming today*
Er hilft uns **nicht**	*He's not helping us*
Ich finde es **nicht**	*I can't find it*

c **nicht can be placed elsewhere in order to emphasise a particular word or phrase**

Normal: Sie will es mir **nicht** geben	*She won't give it to me*
But: Sie will es **nicht** mir geben, sondern meinem Bruder	*It's not me she wants to give it to, but my brother*

d **In subordinate clauses, nicht remains in the same position as above; only the position of the verb changes**

Da sie heute **nicht** kommt, …	*As she's not coming today…*
Weil ich mich **nicht** für diese Musik interessiere, …	*Because I'm not interested in this music, …*
Wenn Sie **nicht** kommen können, …	*If you can't come, …*
Wenn sie **nicht** hätten kommen können, …	*If they hadn't been able to come…*

18.5 Word order with infinitive clauses

a **The infinitive clause must almost always be kept separate from the main clause**

In other words, one verbal idea must be completed before introducing the next. When an infinitive clause forms the subject of the verb, it is placed at the beginning of the sentence; otherwise at the end:

So was zu tun ist nicht meine Sache	*Doing that sort of thing isn't for me*
Ihm dieses Buch zu geben hieße Perlen vor die Säue werfen	*Giving him this book would be like casting pearls before swine*
Hast du Lust **ins Kino zu gehen**?	*Would you like to go to the cinema?*
Sie wiederzusehen wäre fantastisch!	*It would be wonderful to see her again!*

- It is tempting for English learners to combine the infinitive clause into the main clause, especially when there is a past participle or another infinitive in the sentence. This temptation must be avoided (see TIP on p. 197).

Ich habe versucht, das alles zu lernen (**Not** Ich habe das alles zu lernen versucht)	*I tried to learn all of it*
Er muss mir helfen, alles aufzuräumen (**Not** Er muss mir aufzuräumen helfen)	*He must help me clear it all up*

b **There are two exceptions to this rule**

- If the infinitive clause consists *only* of **zu** plus the infinitive it can, in formal German, occasionally be found incorporated into the main clause:

Er hat **zu schreiben** angefangen	*He began to write*
Or Er hat angefangen zu schreiben	

- An infinitive clause which follows on from a relative clause becomes part of the relative clause. This is an exception to the rule above, although in colloquial German this form is avoided:

… die Frau, deren Tochter ich anzurufen versucht hatte	*…the woman whose daughter I had tried to phone*
… sondern ich sah den Knaben, den abzuholen sie gekommen waren	*… but I saw the boy whom they had come to fetch*

19

Word formation

OVERVIEW

> **Simple and complex words**

- **Simple words** consist of just one element:

  das Kind *child*   reich *rich*

- **Complex words** consist of more than one element, created by the addition of a prefix or suffix or joining two or more words together to form a **compound word**:

  kindisch *childish*
  der Kindergarten *kindergarten*
  steinreich *really rich*
  der Reichtum *wealth*
  bereichern *to enrich*

- Often, more than one of these means is used:

  Um / welt / freund / lich / keit *ecofriendliness*

- The root word may be **modified**, usually by changes to the vowel, e.g. sprechen *to speak*:

  der Sprecher *speaker*   der Spruch *saying*
  die Sprache *language*   das Gespräch *conversation*
  die Besprechung *discussion*   das Sprichwort *proverb*
  sprachlich *linguistic*   deutschsprachig *German-speaking*

- One of the characteristics of German is the ease with which new complex words are constantly formed – a true 'Lego language'; it is vital that the learner understands how this happens, as new combinations are encountered all the time.

- It is often easier to understand complex and compound words in German than in English. Start with the root word; in nouns this is usually the last element:

  der Kinder**arzt** *paediatrician* (= children's doctor)
  der Frauen**arzt** *gynaecologist* (= women's doctor)
  unter**schreiben** *to sign* (= to under-write)

19.1 General points

- Learners of German quickly learn that all long words (and it is possible to form some very long words indeed!) are made up from little words or other elements;

breaking a long word down into its component parts usually makes even a daunting word relatively easy to understand. German is highly flexible on this count, and English (which is quite capable of producing its own compounds such as *bookshop* and *caretaker*) sometimes borrows German compounds such as Schadenfreude *schadenfreude (gloating over someone's misfortune)*, or even translates them element by element (Autobahn *motorway*, Verkehrsberuhigung *traffic calming*).

+ Not that compound words are necessarily all that long: it is easy to work out from its elements that a Parkhaus is a *multi-storey car park*, or that an Atomsperrvertrag is a *nuclear non-proliferation treaty* (from sperren *to block* and Vertrag *treaty, contract*).

▶ 19.1.1   Root words

+ **'Root' words are the base words from which 'complex' (=more than one element) words may be formed**

e.g.

die **Liebe** *love:*
   lieben *to love*
sich ver**lieb**en in *to fall in love with*
be**lieb**t *popular*
   die Be**lieb**theit *popularity*
   die be**lieb**ig (viel) *as many (as you wish)*
die Vor**lieb**e *predilection, preference*
lieblos, **lieb**evoll, **lieb**lich *loveless, loving, lovely*
die Tier**liebe** *love of animals*
der/die Ge**lieb**te *lover*
der **Lieb**ling *favourite*
liebhaben *to be fond of*
die Hass**liebe** *love–hate relationship*

▶ 19.1.2   Complex words

+ **'Complex' words may be formed in several ways**

	Root word	Complex word
Prefix	Geduld *patience* alt *old* sprechen *to speak* einfach *simple*	**Un**geduld *impatience* **ur**alt *ancient* **be**sprechen *to discuss* **ver**einfachen *to simplify*
Suffix	Geduld *patience* schön *lovely* meinen *to think* faul *lazy*	geduld**ig** *patient* Schön**heit** *beauty* Mein**ung** *opinion* faul**enzen** *to laze about*
Vowel change	sprechen *to speak* ander *other, different* Gruß *greeting*	die Sprache *language* ändern *to change* begrüßen *to greet*

	Root word	Complex word
Compounding	fahren + Plan *to travel + plan* klein + Geld *small + money* Liebe + voll *love + full* um + Arme *around + arms*	Fahrplan *timetable* Kleingeld *(loose) change* liebevoll *affectionate* umarmen *to embrace*

19.2 Formation of nouns

◆ **Adjective-nouns:** the formation, declension and use of adjectives used as nouns are covered in detail in 5.2. Adjectives may form part of many other nouns, usually by the addition of a suffix – see 19.2.2a, c, g, h, and l–o below.

▷ 19.2.1 Nouns from verbs

a Infinitives as nouns

◆ Almost all infinitives (including those of compound verbs) can be used as nouns. They are always neuter, and refer to the action of the verb (English *-ing* form) (e.g. Lesen refers to the action of reading, while Lektüre refers more to the reading material):

das Einkaufen *shopping*	(cf. die Einkäufe *purchases*)
das Frühaufstehen *getting up early*	
das Singen *singing*	
das Komasaufen *binge drinking*	
das Wandern *hiking, walking*	(cf. die Wanderung *walk, hike*)

b Present and past participles as nouns

Participles used as nouns may be masculine, feminine or neuter; they have the endings of adjectives (see 5.2c).

◆ **Present participles as nouns**

These usually refer to the person or thing performing the action:

der/die Vorsitzende *chair(man)*
der/die Reisende *traveller*
der/die Auszubildende *trainee*
das Entscheidende *the decisive factor*

◆ **Past participles as nouns**

These usually have a passive sense – the person or thing to whom something is being done – or denote a past action:

der/die Geliebte *beloved, sweetheart*
der/die Abgeordnete *delegate*
der/die Angeklagte *accused*
der/die Verwandte *relative*
der/die Interessierte *interested person*
der/die Gefallene *the person who has fallen (e.g. soldier)*
das Bekannte *what's familiar*

c **Nouns from the stem of verbs**

. **Verb stem, often with a vowel change**

Most nouns so formed are masculine:

befehlen – der Befehl *command*	schießen – der Schuß *shot*
fliegen – der Flug *flight*	schreiten – der Schritt *step*
fließen – der Fluß *river*	werfen – der Wurf *throw*
laufen – der Lauf *run, course*	ziehen – der Zug *pull, train, draught*

. **Verb stem less the last letter of the infinitive** (most end in **-e**)

These nouns are all feminine, with the plural:

feiern – die Feier *celebration*   pflanzen – die Pflanze *plant*

Other examples:

die Ausrede *excuse*	die Frage *question*
die Decke *cover, ceiling*	die Rede *speech*
die Durchsage *announcement*	die Regel *rule*
die Eile *haste*	die Ruhe *rest*
die Fliege *fly*	

▶ **19.2.2   Nouns formed using suffixes**

a **A few adjectives can be used as nouns without modification**

blau – das Blau *blue*
fett – das Fett *fat*
gehorsam *obedient* – der Gehorsam *obedience*
hoch *high* – das Hoch *three cheers*
ideal – das Ideal *ideal*

. However, most nouns formed from adjectives, adverbs, other nouns and verbs (apart from those dealt with above) are formed by the addition of a suffix; each suffix is linked to a particular gender, mostly feminine, noted below in brackets.

b **-chen/-lein** (*neuter*) **with umlaut on stem vowel if possible**

. Added to nouns; denotes diminutive. -lein is usually poetic.

das Bäch**lein**	*small stream*
das Bröt**chen**	*bread roll*
das Häus**chen**	*little house, cottage*
das Mäd**chen**	*girl (from die Magd maid (obsolete))*

c **-e** (*feminine*)

. Added to adjectives, often with an umlaut:

die Fern**e**	*distance*	die Näh**e**	*vicinity*
die Frisch**e**	*freshness*	die Stärk**e**	*strength*
die Größ**e**	*size*	die Tief**e**	*depth*
die Kält**e**	*cold(-ness)*	die Wärm**e**	*warmth*

d **-ei (feminine)**

. Denotes where something takes place (often a shop), or a collection of things; or repeated and often tiresome activity:

die Bäcker**ei** *bakery*   die Bücher**ei** *library*
die Dat**ei** *data bank*   die Heuchel**ei** *hypocrisy* (from
die Mecker**ei** *griping, moaning*   heucheln *to be a hypocrite*)
die Nörgel**ei** *nagging*   die Metzger**ei** *butcher's shop*

e -er (sometimes -ler or -ner)/-erin (*feminine*)

+ Added to verb stem, sometimes with an umlaut. These nouns usually denote the person or thing performing the action, or, with place names, an inhabitant.
+ Masculine forms (-er) have the plural -; feminine nouns (-erin) form the plural with -nen.

der Bäck**er** *baker*   der Bastl**er** *DIY enthusiast*
der Berlin**er** *Berliner*   der Besuch**er** *visitor*
der Bohr**er** *drill*   der Einbrech**er** *burglar*
der Einwohn**er** *inhabitant*   der Korkenzieh**er** *corkscrew*
der Lehr**er** *teacher*   der Rentn**er** *pensioner*
der Richt**er** *judge*   der Schriftstell**er** *writer*
der Schweiz**er** *Swiss*   der Zuschau**er** *spectator*
Note der Hannover**aner**   der Weimar**aner**

f -erei (*feminine*)

+ Added to nouns or verbs; denotes repeated or annoying actions:

die Schläg**erei** *brawl, punch-up*
die Schlud**erei** *sloppiness*
die Schwein**erei** *complete mess, scandal*

g -heit (*feminine*)

+ Added to past participles, and many adjectives, including those ending in -en and -ern. Denotes a quality (*-iness, -ity*, etc.):

die Albern**heit** *silliness*   die Beliebt**heit** *popularity*
die Einzel**heit** *detail*   die Frei**heit** *freedom*
die Gesund**heit** *health*   die Gleich**heit** *equality*
die Kind**heit** *childhood*   die Schön**heit** *beauty*
die Verlegen**heit** *embarrassment*   die Verlassen**heit** *desolation*
die Wahr**heit** *truth*   die Sicher**heit** *safety*

h -igkeit (*feminine*)

+ Added to adjectives ending in -haft and -los and a few others:

die Arbeitslos**igkeit** *unemployment*
die Ernsthaft**igkeit** *seriousness*
die Häuf**igkeit** *frequency*
die Müd**igkeit** *tiredness*
die Süß**igkeit** *sweet, sweetness*

i -in (*feminine*)

+ Added to a masculine noun to denote the feminine form. Apart from the examples noted in 19.2.2e and j, note, for instance, the following:

der Koch – die Köchin
der Zahnarzt – die Zahnärztin

j -ist (*masculine*), -istin (*feminine*)
* Denotes a person by their associated skill, activity or belief.
* The resulting masculine noun is a weak noun (see 2.3.2); feminine: nouns add plural -nen:

<table>
<tr><td>der Kommun**ist** Communist</td><td>der Kompon**ist** composer</td></tr>
<tr><td>der Poliz**ist** police officer</td><td>der Rass**ist** racist</td></tr>
<tr><td>die Terror**ist**in terrorist</td><td>die Tour**ist**in tourist</td></tr>
</table>

k -ismus (*masculine*)
* Denotes an ideology, a movement or sometimes a disease:

<table>
<tr><td>der Alkohol**ismus** alcoholism</td><td>der Darwin**ismus** Darwinism</td></tr>
<tr><td>der Impression**ismus** Impressionism</td><td>der Kapital**ismus** capitalism</td></tr>
</table>

Note that the base word sometimes modifies:
totalitär – der Totalit**arismus** *totalitarianism*

l –keit (*feminine*)
* Added to adjectives (especially to those ending in -bar, -ig, -isch, -lich, -sam, and some adjectives ending with -el and -er).
* Denotes a quality:

<table>
<tr><td>die Aufmerksam**keit** attention</td><td>die Bitter**keit** bitterness</td></tr>
<tr><td>die Dankbar**keit** gratitude</td><td>die Einsam**keit** loneliness</td></tr>
<tr><td>die Eitel**keit** vanity</td><td>die Freundlich**keit** friendliness</td></tr>
<tr><td>die Höflich**keit** politeness</td><td>die Langsam**keit** slowness</td></tr>
<tr><td>die Mürrisch**keit** moroseness</td><td>die Sauber**keit** cleanliness</td></tr>
<tr><td>die Schwierig**keit** difficulty</td><td>die Wichtig**keit** importance</td></tr>
</table>

m -ling (*masculine*)
* Added to adjectives or the stem of verbs.
* Usually denotes a person, often negatively:

<table>
<tr><td>der Däum**ling** thumb (of glove);
    Tom Thumb</td><td>der Feig**ling** coward</td></tr>
<tr><td></td><td>der Schwäch**ling** weakling</td></tr>
<tr><td>der Lieb**ling** darling</td><td></td></tr>
<tr><td>der Wider**ling** repulsive creep</td><td></td></tr>
</table>

n -nis (*neuter* or occasionally *feminine*)
* Added to adjectives or verb stems to form abstract nouns:
bilden – das Bild**nis** *image*   finster – die Finster**nis** *darkness*
* Other examples:

<table>
<tr><td>das Bedürf**nis** requirement</td><td>das Erleb**nis** experience</td></tr>
<tr><td>die Fäul**nis** decay, rot</td><td>das Geheim**nis** secret</td></tr>
<tr><td>das Hinder**nis** obstacle</td><td>die Wild**nis** wilderness</td></tr>
</table>

o -schaft (*feminine*)
* Added to nouns and adjectives.
* Often denotes a group of persons:

<table>
<tr><td>die Eigen**schaft** characteristic</td><td>die Freund**schaft** friendship</td></tr>
<tr><td>die Gesell**schaft** society</td><td>die Land**schaft** landscape</td></tr>
<tr><td>die Nachbar**schaft** neighbourhood</td><td>die Studenten**schaft** student body</td></tr>
<tr><td>die Wirt**schaft** economy</td><td>die Wissen**schaft** knowledge, science</td></tr>
</table>

p -tum (*neuter*)

+ Added to nouns or stems of verbs:

> der Beamte – das Beamten**tum** *civil service, civil servants*

+ Other examples:

das Bürger**tum** *middle classes*	das Christen**tum** *Chrisitianity*
das Eigen**tum** *property*	das Fürsten**tum** Liechtenstein *The*
das Wachs**tum** *growth*	*Principality of Liechtenstein*

Note There are two masculine nouns:

> der Irr**tum** *error* der Reich**tum** *wealth*

q -ung (*feminine*)

+ Added to verb stem; often denotes an action (e.g. English *-ing, -tion*).
+ All nouns formed in this way are feminine, with the plural -en:

> heiz~~en~~ – die Heiz**ung** *heating* zahl~~en~~ – die Zahl**ung** *payment*

+ Other examples:

die Ausbild**ung** *training*	die Behandl**ung** *treatment*
die Betreu**ung** *supervision*	die Bestell**ung** *order*
die Einlad**ung** *invitation*	die Entschuldig**ung** *excuse*
die Erklär**ung** *explanation*	die Hoff**nung** *hope*
die Prüf**ung** *examination*	

19.2.3 Nouns formed using prefixes

+ Another way of modifying the meaning of a noun is by the use of prefixes. For the sake of clarity, the only prefixes listed here are those which either have no independent meaning or which might cause confusion. Most prefixes whose meanings are clear from the original (such as nicht, prepositions or verb prefixes) have been omitted.

a Erz- *arch-, out and out*

der **Erz**bischof *archbishop*	der **Erz**verbrecher *out and out*
der **Erz**feind *arch enemy*	*criminal*

b Ge- often denotes collections of something, or a lot of activity

das **Ge**birge *range of mountains*	das **Ge**kicher *giggling*
das **Ge**lächter *laughter*	das **Ge**päck *luggage*

c Haupt- *main*

das **Haupt**fach *main subject*	das **Haupt**quartier *headquarters*
die **Haupt**sache *main thing*	die **Haupt**stadt *capital city*

d Miss- indicates opposite or negative

der **Miss**erfolg *failure, flop*	das **Miss**verständnis *misunderstanding*
der **Miss**brauch *misuse, abuse*	

e Un- *not-* , *un-, abnormal*

die **Un**geduld *impatience*
das **Un**kraut *weeds*
die **Un**moral *immorality*

das **Un**heil *disaster*
die **Un**menge *vast number*
der **Un**sinn *nonsense*

f Ur- *original, ancient*

die **Ur**aufführung *première (of film, play)*
der **Ur**großvater *great grandfather*
die **Ur**sache *cause*

die **Ur**einwohner *original inhabitants*
der **Ur**knall *big bang (astronomy)*
der **Ur**sprung *origin*

19.2.4   Compound nouns

+ The gender of a compound noun is always the gender of its last component.

a Compound nouns may be formed as follows

+ **Noun + noun**[1]   der Zahn + die Pasta: die Zahnpasta *toothpaste*
    die Schule + die Uniform: die Schuluniform *school uniform*
+ **Adjective + noun**[2]   fremd + die Sprache: die Fremdsprache *foreign language*
+ **Adverb + noun**   wieder + die Gabe: die Wiedergabe *reproduction*
+ **Preposition + noun**   aus + der Gang: der Ausgang *exit*
+ **Numeral + noun**   vier + das Eck :   das Viereck *square*
+ **Verb + noun**   fahren + die Karte: die Fahrkarte *ticket*

[1] Care must be taken with the noun + noun group, as there is often an extra letter or syllable added to the first noun; see 19.2.4c below.
[2] Care must be taken with the adjective + noun group, as the resulting noun may mean something quite different from its elements, e.g.

groß (*big*) + der Vater – der Großvater *grandfather*
hoch (*high*) + die Zeit – die Hochzeit *wedding*
weich (*soft*) + das Ei – das Weichei *weakling, wimp*

b Compound nouns may consist of two, three or more elements – rarely more, as more than three put the noun in danger of becoming unintelligible, unless one or more of the elements can be recognised as words in their own right

die Luft / ab / wehr / rakete *anti-aircraft missile*
(die Abwehr *defence*)
die Verkehrs / beruhigungs / maß / nahmen *traffic calming measures*
(die Maßnahmen *measures*)

TIP   **Understanding a new compound noun**

+ The last word in a compound noun is the root or key word, and provides the gender for the whole noun; the words which precede the root word define it:

der Arzt *doctor*
der **Frauen**arzt *gynaecologist*
der **Tier**arzt *vet*

der **Kinder**arzt *paediatrician*
der **Zahn**arzt *dentist*

---

c   Noun + *link* + noun compound words

As outlined at the beginning of the chapter, one of the characteristics of German is the ease with which nouns can be joined together without the need for linking words such as 'of' or 'for'. However, a word of warning: while unknown compound nouns are usually easy to understand, making up new ones accurately can (for beginners at least) be difficult because of the ending, such as -en or -s, which is sometimes added to the first noun. These endings almost always relate to plural or genitive singular endings associated with the first noun.

* **-(e)n-** is used especially on nouns with genitive and plural -en, and nouns ending in -e:

    der Bauer**n**hof *farm*
    das Brille**n**etui *glasses case*
    das Greise**n**alter *extreme old age*
    die Präsident**en**wahl *presidential election*
    die Straße**n**bahn *tram*
    die Student**en**wohnung *student flat/apartment*

* **-(e)s-** relates to the genitive of masculine or neuter nouns; it is also added to some feminine nouns:

    die Ansicht**s**karte *picture postcard*
    die Bund**es**bank *federal bank*
    das Einheit**s**format *standard format*
    der Geburt**s**tag *birthday*
    die Jahr**es**zeit *season* (**but**: das Jahrbuch – *yearbook*)
    das Regierung**s**system *system of government*
    das Tag**es**licht *daylight*

* **-e-** usually relates to plural -e of the first noun, or to a verb:

    das Gäst**e**zimmer *guest room*
    der Getränk**e**automat *drinks machine*
    das Les**e**zeichen *bookmark*
    der Schwein**e**braten *roast pork*
    das Tag**e**buch *diary*
    der Wart**e**saal *waiting room*

* **-er-** is used with nouns which form their plural with -er or ⁼er:

    die Hühn**er**brühe *chicken soup*
    der Kind**er**garten *kindergarten*
    das Länd**er**spiel *international match*
    (cf. die Land**es**grenze *national border* – here Land is thought of as singular)
    der Männ**er**sport *men's sport*

19.3 Formation of adjectives

▶ 19.3.1   Adjectives from the participles of verbs

* **Present and past participles of verbs may be used as adjectives**

    bedeuten**d** *significant*   durchgehen**d** *continuous*
    ein**ge**bild**et** *conceited*   einladen**d** *inviting, welcoming*

erfahren *experienced*
gefragt *in demand*
verlassen *deserted*

geeignet *suitable*
regierend *governing*
wohlhabend *well-off*

19.3.2 Suffixes added to form adjectives

+ **Adjectives may be formed by adding a suffix to a verb stem or noun**

a -bar *-able, -ible*
+ added to the stem of a verb:

brauchbar *usable*
essbar *edible*

erreichbar *attainable*
furchtbar *terrible*

b -(e)n, -ern (sometimes with umlaut added to base word) *made of*

eisern *made of iron*
hölzern *made of wood*

golden *golden*
ledern *made of leather*

But Plastik- *or* aus Plastik *made of plastic*

c -haft
+ added to nouns; denotes a quality:

ernsthaft *serious*
mädchenhaft *girlish*

mangelhaft *unsatisfactory*
vorteilhaft *advantageous*

d -ig (sometimes with an umlaut on the root word)
+ may indicate a quality, or forms adjectives from time-expressions or other parts of speech:

baldig *in the near future*
durstig *thirsty*
fleißig *conscientious*
heutig *modern, of today*
neugierig *curious*
unabhängig *independent*
vierzehnjährig *(lasting) fourteen
    years / fourteen years old*

damalig *of those days*
einig *united, agreed*
geschäftsmäßig *business-like*
mächtig *powerful*
sonstig *other*
viertägig *(lasting) four days*

+ **-(e)rig** is a variant of -ig:

klebrig *sticky*   schläfrig *sleepy*

e -isch (sometimes with an umlaut on the root word)
+ indicates a quality (sometimes pejorative), or forms an adjective from a geographical or proper name; note the use of lower-case letters with these:

alkoholisch *alcoholic*
ausländisch *foreign*
europäisch *European*
mörderisch *murderous*

amerikanisch *American*
bayrisch *Bavarian*
heuchlerisch *hypocritical*
praktisch *practical, convenient*

Note Some names lose the **i**: freudsch *Freudian,* hannoversch *Hanoverian.*

f –lang indicates a substantial length of time

stundenlang *lasting for hours*

tagelang *lasting for days*

g -lich (with umlaut if possible)

ehr**lich** *honest*	n**ö**rd**lich** *northern*
gem**üt**lich *cosy*	ordent**lich** *tidy*
j**ä**hr**lich** *annual*	r**ö**t**lich** *reddish*
nat**ü**r**lich** *natural*	schreck**lich** *terrible*

h -los *un-, non-, -less*

arbeits**los** *unemployed*	leb**los** *lifeless*
bedingungs**los** *unconditional*	obdach**los** *homeless*
hoffnungs**los** *hopeless*	sprach**los** *speechless*
gewalt**los** *non-violent*	

i -mäßig *in accordance with*

alters**mäßig** *corresponding to one's age*	gesetz**mäßig** *legal*
	plan**mäßig** *according to plan*

j -sam added to verb stems and adjectives

bieg**sam** *flexible*	schweig**sam** *silent*
gemein**sam** *mutual, joint*	unaufhalt**sam** *unstoppable*

19.3.3   Prefixes added to adjectives

• **The meaning of adjectives can be varied by prefixes**
This list does not include, for instance, prepositional prefixes such as nach-, über-, unter-, or foreign prefixes such as the negative in-, or multi-, prä-, etc., where the meaning is already clear.

a a-: negative prefix, often with specialist words of foreign origin

amoralisch *amoral, immoral*
anormal *abnormal*
asozial *asocial, antisocial*

b un-: negative prefix

unabhängig *independent*
unabsichtlich *unintentional*
unecht *fake*
unehelich *illegitimate*
unpraktisch *impractical, inconvenient*

c ur-: *original*; also used as intensifier

uralt *ancient*	**ur**komisch *extremely funny*
urdeutsch *ancient Germanic*	**ur**plötzlich *very sudden*
urig *ethnic, special (e.g. pub)*	**ur**sprünglich *original*

19.3.4   Compound adjectives

a Like nouns, adjectives are often formed from more than one element
• **Noun + adjective**

The noun element sometimes adds -(e)s-, -(e)n- in the same way as compound nouns:

der Affe + artig – affen**artig** *ape-like*
der Bund + deutsch – bund**es**deutsch *German Federal*
der Hund + müde – hund**e**müde *dog-tired*
das Kind + sicher – kind**er**sicher *child-safe*
das Wetter + fest – wetterfest *weatherproof*

+ **Verb + adjective:**
gehen + behindert – gehbehindert *disabled*
pflegen + leicht – pflegeleicht *easy-care*

+ **Adjective + adjective:**
minder + wertig – minderwertig *inferior*
voll + schlank – vollschlank *plump*

+ **Adverb + adjective:**
anders + gläubig – andersgläubig *of a different faith*
rechts + radikal – rechtsradikal *right-wing extremist*
selbst + bewusst – selbstbewusst *self-confident*

+ **Pronoun + adjective:**
all + seitig – allseitig *all-round, general*
ich + bezogen – ichbezogen *self-centred*

b **A prefix or other word may be added to intensify the sense of an adjective**

allerschönste *most beautiful of all*   **hyper**aktiv *hyperactive*
erzfaul *bone idle*   **super**leicht *incredibly easy/light*
extrafein *superfine*   **über**sensibel *oversensitive*
grundfalsch *utterly wrong*   **ultra**modern *ultra-modern*
hochaktuell *highly topical*   **ur**komisch *really funny*

+ Some intensifiers are nouns associated with particular adjectives:

affengeil *brilliant, amazing*   **mause**tot *dead as a dodo*
blitzblank *clean as a new pin*   **messer**scharf *very sharp*
blitzschnell *lightning fast*   **nagel**neu *brand new*
felsenfest *rock solid*

19.4 Formation of adverbs

+ **Adverbs and adjectives are normally grammatically identical, at least in their single-word forms, e.g. natürlich *natural, naturally*. There are, however, a number of suffixes that are used specifically to form adverbs**

+ **-ens**	(with superlative)	erst**ens** *firstly*, höchst**ens** *at most*
+ **-falls**	*in the case of*	jeden**falls** *in any case*, gleich**falls** *and the same to you*
+ **-halber**	*for the sake of*	sicherheits**halber** *for safety's sake*
+ **-lich**		ledig**lich** *merely*, neu**lich** *recently*
+ **-lings**	(with parts of body)	bäuch**lings** *on one's stomach*
+ **-mal**	*frequency*	manch**mal** *sometimes*, zwei**mal** *twice*
+ **-mals**	*time*	da**mals** *in those days*, nie**mals** *never*

✦ -(er)massen		einiger**massen** to some extent
		zugegebener**massen** admittedly
✦ -s		morgen**s** in the mornings, größtenteil**s** in the main
✦ -seits	from this point of view	meiner**seits** from my point of view
		anderer**seits** on the other hand
✦ -wärts	-wards	auf**wärts** upwards, heim**wärts** homewards
✦ -wegen	as far as … is concerned	meinet**wegen** as far as I'm concerned
✦ -(s)weise	by (way of)	ausnahm**sweise** as an exception
		beispiels**weise** for example, for instance
		beziehung**weise** or, rather
		möglicher**weise** possibly
		tage**weise** by the day
✦ -willen	for the sake of	seinet**willen** for his sake

19.5 Formation of verbs

- ✦ Verbs in English often change or expand their basic meaning when they are used with another word, commonly a preposition. For instance, *to look* may become *to look after, to look for, to look out for, to look out, to look up, to look to, to overlook.*
- ✦ German verbs can modify in a very similar way by adding a range of **separable and inseparable prefixes** to the verb, e.g.

  'sehen' *to look, to see* may be changed to:

aussehen *to appear*	**be**sehen *to take a look at*
einsehen *to understand*	**über**sehen *to overlook, to see clearly*
versehen *to provide/see to*	**voraus**sehen *to foresee*

Verbs may also be formed from **adjectives** and nouns (see section 19.5.4 below).

TIP   **What sort of prefix is it?**

- ✦ **Separable prefixes** are usually words in their own right, commonly prepositions. In the infinitive, the emphasis in pronunciation falls on the prefix:

  aufräumen *to tidy up*   **aus**gehen *to go out*

  Pronounced: <u>aus</u>gehen, <u>auf</u>räumen

- ✦ **Inseparable prefixes** are not usually words in their own right. In the infinitive, the emphasis in pronunciation falls on the stem of the verb:

  bestellen *to order*   **ver**kaufen *to sell*

  Pronounced: be<u>stell</u>en, ver<u>kauf</u>en

- ✦ **Variable prefixes.** There are, however, some exceptions to the above; some prefixes that are words in their own right may (or may not) be inseparable. The most common are über and unter. These two verbs are inseparable:

  überholen *to overtake*   **unter**schreiben *to sign*

▶ 19.5.1   Separable prefixes

- **Separable prefixes are those which may be detached from the verb (see word order 18.1.1a and 18.1.4a)**

Wir fahren um 6 Uhr **ab**	*We're leaving at 6 o'clock*
Wir wollen um 6 Uhr **ab**fahren	*We want to leave at 6 o'clock*
Wir hoffen, um 6 Uhr **ab**zufahren	*We're hoping to leave at 6 o'clock*
Wir sind um 6 Uhr **ab**gefahren	*We left at 6 o'clock*
Wenn wir um 6 Uhr **ab**fahren, …	*If we leave at 6 o'clock …*

- **Verbs are often used without the prefix if a corresponding preposition is used in the same clause**

  Wir müssen in Köln **aussteigen**
  but *Wir müssen* **aus** *dem Bus* **steigen**

a Common separable prefixes

Prefix	Meaning	Examples	
ab-	*away off, finish, down*	**ab**fahren *to leave* **ab**sagen *to call off* **ab**schleppen *to tow away*	**ab**legen *to put down, lay down* **ab**schalten *to switch off* **ab**seilen *to abseil (let down on a rope)*
an-	*on, at, starting, approach, reach, do partially*	**an**fangen *to start* **an**frieren *to start to freeze* **an**kuscheln *to snuggle up to* **an**schalten *to switch on*	**an**faulen *to begin to rot* **an**kommen *to arrive* **an**probieren *to try on* **an**sehen *to look at*
auf-	*on, up, upon, open*	**auf**decken *to uncover* **auf**machen *to open*	**auf**pumpen *to pump up* **auf**stehen *to get up, stand up*
aus-	*off, out, complete*	**aus**füllen *to fill in (form)* **aus**schalten *to switch off*	**aus**trinken *to finish drinking* **aus**ziehen *to undress, pull out*
ein-	*in, get used to*	sich **ein**arbeiten *to get used to a job* sich **ein**lesen *to get into a book*	**ein**geben *to enter, key in (data)* **ein**steigen *to get in, on*
entgegen-	*against, towards*	**entgegen**arbeiten *to work against* **entgegen**treten *to oppose*	**entgegen**fahren *to drive towards, to meet*
fort-	*away,*[1] *(carry) on*	**fort**bestehen *to continue to exist* **fort**kommen *to get away* **fort**setzen *to continue*	**fort**wollen *to want to leave*
her- [2]	*towards*	**her**bringen *to bring here*	**her**laufen *to come running*
hin- [2]	*away, down*	**hin**fahren *to go there*	**hin**fallen *to fall down*
hinzu-	*addition*	**hinzu**bekommen *to receive as extra*	**hinzu**fügen *to add*
los-	*off, starting*	**los**fahren *to set off*	**los**schießen *to open fire*
mit-	*with*	**mit**arbeiten *to cooperate*	**mit**fahren *to go with*
nach-	*after, imitating*	**nach**ahmen *to imitate* **nach**gehen *to follow*	**nach**prüfen *to check* **nach**sprechen *to repeat*
vor-	*ahead, in front, demonstrating*	**vor**lesen *to read aloud* **vor**sagen *to recite* **vor**sehen *to plan, schedule*	**vor**machen *to demonstrate* **vor**schlagen *to suggest*
weg-	*away*	**weg**werfen *to throw away*	**weg**wollen *to want to leave*

Prefix	Meaning	Examples	
weiter-	*carry on*	**weiter**fahren *to carry on driving*	**weiter**sagen *to pass on*
zu-	*to, towards, closing, addition*	**zu**fahren *to drive towards* **zu**machen *to close* **zu**wenden *to turn towards*	**zu**kleben *to stick down* **zu**nehmen *to increase* **zu**zahlen *to pay extra*
zurück-	*back*	**zurück**geben *to give back*	**zurück**treten *to resign*
zusammen-	*together, down, up*	**zusammen**fassen *to unite, summarise* **zusammen**leben *to live together*	**zusammen**fallen *to collapse* **zusammen**rollen *to roll up*

[1] In the sense of *'away'*, fort is a more refined synonym for weg.
[2] hin and her are most often found attached to another prefix to indicate the direction of the movement in relation to the speaker. See Adverbs, 6.3.3.

Gehen Sie **hinein**!	*Go in!*
Kommen Sie **herein**!	*Come in!*
Er lief die Treppe **hinunter/herunter**	*He ran down the stairs*

b Less common separable prefixes

bei-	*with, to*	**bei**legen *enclose* **bei**tragen *contribute*
da-	*there*	**da**haben *have in stock*
dabei-	*near*	**dabei**sein *be present, involved*
daneben-	*miss*	**daneben**liegen *be quite wrong*
dar-	*there, for a purpose*	**dar**stellen *represent, depict*
davon-	*away*	sich **davon**machen *make off, get away*
empor-	*up*	sich **empor**arbeiten *work one's way up*
fest-	*tight, firm*	**fest**stehen *to be certain* **fest**halten *tie up*
frei-	*free*	**frei**setzen *set free*
inne-	*inside*	**inne**halten *pause*
nieder-	*down*	sich **nieder**lassen *settle down, set up business*
überein-	*agree*	**überein**stimmen *agree*
voraus-	*in advance*	**voraus**sagen *predict*
vorbei-, (**vorüber-**)	*past*	**vorbei**fahren *drive past*

c Other separable verb prefixes may be formed using adjectives, adverbs or nouns

- **Adjectives/adverbs**

fernsehen	*to watch TV*	**wahr**nehmen	*to perceive*
geringschätzen	*to think little of*	**weiter**machen	*to carry on (doing)*
loslassen	*to let go*	**wieder**sehen	*to meet again*

- **Nouns**

achtgeben[1]	*to take care*	**teil**nehmen	*to participate*
haltmachen[1]	*to call a halt*	**stand**halten	*to stand firm*
preisgeben	*to expose*	**statt**finden	*to take place*

[1] These verbs are also written as noun + verb: Acht geben, Halt machen.

▶ 19.5.2 Inseparable prefixes

a Inseparable prefixes share several characteristics

• Most have no existence as separate words. The commonest of them are **ver-** and **be-**.

• In pronunciation inseparable prefixes are always unstressed:

be**stell**en, ver**kauf**en

• Inseparable prefixes remain attached to the verb in all forms and tenses:

Ich **verkaufe** mein Auto	*I'm selling my car*
Ich hoffe mein Auto zu **verkaufen**	*I'm hoping to sell my car*

• The past participle does not add ge-:

Ich habe mein Auto **verkauft**	*I sold my car*

b The inseparable prefixes

Each of the inseparable prefixes except **ge-** and **ver-** has a specific main sense which it brings to the verb, as may be seen in the list below.

• **be-**

– **makes intransitive verbs transitive.** The verb is then used with a direct object in the accusative:

bedienen *to serve*	instead of	jm dienen
beraten *to advise*		jm raten
besprechen *to discuss*		sprechen über
betreten *to enter*		treten in
bewohnen *to inhabit*		wohnen in

Wir haben das Problem **besprochen**	*We discussed the problem*

– **is used to form verbs from nouns or adjectives.** Behind these is the sense of providing with something or a quality. The base word sometimes adds the suffix -ig- before the verb ending:

befreien *to free*	from	frei
befreunden *to befriend*		der Freund
befristen *to limit (time)*		die Frist
begünst**ig**en *to favour, encourage*		die Gunst
benachteil**ig**en *to disadvantage*		der Nachteil
berücksicht**ig**en *to take into account*		die Rücksicht
beruhigen *to calm*		ruhig
beschäd**ig**en *to damage*		der Schaden

Sie versucht, ihn zu **beruhigen**	*She's trying to calm him down*

• **emp-**

– **is used in just three verbs:**

empfangen *to receive*	**emp**fehlen *to recommend*
empfinden *to feel, perceive*	

• **ent-**

– **suggests escaping from, or removing something.** Verbs implying movement used in this way often take the dative:

entdecken *to discover*	**ent**fernen *to remove*

entfliehen + dat. *to flee from*   entführen *to hijack, abduct*
entkommen + dat. *to escape from*   entlassen *to release*
entmenschlichen *to dehumanise*   entschuldigen *to excuse*

+ **er-**
  - **suggests a change of state or the successful completion of an action.** Verbs may be formed from other verbs or from adjectives:
    erfrischen *to refresh*   erklären *to explain*
    erleben *to experience*   erschießen *to shoot someone*

+ **ge-**
  - **has no particular meaning:**
    gebrauchen *to use, apply*   geraten in + acc. *to get into*
                                           (e.g. trouble)
    gefallen *to please*   gewährleisten *to ensure*
    gehorchen *to obey*   gewinnen *to win, earn*
    gehören + dat. *to belong to*   sich gewöhnen an + acc. *to get*
                                           used to

+ **miss-**
  - **is often equivalent to English** *mis-,* **indicating 'wrongly', 'inappropriately':**
    missbrauchen *to misuse*   misstrauen *to mistrust*
    misshandeln *to mistreat*   missverstehen *to misunderstand*

+ **ver-**
  - **indicates change of state ('become' or 'make into') and is formed from nouns or adjectives:**

veralten *to go out of date (= become old)*	from	alt
verändern *to alter (= make different)*		anders
verbleichen *to fade (= become pale)*		bleich
verdeutlichen *to clarify, explain (= make clear)*		deutlich
vergrössern *to enlarge*		grösser
verkleiden *to dress up, disguise*		das Kleid
sich verlieben in *to fall in love with*		die Liebe
vernichten *to destroy (= make nothing)*		nichts
verschärfen *to intensify (= make strict)*		schärf
verschmutzen *to pollute (= make dirty)*		der Schmutz
versichern *to insure, assure*		sicher
versklaven *to enslave*		der Sklave
verspäten *to delay (= make late)*		spät

  - **means add or provide with something** (formed from nouns):
    verkörpern *to embody*   from   der Körper *body*
    vernageln *to nail up*   der Nagel *nail*
    versiegeln *to seal*   der Siegel *seal*

  - **means finish, complete**
    verbrauchen   *to consume*
    verhungern   *to starve, die of hunger*

  - **indicates 'away'; to use all one's time or resources to do something:**

    verführen *to seduce, lead astray*   verrauchen *to spend (money) on smoking*
    verreisen *to go away (on a trip)*   verschlafen *to oversleep, miss by oversleeping*
    versetzen *to transplant, transfer*   verspielen *to gamble away*
    vertrinken *to drink away*

– intensifies the meaning of the base verb:

verfolgen *to pursue, persecute*	from	folgen *to follow*	
verhören *to interrogate, quiz*		hören *to hear*	
versprechen *to promise*		sprechen *to speak*	
verzweifeln *to despair*		zweifeln *to doubt*	

– means do something wrongly or too much:

verbilden *to bring up (child) badly*	sich **ver**hören *to mishear*
sich **ver**kaufen *to make a bad buy*	**ver**kochen *to overcook*
sich **ver**laufen *to lose one's way*	**ver**salzen *to oversalt*
sich **ver**sprechen *to mispronounce*	

– gives opposite meaning of base verb (only a few verbs):

verachten *to despise*	from	achten *to respect*
verkaufen *to sell*		kaufen *to buy*
vermieten *to hire out, rent out*		mieten *to rent, hire*

♦ zer-

– 'into pieces', or sometimes intensifies base meaning:

zerbrechen *to smash*	**zer**knüllen *to scrumple up*
zerfallen *to disintegrate*	**zer**stören *to destroy*
zerfressen *to corrode*	**zer**reißen *to tear*

▶ 19.5.3 Variable prefixes

a Characteristics of variable prefixes

♦ A small group of prefixes can be separable or inseparable. There is a difference in meaning between the two; the sense of the separable verb is usually literal, while the inseparable verb is more figurative in use.

♦ As with other prefixes, separable verbs are stressed on the prefix, while inseparable verbs are stressed on the verb itself.

b The common variable prefixes

Prefix	Separable	Inseparable
durch-[1]	**durch**+blicken *to look through* **durch**+fallen *to fail* **durch**+halten *to survive* **durch**+kommen *to get through, succeed* sich **durch**+finden *to find one's way through*	**durch**leben *to live through* **durch**löchern *to make holes in, shoot down (argument)* **durch**tränken *to soak*
hinter-	**hinter**+haken *to follow sthg up* **hinterher**+laufen *to run after*	**hinter**gehen *to deceive* **hinter**lassen *to bequeath*
über-	Most intransitive; über with literal meaning of *'over'* **über**+fahren *to cross over* **über**+gehen *to change, merge into* sich etw. **über**+hören *to be sick of hearing sthg* **über**+lassen *to leave it (up) to s.o.* **über**+laufen *to overflow*	Mostly transitive **über**fahren *to run over* **über**gehen *to skip, leave out* **über**hören *to ignore, fail to hear* **über**lassen *to leave sthg for s.o.* **über**laufen *to overrun* **über**setzen *to translate* **über**treten *to infringe (law)*

Prefix	Separable	Inseparable
	über+setzen *to ferry across* **über**+treten *to change to*	**über**fallen *to attack* **über**holen *to overtake* **über**nachten *to stay the night* **über**raschen *to surprise* **über**treiben *to exaggerate* **über**winden *to overcome*

um-	Usually indicating *turning round/over,*
	  or change of state
	um+bauen *to rebuild*
	um+fahren *to run over*
	um+gehen *to circulate; get on with*
	um+schreiben *to rewrite, adapt*
	um+fallen *to fall over*
	um+gestalten *to alter, remodel*
	um+kippen *to overturn, knock over*
	um+leiten *to divert*
	um+lernen *to retrain*
		Often indicating *around*
		
		umbauen *to enclose*
		umfahren *to drive round, detour*
		umgehen *to avoid, bypass*
		umschreiben *to paraphrase, outline*
		umfassen *to embrace; cover, deal*
		  with
		umgeben *to surround*
		umsegeln *to sail round*

unter-	unter usually has literal meaning of
	  under
	unter+halten *to hold underneath*
	unter+legen *to put underneath; to*
	  attribute
	unter+schlagen *to cross (one's*
	  legs)
	unter+bringen *to accommodate (i.e.*
	  bring under one's roof)
	unter+gehen *to decline, sink*
	unter+kommen *to find*
	  accommodation
		unterhalten *to entertain*
		unterlegen *to underlay, line*
		unterschlagen *to embezzle*
		unterbrechen *to interrupt*
		unterdrücken *to oppress*
		unterlassen *to refrain from*
		unterliegen *to lose to, be subject to*
		unternehmen *to do, undertake*
		unterrichten *to teach*
		untersagen *to prohibit*
		unterschätzen *to underestimate*
		unterscheiden *to distinguish, tell*
		  apart
		unterschreiben *to sign*
		unterstützen *to support*
		untersuchen *to investigate*
		untertauchen *to submerge*

voll-	usually with literal meaning of *fully* **voll**+schmieren *to mess up* **voll**+stopfen *to stuff* **voll**+tanken *to fill up car with fuel*	**voll**enden *to complete* **voll**strecken *to carry out, execute* **voll**ziehen *to carry out, execute*
wider-	usually indicates *against* **wider**+hallen *to echo* **wider**+spiegeln *to reflect, mirror*	**wider**legen *to refute, disprove* **wider**rufen *to cancel, revoke* **wider**sprechen *to contradict* **wider**stehen *to resist* **wider**streben *to oppose*
wieder-	**wieder**+sehen *to see again* **wieder**+erkennen *to recognise* **wieder**+geben *to give back; reproduce* *(sound)*	**wieder**holen *to repeat*

Er hat den Igel **über**fahren   *He drove over the hedgehog*
Er ist mit der Fähre **über**gefahren   *He crossed by ferry*
Wir hoffen, die Küche   *We're hoping to change the*
  umzubauen   *kitchen*

Wir hoffen, den Garten zu **um**bauen	*We're hoping to build a wall round the garden*

▷ 19.5.4 Verbs formed from adjectives and nouns

+ **Verbs can be formed from adjectives and nouns by adding -(e)n to the noun or adjective**

Occasionally a link is added, such as **-ig-** to an adjective, and an umlaut to the root word.

beginnen *to begin*	from	der Beginn	fertigen *to manufacture*	from	fertig
fr**ö**ste**l**n *to shiver*		der Frost	k**ü**rzen *to shorten*		kurz
kochen *to cook*		der Koch	**ö**ffnen *to open*		offen
teilen *to share*		der Teil	rein**ig**en *to clean, purify*		rein

20

Numbers, spelling and punctuation

▶ 20.1.1 Cardinal numbers

0 null	10 zehn	20 zwanzig	80 achtzig
1 eins	11 elf	21 einundzwanzig	90 neunzig
2 zwei	12 zwölf	22 zweiundzwanzig	100 hundert
3 drei	13 dreizehn	26 sechsundzwanzig	101 hundert(und)eins
4 vier	14 vierzehn	27 siebenundzwanzig	
5 fünf	15 fünfzehn	30 dreißig	102 (ein)hundertzwei
6 sechs	16 sechzehn	40 vierzig	
7 sieben	17 siebzehn	50 fünfzig	
8 acht	18 achtzehn	60 sechzig	
9 neun	19 neunzehn	70 siebzig	

120 (ein)hundertzwanzig	1000 (ein)tausend
121 hunderteinundzwanzig	1066 tausendsechsundsechzig
215 zweihundertfünfzehn	1300 (ein)tausenddreihundert/ dreizehnhundert
	2010 zweitausendzehn

1 000 000 eine Million	1 000 000 000 eine Milliarde (Eng: billion)
2 000 000 zwei Millionen	1 000 000 000 000 eine Billion

a **eins becomes the indefinite article ein when used with a dependent following noun, and declines according to gender, number and case (see 3.1.2)**
Exceptions to this rule are a few idiomatic phrases:
ein Uhr *one o'clock* (**cf.** eine Uhr *a clock, one clock*)
vor ein oder zwei Tagen *one or two days ago*

b **zwei and drei have a genitive form, zweier and dreier**
These are used in formal written German; less formal language uses von + dative:
die Aussagen **zweier** *the statements of two reliable*
zuverlässiger Augenzeugen *eyewitnesses*
Or… von zwei zuverlässigen Augenzeugen
das Leben **dreier** Kinder *the lives of three children*
Or das Leben von drei Kindern

c **zwo is sometimes used in speech instead of zwei where its sound might be confused with drei (e.g. on the phone or in radio communications)**

d Phone numbers are usually given in pairs after the dialling code

Null zwei vier acht,   *0248 82 39 14*
  zwoundachtzig,
  neununddreißig, vierzehn
Die Vorwahl ist null null vier neun   *The dialling code is 0049*

e Years up to 1999 are given in hundreds

im Jahr neunzehnhundertachtundneunzig   *in 1989*
Note in + year: im Jahr 1989, or simply: 1989

f Long numbers are written out in full only on cheques; most numbers are normally written as numerals

g Numbers from 10 000 upwards are usually written with a space every three digits; occasionally, a point is used instead: 120 372 or 120.372

h eine Million (-en), eine Milliarde[1] (-n) and eine Billion[2] (-en) always stand as separate nouns

drei Millionen Euro   zweieinhalb Milliarden Dollar
eine Million Euro
But eins Komma zwei Million**en** Euro

[1] eine Milliarde = a thousand million
[2] eine Billion = a million million

i Cardinal numbers may be used as nouns; they take the feminine gender

Im Abi hat er eine glatte **Eins**   *He got a straight A in his Abitur*
  bekommen
Wir fahren mit der **Sechzehn**   *We go on the (number) 16 (bus/*
Or … mit der Linie sechzehn   * tram)*
die Nationalelf   *the national (football) team*

j Multiplication

Vier **mal** zwei ist acht   *four twos are eight*
Der Teppich ist drei **mal** sechs   *The carpet is three metres by six*
  Meter
Das habe ich dir schon   *I've told you that a hundred times*
  hundertmal gesagt!   * already!*
eine **einfache** Karte   *a single ticket*
der **dreifache** Sieger   *the three-times winner*
Dieses Buch habe ich **dreifach**   *I've got three copies of this book*
zweimal die Woche   *twice a week*
alle zehn Minuten   *every ten minutes*

k Other constructions with cardinal numbers

ihre beiden Söhne   *their two sons*
welcher von beiden?   *which of the two?*
Hast du einen Zwanziger?   *Have you got a 20-euro note?*
die sechziger Jahre   *the sixties (i.e. 1960s)*
eine Frau in den Sechzigern   *a woman in her sixties*
Gehen wir zu dritt?   *Shall we go as a (group of) three?*
Sie gehen zu viert   *They go in groups of four*
Sie gehen auf allen vieren   *They walk on all fours*

▷ 20.1.2 Ordinal numbers

+ Ordinal numbers are the adjectival forms of numbers, and are used when placing things in numerical order; they take the appropriate adjective endings:

am neun**ten** Oktober	am dreißig**sten** Mai
zum vier**ten** Mal	der zwanzig**ste** Präsident

a Numbers 1–19 add -te, followed by the adjective ending

der fünf**te** *fifth*	der siebzehn**te** *seventeenth*
am fünf**ten** März	der hundertzwei**te** *hundred-and-second*

+ There are four irregular forms:

der **erste** *first*   der **dritte** *third*   der **siebte** *seventh*   der ach**te** *eight*

+ Note also:

der **viert**größte Staat	the fourth largest state
die **zweit**beste Sportlerin	the second best sportswoman

b Numbers 20 and above add -sten, followed by the adjective ending

der einundvierzig**ste** *forty-first*	der tausend**ste** *thousandth*
am einundzwanzig**sten** Juli *on 21 July*	

c In their written form, ordinal numbers are followed by a point

am 1. November	zum 40. Geburtstag
die 13. Klasse	im 2. Stock

d Ordinal numbers may be used as nouns; as they are adjective-nouns they may be any gender

jeder **Zehnte**	*one in ten*
heute ist der **Zweite**	*today is the second (of the month)*
die **Vierzigste** von Mozart	*Mozart's 40th (symphony)*
Die Chinesen waren die **Ersten**, die …	*the Chinese were the first to …*

▷ 20.1.3 Fractions and decimals

a Fractions are usually formed by adding -el to the ordinal number to form a neuter noun

ein Viert**el**	*a quarter*
ein Dritt**el**	*a third*
zwei Dritt**el**	*two thirds*
ein Drittelliter	*a third of a litre*
or ein drittel Liter	
eine Viertelstunde	*a quarter of an hour*
eine Dreiviertelstunde	*three quarters of an hour*

b The exception is *half a*, for which the adjective halb is used

eine **halbe** Flasche Wein	*half a bottle of wine*
Das habe ich zum **halben** Preis gekauft	*I bought it at half price*
Der Bus kommt alle **halbe** Stunde	*The bus comes every half an hour*

- With place names not requiring the article, uninflected **halb** is used:

halb Österreich	*half (of) Austria*

- The noun *half (of) the* is **die Hälfte** + genitive:

die Hälfte des Brotes	*half (of) the loaf*
die Hälfte aller Engländer	*half of all English people*
die Hälfte seines Vermögens	*half (of) his fortune*
Ich habe das Buch nur **zur Hälfte** gelesen	*I've only read half the book*

- *one and a half, two and a half* are expressed by the indeclinable **eineinhalb/anderthalb, zweieinhalb**, etc.:

nur noch **eineinhalb/anderthalb** Wochen!	*Only one and a half weeks to go!*
Ich habe sie seit **viereinhalb** Jahren nicht mehr gesehen	*I haven't seen her for four and a half years*

c Decimals are written with a comma, not a point

0,8 null Komma acht
1,3 eins Komma drei
5,75 fünf Komma sieben fünf

▶ 20.1.4 Expressions of quantity and money

a Masculine and neuter quantities retain their singular forms even in plural quantities

hundert Cent ergeben einen Euro	*a hundred cents make a/one euro*
zehn Euro; vier Pfund; drei Dollar	*ten euros; four pounds; three dollars*
ein Glas Bier; drei Glas Bier	*a glass of beer; three glasses of beer*
mit zwei Paar Schuhen	*with two pairs of shoes*
zehn Euro das Meter	*ten euros a metre*
Er gab uns je zehn Euro	*He gave us ten euros each*
fünf Euro neunzig	*five euros ninety (cents)*
alle paar Meter	*every few metres*

b Feminine nouns take plural forms in plural quantities (see also 2.2.11b)

wir trinken eine Flasche deutschen Wein	*We're drinking a bottle of German wine*
zwei Flaschen Wein	*two bottles of wine*
eine Tasse Kaffee; zwei Tassen Kaffee	*one cup of coffee; two cups of coffee*
drei Briefmarken zu einem Euro	*three one-euro stamps*

20.2 Spelling

▶ 20.2.1 Capitals or small letters?

Students will already be familiar with the use of initial capital letters for:

- **proper names** (Köln *Cologne*, der Schwarzwald *The Black Forest*, Karl der Große *Charlemagne*, der Blaue Planet *The Blue Planet (Earth)*)

♦ **nouns** (der Mann, die Alte)
♦ the polite word for **you** and all its forms (Sie, Ihnen, Ihr-)
♦ the **first word in a sentence**.

The following points can, however, cause confusion.

a Any word used as a noun starts with a capital letter

eine Eins	das Ich	im Großen und Ganzen
das Aus	das Beste	im Voraus
beim Essen	im Allgemeinen	das Nichts
Recht haben	das Autofahren	
Radfahren	nichts Neues	

b Adjectives referring to 'understood' (i.e. non-repeated) nouns do not start with a capital letter

Er fährt ein blaues Auto, und sie *He drives a blue car, and she a*
  ein graues *grey one*
Ist das dein erster Besuch? *Is this your first visit?*
– Nein, mein zweiter *– No, my second (one)*

c Adjectives of nationality start with a small letter, unless they apply to a proper noun

deutsche Romane *German novels*
französische Weine *French wines*
die Deutsche Bahn *German railways*
der Deutsch-französische Krieg *The Franco-Prussian War*

▶ **TIP** **Deutsch with a capital or a small letter?**

♦ When referring to a language, **Deutsch** and words for other languages start with a capital letter when used as a noun, including where the idea of learning the language is concerned:

ich lerne Deutsch *I'm learning German*
ein Buch auf Deutsch *a book in German*
Sie kann gut Deutsch *She can speak German well*
Auf Deutsch sagt man … *In German we say …*
Ich habe eine Eins in Deutsch *I've got an A grade in German*

♦ **But** they start with a small letter when used as an adverb in combination with a verb (i.e., they answer the question 'how?'):

Sollen wir deutsch oder englisch *Should we speak German or*
  reden? *English?*
Die E-mail ist deutsch *The e-mail is in German*

---

d Adjectives formed from the names of persons may be written in two ways

die einsteinsche Relativitätstheorie **Or** die Einstein'sche
  Relativitätstheorie
die wagnerschen Oper **Or** die Wagner'schen Oper

♦ Often, however, a simpler form of language will be preferred altogether:

Einsteins Relativitätstheorie *Wagners Oper*

e The pronoun Sie and its related forms (Ihnen, Ihr-) always begin with capitals

Vielen Dank für **Ihren** Brief

Wie wir **Ihnen** schon mitgeteilt haben, können wir **Sie** …

♦ This rule formerly applied also to du, ihr and their various forms (dich, dir, dein-; euch, euer-) in letter-writing, and although this is no longer the rule since the recent spelling reform, many German-speakers continue to write them the old way:

Vielen Dank für deinen (formerly: Deinen) Brief

Wie geht es euch? (formerly: Euch)

f Infinitives as nouns: it is usually obvious where infinitives are being used as nouns (and therefore start with a capital letter)

Note these examples, where the infinitive may start with either a capital or a small letter:

Sie liebt reiten/Reiten

Ich lerne segeln/Segeln und windsurfen/Windsurfen

20.3 One word or two?

♦ Deciding whether words should be written as one word or two can be problematic, especially as older German writers and books will use forms which are no longer current since spelling reform.

♦ While the rules are rather more flexible than there is space to describe here, the basic principle is this:

If compounds are viewed as a single idea, they are written together; otherwise they are written separately:

Die Autos sind zusammengefahren	*The cars collided*
Wir sind zusammen gefahren	*We travelled together*

▶ 20.3.1 Separable verbs

Separable verbs are normally written with the prefix and verb as one word in the infinitive. See 19.5.1 and 19.5.3. The following notes cover those verbs where it may be unclear whether the prefix should be a completely separate word.

a Noun + verb compounds are usually written separately

Rad fahren *to cycle*		Ski laufen *to ski*	
Schlange stehen *to queue*			

Note When these infinitives are used as nouns, they are written as one word:

das Radfahren, das Skilaufen, das Schlangestehen

Note Noun prefixes which are now regarded as part of the verb idiom are prefixed to the infinitive, e.g.

eislaufen	*to ice skate*	leidtun	*to feel sorry for*
preisgeben	*to betray, expose*	standhalten	*to stand firm*
stattfinden	*to take place*	teilnehmen	*to take part*

verbs beginning with heim-, and irre-:

heimfahren	to drive home
heimkehren	to return home
heimkommen	to come home
heimleuchten	to give a piece of one's, mind
heimzahlen	to pay back
irreführen	to mislead
irreleiten	to mislead
irrereden	to rave

b Adjective + verb compounds are written *together* in the infinitive and participles with the adjective as separable prefix, if together they form a new idiomatic verb

rotsehen *to be furious, see red*	schwerfallen *to be hard for*
sich totlachen *to laugh one's head off*	schwarzfahren *to travel without paying*

+ They are written *separately* if the adjective is complex (i.e. has more than one element), or is qualified by an adverb, or is linked to an already separable verb:

complex:	bewusstlos schlagen	*to knock out*
adj. + adverb:	sehr fein mahlen	*to grind very finely*
adj. + separable vb:	schwarz fernsehen	*to watch television without a licence*

+ In some instances they may be written *together* or *separately*:

feinmahlen **or** fein mahlen	*to grind finely*
kaputtmachen **or** kaputt machen	*to smash*
liebhaben **or** lieb haben	*to love, to be fond of*
rotstreichen **or** rot streichen	*to paint red*

c Verbs formed from an adjective + sein are written separately

aus sein	*to be over, out*
los sein	*to be rid of*
zu sein	*to be shut*
zufrieden sein	*to be satisfied*

d Verbs formed from verb + verb are usually written separately

fallen lassen	*to drop*
kennen lernen	*to meet, get to know*
liegen lassen	*to leave*
sitzen bleiben	*to repeat a year*
spazieren gehen	*to go for a walk*

20.3.2 Nouns

a Nouns which involve a name may be written together or, for clarity or emphasis, joined with a hyphen

das Goethehaus **or**	das Goethe-Haus
der Suezkanal **or**	der Suez-Kanal
die Bordeauxweine **or**	die Bordeaux-Weine

Compounds formed with longer geographical names are linked by hyphens:

der Rio-de-Janeiro-Flug

Note Geographical names used adjectivally and ending in -er never become part of the noun:

> Wiener Schnitzel
> Genfer See *Lake Geneva* (but Swiss German: Genfersee)

b Longer phrases used as nouns are usually joined by hyphens

in einem Dritte-Welt-Land	*in a Third World country*
ein Atom-U-Boot	*an atomic submarine*
Das ist zum Aus-der-Haut-Fahren!	*It's enough to drive you up the wall!*

20.4 ss or ß ?

a ss is used after a short vowel

> der Fluss, die Flüsse, müssen, er muss, die Massage, wissen, der Pass, essen

b ß is used after a long vowel or a diphthong

> der Fuß, die Füße, groß, weiß, sie weiß, die Maße, die Straße, sie aß

Note ß is not normally used in words written in capitals:

> Er wohnt in Gießen **but** GIESSEN

20.5 Punctuation

20.5.1 The comma

a The comma is used to mark off clauses

Als er nach Hause kam, war es schon spät	*When he got home, it was already late*
Ich gehe ins Kino, aber er bleibt hier	*I'm going to the cinema, but he's staying here*

Note The comma is *not* used to provide a breathing space or to mark off adverbs as in English:

Um 5 Uhr verließ er das Haus und ging zum Bahnhof	*At 5 o'clock, he left the house and walked to the station*
Es war aber schon zu spät für mich	*It was, however, too late for me*

b A comma is needed between two or more adjectives where both relate equally to the noun, but not where one adjective qualifies the other

• The key is that, where both adjectives qualify the noun equally, they could be joined by **und**:

> eine nette, interessante Frau
> **or** eine nette und interessante Frau
> Ein neuer deutscher Film
> (Not possible: ein neuer und deutscher Film)

Compare the following:

> neue, umweltfreundliche Autos (i.e. the new cars are environmentally friendly, unlike the old ones)

neue umweltfreundliche Autos (i.e. there are new cars which are environmentally friendly, just like some already on the market)

c A comma is needed before conjunctions introducing a contrast, e.g. aber, doch, jedoch, sondern

Der Tag war schön, aber kalt	*The day was beautiful but cold*
Mein Bruder blieb nicht zu Hause, sondern (er) ging ins Kino	*My brother didn't stay at home, but went to the cinema*
Ich wollte ihn besuchen, aber er war nicht zu Hause	*I wanted to visit him, but he wasn't at home*

d Clauses beginning with co-ordinating conjunctions und and oder need no comma

Ich gehe ins Kino und sie bleibt hier
Peter kann hier bleiben oder er kann mitkommen
Wir fahren entweder mit der Bahn oder mit dem Flugzeug

However, the writer may choose to add a comma for the sake of clarity:

Sie trank nur Wasser, und den Wein ließ sie im Kühlschrank	*She drank only water, and left the wine in the fridge*

(i.e. to make it clear that she didn't drink the wine as well)

Im Dorf, und das ist allgemein bekannt, leben zwei Hundertjährige	*In the village – and this is well known – live two centenarians*

e Exclamations, clauses and phrases in apposition, explanations, etc. are marked by commas

Ja, natürlich!	*Yes, of course!*
Peter, kannst du mir bitte mal helfen?	*Could you help me please, Peter?*
Bach, der große Komponist, lebte in Leipzig	*Bach, the great composer, lived in Leipzig*
Ich trinke gern Wein, besonders Rotwein	*I enjoy drinking wine, especially red wine*
Wir fahren am Montag, und zwar um 10 Uhr	*We're going on Monday, at 10 o'clock, in fact*

f A comma is needed before clauses with zu + infinitive

Ich habe vor, ins Kino zu gehen	*I'm intending to go to the cinema*
Er verließ das Haus, ohne mich zu sehen	*He left the house without seeing me*
Ich gehe in die Stadt, um Milch zu kaufen	*I'm going into town to buy milk*
Wir freuen uns darauf, euch zu besuchen	*We're looking forward to visiting you*
Es war uns möglich, ihm zu helfen	*It was possible for us to help him*

• **Compare** how the placing of the comma affects the meanings of these two sentences:

Er versuchte, täglich 10 Km zu laufen	*He tried to run 10 km every day*
Er versuchte täglich, 10 Km zu laufen	*He tried every day to run 10 km*

20.5.2 Inverted commas (speech marks) and colons

a The opening set of inverted commas is placed at the bottom of the line, facing outwards, while the closing set is placed at the top, also facing outwards

A colon is used after a verb of saying, and it is followed by a capital letter:

Dann sagte er mir: „Ich verstehe kein Wort davon."	*Then he said to me, 'I don't understand a word of it.'*
Ich fragte sie: „Woher kommst du?"	*I asked her, 'Where do you come from?'*

• If the verb of saying stands after the speech marks, a comma is used and stands after the speech marks:

„Woher soll ich das wissen?", fragte er	*'How am I supposed to know that?' he asked*
„Es ist schön", dachte er, „dass sie zurückgekommen ist."	*'It's nice', he thought, 'that she's come back.'*

20.5.3 The apostrophe

a The apostrophe is used to denote an abbreviated es or an omitted beginning of a word in written representations of colloquial spoken German

Wie geht's?	*How are you?*
Sie hat 'nen Bruder	*She's got a brother*
's ist nicht leicht mit 'nem Kater	*It's not easy with a hangover*

b. The apostrophe is not used for the omitted ends of words, or for the possessive

Ich hab keine Zeit	*I have no time*
Stefans Weinkeller	*Stefan's wine cellar*
Bachs Werke	*Bach's works*
bei Theissens	*at the Theissens' house*

20.5.4 The exclamation mark

a The exclamation mark is used, as expected, for exclamations and commands

Oh nein!	Hallo!	Du meine Güte!
Gib mir das Buch!		Bleiben Sie hier!

However, the exclamation mark is gradually being replaced with a full stop, unless the command is a forceful one.

b It is also used after the opening address of a letter. The first word of the letter after the exclamation mark begins with a capital letter

Lieber Theo!	Sehr geehrte Frau Oswald!

Here too, the exclamation mark is being replaced by a comma, as in English, and then the first word of the letter starts with a small letter.

21

List of strong and irregular verbs

- See 12.4 for a list of irregular verbs and 12.1 for mixed verbs; their irregular parts are also noted below.
- It is worth remembering that, with the exception of **sein,** the present tense plural forms of verbs (**wir, ihr, sie/Sie**) are never irregular.

In the following list:
- The present tense form is included only if the stem vowel changes from the infinitive.
- Vowel changes from the infinitive are in bold; where there are other changes (e.g. singling or doubling of the following consonant or some other change to the following consonant), the whole word is in bold.
- Verbs marked with * are always intransitive, and so are conjugated with **sein** in the perfect tense.
- Verbs marked with (*) are conjugated with **sein** in the perfect tense if they are intransitive and with **haben** if they are transitive. See 10.3.4.

Infinitive	er - Present	er - Imperfect	Past participle	Meaning
backen	bäckt	backte	gebacken	to bake
befehlen	befiehlt	befahl	befohlen	to command/order
beginnen		begann	begonnen	to begin
beißen		biss	gebissen	to bite
bergen	birgt	barg	geborgen	to save/shelter
bersten	birst	barst	* geborsten	to burst
betrügen		betrog	betrogen	to deceive/cheat
biegen		bog	(*) gebogen	to bend/turn
bieten		bot	geboten	to offer
binden		band	gebunden	to tie/bind
bitten		**bat**	**gebeten**	to ask/request
blasen	bläst	blies	geblasen	to blow
bleiben		blieb	* geblieben	to stay/remain
braten	brät	briet	gebraten	to roast
brechen	bricht	brach	(*) gebrochen	to break
brennen		brannte	gebrannt	to burn
bringen		**brachte**	**gebracht**	to bring

Infinitive	*er* - Present	*er* - Imperfect	Past participle	Meaning
denken		dachte	gedacht	*to think*
dringen		drang	(*) gedrungen	*to force one's way*
dürfen	darf	durfte	gedurft / dürfen	*to be allowed to*
empfangen	empfängt	empfing	empfangen	*to receive, welcome*
empfehlen	empfiehlt	empfahl	empfohlen	*to recommend*
empfinden		empfand	empfunden	*to feel*
erlöschen	erlischt	erlosch	* erloschen	*to go out (fire)*
erschrecken	erschrickt	erschrak	* erschrocken	*to be frightened*
essen	isst	aß	gegessen	*to eat*
fahren	fährt	fuhr	(*) gefahren	*to go (by vehicle)/ to drive*
fallen	fällt	fiel	*gefallen	*to fall*
fangen	fängt	fing	gefangen	*to catch*
fechten	ficht	focht	gefochten	*to fence/fight*
finden		fand	gefunden	*to find*
fliegen		flog	(*) geflogen	*to fly*
fliehen		floh	(*) geflohen	*to flee, run away*
fließen		floss	* geflossen	*to flow*
fressen	frißt	fraß	gefressen	*to eat (of animals)*
frieren		fror	(*) gefroren	*to freeze /be cold*
gären		gor	* gegoren	*to ferment*
gebären	gebiert	gebar	geboren	*to give birth to/bear*
geben	gibt	gab	gegeben	*to give*
gedeihen		gedieh	* gediehen	*to prosper, thrive*
gehen		ging	* gegangen	*to go/walk*
gelingen		gelang	* gelungen	*to succeed/manage*
gelten	gilt	galt	gegolten	*to be valid/worth*
genießen		genoss	genossen	*to enjoy/relish*
geschehen	geschieht	geschah	* geschehen	*to happen*
gewinnen		gewann	gewonnen	*to win/gain*
gießen		goss	gegossen	*to pour*
gleichen		glich	geglichen	*to resemble*
gleiten		glitt	* geglitten	*to glide/slide*
graben	gräbt	grub	gegraben	*to dig*
greifen		griff	gegriffen	*to grasp/seize*
haben	hat	hatte	gehabt	*to have*
halten	hält	hielt	gehalten	*to hold/stop*
hängen		hing	gehangen	*to hang (intrans.)*

Infinitive	er - Present	er - Imperfect	Past participle	Meaning
hauen		haute/**hieb**	gehauen	to hit, clobber
heben		hob	gehoben	to lift/raise
heißen		hieß	geheißen	to be called
helfen	hilft	half	geholfen	to help
kennen		kannte	gekannt	to know (person/place)
klingen		klang	geklungen	to sound
kneifen		**kniff**	**gekniffen**	to pinch
kommen		**kam**	* gekommen	to come
können	**kann**	**konnte**	**gekonnt/können**	can/to be able
kriechen		kroch	* gekrochen	to creep/crawl
laden	lädt	lud	geladen	to load
lassen	lässt	ließ	gelassen	to let/leave
laufen	läuft	lief	* gelaufen	to run
leiden	.	**litt**	**gelitten**	to suffer
leihen		lieh	geliehen	to lend/borrow
lesen	liest	las	gelesen	to read
liegen		lag	gelegen	to lie
lügen		log	gelogen	to (tell a) lie
mahlen		mahlte	gemahlen	to grind
meiden		mied	gemieden	to avoid
melken		melkte	gemolken	to milk
messen	misst	maß	gemessen	to measure
mögen	**mag**	**mochte**	**gemocht/mögen**	to like
müssen	**muss**	**musste**	**gemusst/müssen**	to have to/must
nehmen	**nimmt**	nahm	**genommen**	to take
nennen		nannte	genannt	to name
pfeifen		**pfiff**	**gepfiffen**	to whistle
preisen		pries	gepriesen	to praise
quellen	quillt	quoll	* gequollen	to gush out/spring
raten	rät	riet	geraten	to advise
reiben		rieb	gerieben	to rub
reißen		riss	(*) gerissen	to tear
reiten		**ritt**	(*) **geritten**	to ride
rennen		rannte	* gerannt	to run/race
riechen		roch	gerochen	to smell
ringen		rang	gerungen	to wrestle/struggle
rinnen		rann	* geronnen	to run, flow
rufen		rief	gerufen	to call

Infinitive	er - Present	er - Imperfect	Past participle	Meaning
saufen	säuft	soff	gesoffen	to drink (of animal)
schaffen[1]		schuf	geschaffen	to create
scheiden		schied	(*) geschieden	to part/separate
scheinen		schien	geschienen	to shine/seem
scheißen		schiss	geschissen	to shit
schelten	schilt	schalt	gescholten	to scold
schieben		schob	geschoben	to push/shove
schießen		schoss	(*) geschossen	to shoot/fire
schlafen	schläft	schlief	geschlafen	to sleep
schlagen	schlägt	schlug	geschlagen	to hit/strike/beat
schleichen		schlich	* geschlichen	to creep
schleifen		schliff	geschliffen	to grind, sharpen
schließen		schloss	geschlossen	to shut
schlingen		schlang	geschlungen	to coil; to gulp
schmeißen		schmiss	geschmissen	to fling/chuck
schmelzen	schmilzt	schmolz	(*) geschmolzen	to melt
schneiden		schnitt	geschnitten	to cut
schreiben		schrieb	geschrieben	to write
schreien		schrie	geschrie(e)n	to shout/scream
schreiten		schritt	* geschritten	to stride/proceed
schweigen		schwieg	geschwiegen	to be silent
schwellen	schwillt	schwoll	*geschwollen	to swell
schwimmen		schwamm	(*) geschwommen	to swim
schwinden		schwand	* geschwinden	to disappear
schwingen		schwang	geschwungen	to swing
schwören		schwor	geschworen	to swear (an oath)
sehen	sieht	sah	gesehen	to see
sein	ist	war	* gewesen	to be
senden[2]		sandte	gesandt	to send
singen		sang	gesungen	to sing
sinken		sank	*gesunken	to sink
sitzen		saß	gesessen	to sit/be seated
sollen	soll	sollte	gesollt/sollen	should
spalten		spaltete	gespalten	to split
speien		spie	gespien	to spew, vomit
spinnen		spann	gesponnen	to spin/be crazy
sprechen	spricht	sprach	gesprochen	to speak
springen		sprang	* gesprungen	to jump

Infinitive	*er* - Present	*er* - Imperfect	Past participle	Meaning
stechen	sticht	stach	gestochen	*to sting/prick*
stehen		**stand**	**gestanden**	*to stand*
stehlen	stiehlt	stahl	gestohlen	*to steal*
steigen		stieg	* gestiegen	*to climb/mount*
sterben	stirbt	starb	* gestorben	*to die*
stinken		stank	gestunken	*to stink, smell bad*
stoßen	stößt	stieß	(*) gestoßen	*push; knock, encounter*
streichen		strich	(*) gestrichen	*stroke/roam/paint*
streiten		**stritt**	**gestritten**	*to argue/quarrel*
tragen	trägt	trug	getragen	*to carry/wear*
treffen	trifft	**traf**	getroffen	*to meet; hit (target)*
treiben		trieb	(*) getrieben	*to drive/do; drift*
treten	**tritt**	trat	(*) getreten	*to step/go*
trinken		trank	getrunken	*to drink*
trügen		trog	getrogen	*to deceive*
tun	**tut**	**tat**	**getan**	*to do*
verbergen	verbirgt	verbarg	verborgen	*to hide*
verderben	verdirbt	verdarb	(*) verdorben	*to spoil/ruin/go bad*
vergessen	vergisst	vergaß	vergessen	*to forget*
verlieren		verlor	verloren	*to lose*
vermeiden		vermied	vermieden	*to avoid*
verschwinden		verschwand	* verschwunden	*to disappear*
verzeihen		verzieh	verziehen	*to pardon*
wachsen	wächst	wuchs	* gewachsen	*to grow*
waschen	wäscht	wusch	gewaschen	*to wash*
weichen		wich	gewichen	*to give way, yield*
weisen		wies	gewiesen	*to point/show*
werben	wirbt	warb	geworben	*to advertise*
werden	**wird**	**wurde**	* **geworden**	*to become*
werfen	wirft	warf	geworfen	*to throw*
wiegen		wog	gewogen	*to weigh*
winden		wand	gewunden	*to wind*
wissen	**weiß**	**wusste**	**gewusst**	*to know (fact)*
wollen	**will**	**wollte**	**gewollt / wollen**	*to want to/wish*
ziehen		**zog**	(*) **gezogen**	*to pull; move (away)*
zwingen		zwang	gezwungen	*to force/compel*

[1] cf. schaffen **as a weak verb** (schafft, schaffte, hat … geschafft) = *to manage, work.*
[2] cf. senden **as a weak verb** (sendet, sendete, hat …gesendet) = *to broadcast.*

22

Guide to tenses

Infinitive	Weak	Strong	Modal		
	sagen	geben	können	sein	werden
Present	ich sage	ich gebe	ich kann	ich bin	ich werde
	du sagst	du gibst	du kannst	du bist	du wirst
	er sagt	er gibt	er kann	er ist	er wird
	wir sagen	wir geben	wir können	wir sind	wir werden
	ihr sagt	ihr gebt	ihr könnt	ihr seid	ihr werdet
	sie sagen	sie geben	sie können	sie sind	sie werden
Simple past	ich sagte	ich gab	ich konnte	ich war	ich wurde
	du sagtest	du gabst	du konntest	du warst	du wurdest
	er sagte	er gab	er konnte	er war	er wurde
	wir sagten	wir gaben	wir konnten	wir waren	wir wurden
	ihr sagtet	ihr gabt	ihr konntet	ihr wart	ihr wurdet
	sie sagten	sie gaben	sie konnten	sie waren	sie wurden
Perfect	ich habe gesagt	ich habe gegeben	ich habe … können	ich bin gewesen	ich bin geworden
	du hast gesagt	du hast gegeben	du hast … können	du bist gewesen	du bist geworden
	er hat gesagt	er hat gegeben	er hat … können	er ist gewesen	er ist geworden
	wir haben gesagt	wir haben gegeben	wir haben … können	wir sind gewesen	wir sind geworden
	ihr habt gesagt	ihr habt gegeben	ihr habt … können	ihr seid gewesen	ihr seid geworden
	sie haben gesagt	sie haben gegeben	sie haben … können	sie sind gewesen	sie sind geworden
Pluperfect	ich hatte gesagt	ich hatte gegeben	ich hatte … können	ich war gewesen	ich war geworden
	du hattest gesagt	du hattest gegeben	du hattest … können	du warst gewesen	du warst geworden
	er hatte gesagt	er hatte gegeben	er hatte … können	er war gewesen	er war geworden
	wir hatten gesagt	wir hatten gegeben	wir hatten … können	wir waren gewesen	wir waren geworden
	ihr hattet gesagt	ihr hattet gegeben	ihr hattet … können	ihr wart gewesen	ihr wart geworden
	sie hatten gesagt	sie hatten gegeben	sie hatten … können	sie waren gewesen	sie waren geworden

Infinitive	Weak sagen	Strong geben	Modal können	sein	werden
Future	ich werde sagen du wirst sagen er wird sagen wir werden sagen ihr werdet sagen sie werden sagen	ich werde geben du wirst geben er wird geben wir werden geben ihr werdet geben sie werden geben	ich werde … können du wirst … können er wird … können wir werden … können ihr werdet … können sie werden … können	ich werde sein du wirst sein er wird sein wir werden sein ihr werdet sein sie werden sein	ich werde werden du wirst werden er wird werden wir werden werden ihr werdet werden sie werden werden
Future perfect	ich werde gesagt haben du wirst gesagt haben er wird gesagt haben wir werden gesagt haben ihr werdet gesagt haben sie werden gesagt haben	ich werde gegeben haben du wirst gegeben haben er wird gegeben haben wir werden gegeben haben ihr werdet gegeben haben sie werden gegeben haben		ich werde gewesen sein du wirst gewesen sein er wird gewesen sein wir werden gewesen sein ihr werdet gewesen sein sie werden gewesen sein	
Subjunctive 1/ *Konjunktiv I*	ich sage du sagest er sage wir sagen ihr saget sie sagen	ich gebe du gebest er gebe wir geben ihr gebet sie geben	ich könne du könnest er könne wir können ihr könnet sie können	ich sei du seist er sei wir seien ihr seiet sie seien	ich werde du werdest er werde wir werden ihr werdet sie werden
Subjunctive 1/ *Konjunktiv II*	ich sagte du sagtest er sagte wir sagten ihr sagtet sie sagten	ich gäbe du gäbest er gäbe wir gäben ihr gäbet sie gäben	ich könnte du könntest er könnte wir könnten ihr könntet sie könnten	ich wäre du wärst er wäre wir wären ihr wäret sie wären	ich würde du würdest er würde wir würden ihr würdet sie würden

Infinitive	Weak	Strong	Modal		
	sagen	geben	können	sein	werden
würde-conditional	ich würde sagen	ich würde geben			ich würde werden
	du würdest sagen	du würdest geben			du würdest werden
	er würde sagen	er würde geben			er würde werden
	wir würden sagen	wir würden geben			wir würden werden
	ihr würdet sagen	ihr würdet geben			ihr würdet werden
	sie würden sagen	sie würden geben			sie würden werden
'Conditional in the past' (pluperfect subjunctive)	ich hätte gesagt	ich hätte gegeben	ich hätte … können	ich wäre gewesen	ich wäre geworden
	du hättest gesagt	du hättest gegeben	du hättest … können	du wärst gewesen	du wärst geworden
	er hätte gesagt	er hätte gegeben	er hätte … können	er wäre gewesen	er wäre geworden
	wir hätten gesagt	wir hätten gegeben	wir hätten … können	wir wären gewesen	wir wären geworden
	ihr hättet gesagt	ihr hättet gegeben	ihr hättet … können	ihr wäret gewesen	ihr wäret geworden
	sie hätten gesagt	sie hätten gegeben	sie hätten … können	sie wären gewesen	sie wären geworden
Imperative	Sag!	Gib!		Sei!	Werde!
	Sagt!	Gebt!		Seid!	Werdet!
	Sagen Sie!	Geben Sie!		Seien Sie!	Werden Sie!

Glossary

accusative	One of the four CASES (Chapter 1); it indicates the DIRECT OBJECT (1.1.2a), and is used after certain PREPOSITIONS (1.1.2b, 9.1): Meine Schwester ruft **ihren Freund** an.
active voice	One of two VOICES (Chapter 15 overview) in German; the most common is the active voice, in which the person or thing which performs the action is the SUBJECT of the VERB: **Mein Bruder** fährt das Auto.
adjective	A word which describes a noun (Chapter 5). An **attributive** adjective stands before the noun: Der **alte** Mann. A **predicative** adjective stands after a verb such as sein: Der Mann ist **alt**.
adjective-noun (or **adjectival noun**)	An adjective used as a noun (5.2): der **Fremde**, das **Gute**.
adverb	A word which modifies a VERB, ADJECTIVE, another adverb, or a clause (Chapter 6), often indicating **when, where, how** or **why**: Sie spielt **ganz toll**. Er ist **sehr** alt. **Leider** geht das **nicht**.
adverbial	A word or phrase used as an ADVERB: Sie spielt **im Garten**. Er hat Hunger, **wenn er nach Hause kommt**.
agent	The person or thing performing the action of the VERB in the PASSIVE (15.1.2): Das Stück wurde von **Shakespeare** geschrieben.
agreement	Matching appropriate grammatical characteristics of one item with another; for example, DETERMINERS and attributive ADJECTIVES 'agree' with the NOUN in gender, number and case (5.1): **der alte** Mann; **die alten** Männer. VERBS 'agree' with their SUBJECTS: ich **gehe**, wir **gehen**.
apposition	A noun phrase which explains or adds information about the noun next to which it stands (1.2): die Musik von Bach, **dem großen Komponisten**.
article	A type of DETERMINER; der, die, das, etc. (the **definite** article) (3.1.1), and ein, eine, etc. (the **indefinite** article) (3.1.2).
auxiliary verb	A verb used with the INFINITIVE or PAST PARTICIPLE of another verb, often to form a COMPOUND TENSE (10.3, 10.4, 10.5, 10.6) or the PASSIVE (15.1): Ich **habe** gelesen; Sie **musste** ins Haus gehen; Er **wurde** verletzt. The auxiliaries are haben, sein, werden and the MODAL VERBS such as wollen and können.
case	DECLENSIONS which indicate how certain words (e.g. PRONOUNS, NOUN PHRASES) function in a CLAUSE (Chapter 1). German has four cases: NOMINATIVE (**der** Mann), ACCUSATIVE (**den** Mann), GENITIVE (**des** Mannes) and DATIVE (**dem** Mann).

clause	A verb with its COMPLEMENTS such as SUBJECT and OBJECT (18.1): **Ich lese ein Buch.** A **main clause** makes sense on its own: Ich habe kein Geld. A **subordinate clause** needs a **main clause** in order to make sense, and starts with a CONJUNCTION: Weil ich kein Geld habe, … See also PHRASE.
comparative	A form of the adjective or adverb used when comparing people and things (Chapter 8): ein **besserer** Film; ich koche **langsamer.**
complement	Sometimes called the **completion**; the word or group of words, especially the SUBJECT or OBJECT, required to complete the meaning of the VERB.
compound tense	A tense made up of an auxiliary plus an INFINITIVE or PAST PARTICIPLE, specifically, the PERFECT, PLUPERFECT and FUTURE. See also SIMPLE TENSE.
compound word	A word made by joining two or more other words (Chapter 19): Autobahn, altmodisch.
conditional	A form of SUBJUNCTIVE 2 (*KONJUNKTIV II*) made up of würde + INFINITIVE (17.2.3b, 17.4.1): Ich würde kaufen.
conjugation	The pattern of forms of a VERB in each TENSE and for each person. The main conjugations in German are WEAK and STRONG (Chapter 10).
conjunction	A word which links CLAUSES in a SENTENCE. **Co-ordinating conjunctions** (und, aber, oder, etc.) usually link MAIN CLAUSES (18.2.1); **subordinating conjunctions** (wenn, weil, dass, etc.) link a SUBORDINATE CLAUSE to a MAIN CLAUSE (18.2.2).
copular verb	Sometimes called a **linking** verb. It does not describe an action, but connects the SUBJECT to its nominative COMPLEMENT, e.g. sein, werden (1.1.1b): Er **war** ein alter Mann.
dative	One of the four CASES; it indicates the INDIRECT OBJECT of a VERB (Sie gibt **mir** ein Geschenk) (1.1.5); it is also used after certain PREPOSITIONS (9.2, 9.3), VERBS (12.6.1, 13.3.1) and ADJECTIVES (5.3.3).
declension	The pattern of endings on a DETERMINER, ADJECTIVE or NOUN used to indicate GENDER, NUMBER and CASE.
demonstrative	A word which indicates a particular person or thing as if in answer to the question 'Which one?' (3.3, 4.3): e.g. dieser, jener.
determiner	A word used with a NOUN, such as the ARTICLE (der, ein) or DEMONSTRATIVE (dieser) (Chapter 3).
diphthong	A pair of vowels sounded as one: Haus, mein, viel.
direct object	The person or thing directly affected by the action of the verb (1.1.2a): Ich esse **Käse.**
direct speech	Statements, questions, and IMPERATIVES given in their original form inside quotation marks: **„Wie spät ist es?"** fragte er. See also INDIRECT QUESTION, INDIRECT SPEECH.
ending	The suffix added to a DETERMINER, ADJECTIVE or NOUN to help show the CASE, GENDER or NUMBER; or to the verb STEM to indicate the TENSE, PERSON, NUMBER and MOOD of the word.

finite verb	The conjugated form of the VERB with its ending for PERSON, TENSE, NUMBER and MOOD: ich **kaufe**, wir **kaufen**. See also INFINITIVE.
future perfect	The TENSE that refers to an event which will have happened before another (10.6, 11.5): Sie wird schon nach Hause gekommen sein. It is not much used in German.
future tense	A TENSE referring to the future, formed from the AUXILIARY werden + an infinitive (10.5.1, 11.4): Ich werde nach Berlin fahren. See also PRESENT TENSE.
gender	All NOUNS fall into one of three groups depending on the word used for *the*: der (masculine), die (feminine) and das (neuter).
genitive	One of the four CASES; it is used to show possession (1.1.3a) and after some PREPOSITIONS (9.4).
gerund	The INFINITIVE used as a NOUN. It is always neuter (14.1.3, 14.4.2a): das Wandern, das Autofahren.
imperative	The MOOD used when giving commands, etc. (Chapter 16): Bleiben Sie hier!
indefinite	A PRONOUN (e.g. etwas) (4.5) or DETERMINER (e.g. eine) (3.6) which is not specific to one thing or person.
indicative	The most common of the three MOODS in German; it is used for straightforward factual statements and questions (Chapter 11): Ich gehe ins Bett.
indirect object	If a VERB (such as geben) has two OBJECTS, one of them will usually be indirectly affected by the action; this is the indirect object (1.1.5a, 18.3.2): Ich gebe **meinem Bruder** ein Geschenk. See also DIRECT OBJECT.
indirect question	A question that is reported rather than given in the original (17.3.3): Er fragte mich, **wie spät es sei**. See also DIRECT SPEECH.
indirect speech	A statement that is reported rather than given inside quotation marks (17.3.1). Compare DIRECT SPEECH: „Es ist schon spät," sagte er with INDIRECT SPEECH: Er sagte, **es sei schon spät**.
infinitive	The basic, dictionary form of the verb: haben, sehen, abfahren.
infinitive clause	A clause in which the verb is an infinitive rather than a conjugated form (14.1, 18.5): Ich habe vor, **in die Stadt zu fahren**.
inflection	A general word for CONJUGATION (applied to VERBS) and DECLENSION (for NOUNS).
inseparable verb	A verb that has a prefix which is not separated from the verb when conjugated (19.5.2): bestellen, verkaufen.
interrogative	DETERMINERS, ADVERBS and PRONOUNS used to ask questions (3.5, 4.6, 6.7). **Welches** Haus ist deins? **Woher** kommst du? **Wer** ist das?
intransitive verb	A verb with no DIRECT OBJECT (12.5): Ich schlafe. Er folgte mir. Du siehst dumm aus. Denkst du an mich?
irregular verb	A verb whose CONJUGATION does not follow fully the patterns of one of the standard WEAK or STRONG groups of verbs (12.4, Chapter 21), e.g. sein, werden.
Konjunktiv	The German word for the SUBJUNCTIVE.
mixed verb	One of a small group of verbs which have WEAK VERB endings and certain STRONG VERB vowel changes (12.1), e.g. brennen, nennen.

modal particle	A small word such as doch, eben or mal used particularly in spoken German to indicate the attitude of the speaker (Chapter 7): Hilf mir **doch mal**!
modal verb	The verbs dürfen, können, mögen, müssen, sollen and wollen; usually used as AUXILIARY verbs together with an INFINITIVE (12.2, 12.3).
mood	Verbs are used in one of the three moods to indicate the attitude of the speaker or writer to the action described. See INDICATIVE, IMPERATIVE and SUBJUNCTIVE.
nominative	One of the four CASES; it is usually used to indicate the SUBJECT of the verb (1.1.1): **Meine Schwester** ruft ihren Freund an.
non-finite	The INFINITIVE and the PRESENT and PAST PARTICIPLES, i.e. the forms of the verb that do not vary according to the SUBJECT: parken, parkend, geparkt.
noun	A word for a person, thing or idea (Chapter 2): das Kind, die Stadt, die Liebe.
noun phrase	The NOUN with its connected words, e.g. a DETERMINER and/or an ADJECTIVE.
number	NOUNS, PRONOUNS, etc. are all either singular or plural in number.
object	COMPLEMENTS of the VERB. See DIRECT OBJECT, INDIRECT OBJECT and PREPOSITIONAL OBJECT.
participle	One of the NON-FINITE forms of the verb. German verbs have two participles, the PRESENT PARTICIPLE (14.3) and the PAST PARTICIPLE (14.2).
passive voice	One of the two VOICES in German. In the passive, the SUBJECT of the VERB is the object of the action (Chapter 15), e.g. Das Auto wird von meinem Bruder gefahren.
past participle	The NON-FINITE form of the verb used to form some COMPOUND TENSES such as the PERFECT TENSE: gewohnt, gefahren (10.3.1, 10.3.2, 14.2) and the PASSIVE (15.1).
past tense	The tense (usually called the SIMPLE PAST) which indicates actions or states in the past (10.2, 11.2, 12.2.2b, Chapter 22): Ich **fuhr** nach Hamburg; es **war** kalt.
perfect tense	A COMPOUND TENSE used to indicate past actions or states (10.3, 11.2, Chapter 22): Ich **habe** früher in Berlin **gewohnt**. Sie **sind** nach Berlin **gefahren**.
personal pronoun	A word which refers to or replaces a NOUN PHRASE or referring to persons (4.1): ich, mich, mir.
phrase	A meaningful group of words which does not contain a FINITE VERB: um sechs Uhr; vor dem Bahnhof. See also CLAUSE.
pluperfect tense	A COMPOUND TENSE used to indicate an action which preceded another in the past (10.4, 11.3): Als ich angekommen bin, **waren** sie schon **abgefahren**.
possessive	A DETERMINER or PRONOUN which indicates possession (3.4, 4.4): Das ist **mein** Haus; **seines** ist größer.
prefix	One or more syllables added to the front of a word to form another (Chapter 19): **ver**kaufen, **an**kommen, **Alt**stadt, **un**wichtig.

preposition	A word which usually stands before a NOUN PHRASE and which indicates the relationship of the noun phrase to another in terms of time, place, etc. (Chapter 9): **um** 6 Uhr/**vor** 6 Uhr; **mit** ihm/**für** ihn.
prepositional adverb	A word formed from da(r)- and a PREPOSITION, and used in place of a PREPOSITION plus a PRONOUN to refer to things (13.2): **damit** *with it, with them,* **darunter** *underneath it, among them.*
prepositional object	A COMPLEMENT of the verb beginning with a PREPOSITION which is required by the individual verb: Ich interessiere mich **für** Musik. Das schmeckt **nach** Zitronen.
prepositional phrase	A PHRASE made up of a PREPOSITION followed by a NOUN PHRASE: mit ihrem Vater; am Donnerstag.
present participle	The INFINITIVE with the suffix **-d**. Unlike English *-ing* forms, it is used mostly as an ADJECTIVE (14.3): die **tanzenden** Teenager.
present tense	The SIMPLE TENSE which indicates an event which is taking place now, or which takes place regularly (10.1, 11.1): Normalerweise **trinke** ich Kaffee, aber heute **trinke** ich Tee.
pronoun	A word which refers to or replaces a NOUN PHRASE (Chapter 4). See also DEMONSTRATIVE, INTERROGATIVE, PERSONAL PRONOUN, REFLEXIVE PRONOUN and RELATIVE PRONOUN.
reflexive pronoun	A PRONOUN which refers back to the SUBJECT of the VERB (4.2): Ich wasche **mich**. Ich wasche **mir** die Hände.
reflexive verb	A verb used with a REFLEXIVE PRONOUN (4.2, 12.7): sich interessieren, sich ausruhen.
register	The forms and vocabulary of language used depending on whether the language is, for instance, spoken or written, and whether the situation is formal or informal.
relative clause	A CLAUSE which starts with a RELATIVE PRONOUN and is used to describe the preceding noun (4.7): das Kind, **das im Garten spielt**; mein Bruder, **mit dem ich ins Kino gehe**.
relative pronoun	The PRONOUN which starts a RELATIVE CLAUSE; cf. *who, which, what* in English (which sometimes omits the relative pronoun) (4.7): das Kind, **das** im Garten spielt; mein Bruder, mit **dem** ich ins Kino gehe.
reported speech	See INDIRECT SPEECH.
separable verb	A verb which, in the INFINITIVE form, has a PREFIX which is detached from the VERB in MAIN CLAUSES (19.5.1): **auf**stehen: ich stehe früh **auf**.
simple tense	A tense formed from a single word (cf. COMPOUND TENSE). The two simple tenses in German are the PRESENT and the PAST.
stem	The root part of the VERB which contains the meaning; to this is added the ENDING, which indicates the PERSON, NUMBER, TENSE and MOOD: the stem of sagen, sagst, sagt, etc. is **sag-**.
strong verb	A verb which changes not only its endings but also its STEM vowel in certain forms, notably in the PAST TENSE, and whose past participle has the ending **-en** (10.1.2, 10.2.2, 10.3): fahren: fährt – fuhr – ist gefahren.
subject	The person or thing carrying out the action expressed by the VERB: **Ich** spiele Fußball.

subjunctive (*Konjunktiv*)	The MOOD used to indicate that the action or state may not be factual, e.g. in INDIRECT SPEECH, where *Konjunktiv I* is used (17.1, 17.3): Er sagte, sie **sei** krank. *Konjunktiv II* is usually used to express possibility, wishes or conditions which are unlikely to be met (17.2, 17.4): Ich **könnte** dir helfen; Ich **würde** gern dorthin fahren; Wenn er nur hier **wäre, …**
suffix	An addition to the end of a word, resulting in a new word or different forms of a given word (Chapter 19): Schmutz – schmutz**ig**; unhöflich – Unhöflich**keit**; komm**en** – komm**t** – komm**e**.
superlative	The form of ADJECTIVES and ADVERBS expressing the highest (or lowest) degree (Chapter 8): der **faulste** Student; sie singt **am schönsten**.
tense	The form of the verb which expresses the particular time of the action. See COMPOUND TENSE, SIMPLE TENSE.
transitive verb	A verb which takes a DIRECT OBJECT: Ich **sehe** einen Film.
verb	A word which indicates an action, state or process: laufen, geschehen, werden, sein.
voice	Denotes the relationship between the VERB and its SUBJECT. See ACTIVE VOICE and PASSIVE VOICE.
weak masculine noun	One of a small group of nouns which add **-(e)n** in all cases except the NOMINATIVE SINGULAR (2.3.2): der Junge, den Jungen, des Jungen, dem Jungen, pl. die Jungen.
weak verb	A regular VERB which changes only its endings, and has a past participle ending in **-t** (10.1.1, 10.2.1, 10.3): sagen, sagt, sagte, hat gesagt.

Further study

This list contains a selection of books and websites which may be found useful for further study.

Grammars

Dodd, Bill, Eckhard-Black, Christine, Klapper, John and Whittle, Ruth, *Modern German Grammar*, Routledge, 2003 (particularly for its coverage of language functions)

Dreyer, Hilke and Schmitt, Richard, *A Practice Grammar of German*, Verlag für Deutsch, 2001 (particularly useful for its grammar exercises; the exercise key has to be purchased separately)

Duden 4, *Grammatik der deutschen Gegenwartssprache*, Dudenverlag, 2009 (for the most advanced students; comprehensive, and with interesting articles on many aspects of language, not just grammar, but not easily accessible)

Durrell, M., *Hammer's German Grammar and Usage*, Hodder Headline, 2011 (exhaustive; for advanced users)

www.ids-mannheim.de/grammis (a useful website, in German, maintained by the Institut für deutsche Sprache)

Usage

Duden, *Im Zweifel für den Genitiv*, Dudenverlag, 2008 (FAQs on German language usage; in German, but not difficult)

Duden 9, *Richtiges und gutes Deutsch*, Dudenverlag, 2007 (a handbook of German usage; much more comprehensive than the volume above – and more difficult)

Duden 2, *Stilwörterbuch*, Dudenverlag, 2010 (brief dictionary definitions followed by numerous examples of how words are used in context)

Durrell, M., *Using German*, Cambridge University Press, 2nd edn, 2003 (with a focus on contemporary usage, including register, i.e. levels of language)

Sick, B., *Der Dativ ist dem Genitiv sein Tod*, Kiepenheuer & Witsch, 2006 (four collections of witty and sometimes controversial observations on German grammar and usage, taken from the *Babelfisch* columns of *Der Spiegel* online)

Dictionaries

Collins German Dictionary, Collins, 2007; regularly updated (excellent coverage and clear explanations)

Duden, *Deutsches Universalwörterbuch*, 6th edn, Dudenverlag, 2006 (the standard monolingual dictionary)

www.leo.de (needs to be used with caution, like all on-line dictionaries, but is particularly interesting for the discussions of language usage and new vocabulary)

General

Johnson, Sally and Braber, Natalie, *Exploring the German Language*, 2nd edn, Cambridge University Press, 2008 (an excellent introduction to the German language in its linguistic and cultural context)

Index

Numbers in bold type refer to Chapters.

ab (preposition) 9.2.10a
aber
  co-ordinating conjunction 18.2.1
  modal particle 7.2.1
accusative case 1.1.2
  after prepositions 1.1.2b, 9.1, 9.3
  direct object of verb 1.1.2a
  in phrases 1.1.2f
  verbs with double accusative 1.1.2d, 13.3.3
  with adjectives 1.1.2c, 5.3.1
adjectival phrase 5.5, 14.2.2b, 14.3.2a
adjective **5**
  attributive 5.1
  comparative **8**
  compound 19.3.4
  declension 5.1
  declension after indefinite determiners 5.1.3
  derived from place names 5.1.4d
  formation 19.3
  in titles 5.1.5
  indeclinable adjectives 5.1.4
  irregular adjectives 5.1.6
  mixed declension 5.1.2
  noun compounds 5.1.4b
  participle as adjective 19.3.1
  predicative (word order) 18.3.1
  prefixes 19.3.3
  and prepositions 5.4
  strong declension 5.1.3
  suffixes 19.3.2
  superlative **8**
  used as noun 2.1.8a, 5.2, TIP p. 68, 14.3.2b
  weak declension 5.1.1
adjectives and cases 5.3
  + accusative 5.3.1
  + dative 5.3.3
  + genitive 5.3.2
adverbs **6**
  comparative and superlative **8**
  formation 19.4
  hin/her 6.3.3
  interrogative 6.7
  linking clauses 18.2.5
  of comment/attitude 6.4
  of degree 6.5

  of manner 6.2
  of place 6.3
  of qualification/contrast 6.6.2
  of reason 6.6
  of time 1.1.2f, 6.1
  position in clause 18.3.3–4
  prepositional (darauf, etc.) 4.1.4, 13.2
  Time–Manner–Place rule 18.3.3
agent (in passive) 15.1.2
agreement
  collective nouns with verb TIP p. 26
  festivals 2.2.11c
  gender with possessives 2.1.8d
  gender with pronouns 2.1.7
all, alles, alle 3.6.1, TIP p. 39, 3.6.15, 4.5.1
als
  in comparative 8.3
  conjunction 18.2.2e
als dass 17.4.6d
als ob 17.4.6
also 18.2.5
am …-sten 8
an 9.3.1, 9.5.1d, 9.5.3a, 9.6.1, 13.1.1
anstatt 9.4.1a
  anstatt dass 14.1.1d, 17.4.6d
  anstatt … zu 14.1.1d
apposition 1.2
  dates 1.2b
  geographical names 1.2d
  marked by commas 20.5.1e
  with names & titles 1.2.c
article 3.1–3
  use/omission of 3.2
  with names 3.2.1c–g
  see also definite article, indefinite
     article
auch 7.2.2, 18.2.5
auch wenn 17.4.2c
auf 9.3.2, 13.1.2
aus 9.2.1, 13.1.3
aus or **von**? TIP p. 97
außer 9.2.2
außer dass 14.1.1d
außer … zu 14.1.1d
außerdem 18.2.5

auxiliary verb
  haben/sein in perfect/pluperfect tenses 10.3.3, 10.4
  werden in future/future perfect 10.5, 10.6
  werden in passive 15.1.1

bald ... bald ... 18.2.3e
bei 9.2.3, 9.6.1, 13.1.4
beide 3.6.3, 3.6.15b, 4.5.2
bekommen 15.2g
bevor 18.2.2
bis
  conjunction 18.2.2
  preposition 9.1.1
bleiben 14.1.2c
  copular verb 1.1.1b
bloß 7.2.3
bringen 12.4, **21**
by (passive) 15.1.2

capital letters 20.2.1
cardinal numbers 20.1.1
cases **1**
  and adjectives 5.1, 5.3
  and demonstratives 3.3
  and determiners **3**
  endings on nouns 2.3
  and possessives 3.4, 4.4
  prepositions **9**, 13.1
  and pronouns 4.1.1, 4.2
  and relative pronouns 4.7
  and verbs 13.3
  see also nominative, accusative, genitive, dative
clause
  and conjunctions 18.2
  infinitive 18.5, 14.1.1c–d
  main 18.1.1
  relative 4.7
  separated by comma 20.5.1
  subordinate 14.4.3, 18.1.4
  word order **18**
colon 20.5.2
comma 20.5.1
commands **16**, 17.3.2, 17.3.5
  word order 18.1.3b
comparative and superlative of adjectives and adverbs **8**
  'absolute' 8.3g
  adjectives: formation 8.1
    compound adjectives 8.1.3
    irregular forms 8.1.2
  adverbs: formation 8.2
  als *or* **wie?** TIP p. 91
  comparison 8.3a
  equality (*as ... as*) 8.3c
  progression (*more and more*) 8.3d
  proportion (*the more ... the more*) 8.3e
  relative (*fairly ...*) 8.3f

superlative 8.3b
complex sentences 18.1.5
complex words 19.1.2
compound adjectives 19.3.4
compound nouns 19.2.4
compound tenses, *see* tense
conditional 17.2.3, **22**
conditional in the past 17.2.4, 17.5, **22**
conditions: 'real' and 'unlikely' 17.4.2
conjugation of verb **10**, **12**, **22**
conjunctions 18.2
  adverbs used as 18.2.5
  co-ordinating 18.2.1
  correlative (two-part) 18.2.3
  subordinating 18.2.2
copular verb 1.1.1b

da 18.2.2
dadurch..., dass ... 14.4.3a
daher 18.2.5
damit 18.2.2
danach 18.2.5
dank 9.2.10b
dann 18.2.5
da(r)- + preposition 13.2.1
darum 18.2.5
dative case 1.5
  after adjectives 1.1.5d, 5.3.3
  after prepositions 1.1.5b, 9.2, 9.3
  after verbs 1.1.5c, 12.6.1, 13.3.1
  in phrases 1.1.5g
  possession 1.1.5e
dative object 13.3.1
  indirect object 1.1.5a, TIP p. 8, 18.3.2
  in passive 15.1.3
decimals 20.1.3c
declension
  of adjectives 5.1
  of adjective-nouns 5.2
  of determiners **3**
  of pronouns **4**
  case endings on nouns 2.3.1
  names and proper nouns 2.3.3
  weak masculine nouns 2.3.2
  weak masculine nouns: feminine forms 2.3.2b
  weak masculine nouns: how to recognise TIP p. 28
definite article (*the*) 3.1.1, 3.2
  as pronoun 4.3.1
demonstrative (*this*)
  determiners 3.3
  pronoun 4.3
denken 12.4, **21**
denn
  co-ordinating conjunction 18.2.1a
  modal particle 7.2.4

dennoch 18.2.5
der, die, das
   definite article 3.1.1, 3.1.1–3
      with names 3.2.1f–g
   demonstrative determiner 3.3.1a,
   demonstrative pronoun 4.3.1
   relative pronoun 4.7
derjenige 3.3.3, 4.3.4
   replaced by **der** 3.3.3
derselbe 3.3.4
deshalb 18.2.5
deswegen 18.2.5
determiner **3**
   see also definite article, demonstrative, indefinite;
      interrogative
   determiners and pronouns – summary 3.7
deutsch or **Deutsch** TIP p. 231
dies 4.3.2c
dieser 3.3.1, 4.3.2
   replaced by **der** 4.3.1
direct object
   accusative case 1.1.2
   word order 18.3
direct speech 17.3.1
doch 7.2.5, 18.2.5
double infinitive
   modal verbs 12.2.2c, 12.2.2e, 12.2.4, 18.1.4b
   word order 18.1.4b
du/ihr or **Sie**? TIP p. 47
durch 9.1.2, 15.1.2
dürfen 12.2, 12.3.1

eben 7.2.6
eigentlich 7.2.7
ein, eine (indefinite article) 3.1
ein bisschen 3.6.5, 4.5.3
ein paar 3.6.6
ein wenig 3.6.5, 4.5.3
einander 4.2.3
einer (pronoun) 4.5.4
einige 3.6.4, 3.6.15, 4.5.5
einzelne 3.6.15
entgegen 9.2.10c
entlang 9.1.3
entweder ... oder ... 18.2.3b
erst 7.2.8
es
   impersonal constructions 12.6
   replaced by **das** 4.3.1b
   'subjectless' passive 15.1.4
   translating *it* 4.1.2a,
   uses 4.1.3
es gibt 1.1.2f, 12.6.3
   avoiding, TIP p. 143
es ist/sind 12.6.3
etliche 3.6.15
etwa 7.2.9
etwas 3.6.7, 4.5.6

even if 17.4.2c
exclamation 20.5.1e

fahren 14.1.2e, **21**
feminine noun 2.1.3, 2.2.3
finden 21
finite verb
   word order **18**
   see also tenses
first position in main clause 18.1.2
folgende 3.6.15
for + time 6.1.4
fractions 20.1.3
fühlen 14.1.2d
für 9.1.4, 13.1.5
future in the past 17.4.5
future perfect tense, *see* tense
future tense, *see* tense
ganz 3.6.2

geboren 15.1.5c
gegen 9.1.5
gegenüber 9.2.4
gehen 12.4, 14.1.2e, **21**
gemäß 9.2.10d
gender of nouns 2.1
   compound nouns TIP p. 12
   dual gender 2.1.6b
   gender agreement with possessives 2.1.8d
   gender agreement with pronouns 2.1.7
   gender issues 2.1.8
   homonyms 2.1.6
   linked to form 2.1.2b, 2.1.3b, 2.1.4b, 2.1.5
   linked to meaning 2.1.2a, 2.1.3a, 2.1.4a
   regional variations 2.1.6c
gender of personal pronouns 4.1.2, 2.1.7
genitive case 1.1.3
   after adjectives 1.1.3c, 5.3.2
   after prepositions 1.1.3b
   after verbs 1.1.3c, 13.3.4
   endings on nouns 2.3.1b
   with names/proper nouns 2.3.3
   in phrases 1.1.3d
   possession 1.1.3a, 2.3.3
   replaced by dative 1.1.3b, 1.1.4
gleich 7.2.10

haben
   auxiliary 10.3.3
   conjugation 12.4, **21**
haben + **zu** + infinitive 12.3.4e, 16.3e
halt (modal particle) 7.2.11
helfen 14.1.2f
-her 6.3.3
-hin 6.3.3
hinter 9.3.3
hoch 5.1.6b
hören 14.1.2d

imperative mood **16**
  du forms 16.1.3
  formation 16.1.2, **22**
  ich form used as 16.3b
  infinitive used as 16.2
  nouns used as 16.3a
  polite forms 16.1.4
  wir forms 16.1.6
imperfect tense *see* tense (simple past)
impersonal verb 12.6
  reflexive verbs 12.7.6
in 9.3.4, 9.5.1a, 9.5.2b, 9.6.1, 13.1.6
indefinite article (*a, an*) 3.1
indefinite determiner 3.6
  + adjective + noun 3.6.15
indefinite pronoun 4.5
indem 14.4.3a, 18.2.2
indicative mood **11**, 17.4.2a, 17.4.6c
indirect object
  dative case 1.1.5
  word order 18.3.2
indirect questions 17.3.3
indirect speech 17.1.4
infinitive 14.1
  as noun 14.1.3a, 14.4.2, 19.2.1a
  as past participle (modal verbs) 14.1.3b
  conjunctions + **zu** + infinitive 14.1.1d
  in imperative 14.1.3c, 16.2
  in passive 15.1.7
  infinitive clause 14.1, 18.5
  omitted after modal verb 12.2.5
  verb + **darauf** etc. + infinitive clause 14.1.1c
  with/without **zu** 14.1.1, 14.1.2, TIP p. 161
-ing, English forms ending in 14.4
inseparable verb 10.3.2b, TIP p. 219, 19.5.2, 19.5.3
interjection 18.1.1b
interrogative (*which, what kind of*)
  adverbs 6.7
  determiner 3.5
  pronouns 4.6
  used as conjunctions 18.2.2f
intransitive verb 12.5, TIP p. 114
inwiefern 6.7, 18.2.2f
inwieweit 6.7, 18.2.2f
irgend- 3.6.8, 4.5.7
irregular verbs 12.4, **22**

ja 7.2.12
je... desto/um so 8.3e, 18.2.2, 18.2.3a
jeder 3.6.9, 4.5.8
jemand 4.5.9
jener 3.3.1, 4.3.2

kein 3.1.2
kommen 14.1.2e, 14.4.4b
Konjunktiv, see subjunctive
können 12.2, 12.3.2
kriegen 15.2g

lassen 10.3.2c, 14.1.2b, 15.2f
laut 9.2.10d
lehren 14.1.2f
leiden 12.4, **21**
lernen 14.1.2f

main clause, *see* word order
mal 7.2.13
mal ... mal ... 18.2.3f
man 4.5.10, 15.2a
mancher 3.6.10, 3.6.15, 4.5.11
masculine noun 2.1.2, 2.2.2, 2.3.2
mehrere 3.6.11, 3.6.15, 4.5.12
meist- 3.2.1h
mit 9.2.5, 13.1.7, 15.1.2
mixed adjective declension 5.1.2
modal particles **7**
modal verbs 12.2
  and polite requests 16.1.4c, 17.4.4
  and subjunctive 17.1, 17.2, 17.4.4
  and word order 14.1.2a, 18.1.4b
  future tense 12.2.2e
  perfect tense 12.2.2c–d
  pluperfect tense 12.2.2c–d
  present tense 12.2.2a
  simple past tense 12.2.2b
  two modal verbs in same clause 12.2.4
mögen 12.2, 12.3.3
mood, *see* imperative, indicative, subjunctive
müssen 12.2, 12.3.4

nach 6.3.3, 9.2.6, 9.5.2a, 13.1.8
nachdem 18.2.2
neben 9.3.5
negatives, *see* kein, nicht, nichts, niemand
nehmen 12.4, **21**
neuter noun 2.1.4, 2.2.4
nicht, position of 18.4
nicht dass 17.4.6d
nicht nur ... sondern auch ... 18.2.3d
nichts 4.5.13
niemand 4.5.9
nominative case 1.1.1
  after **sein, werden, bleiben** 1.1.1b
  subject of verb 1.1.1a
noun **2**, 19.2
  adjective used as noun 5.2, TIP p. 69, 14.3.2b
  collective TIP p. 26
  compound 19.2.4, 20.3.2
  declension 2.3.1
  feminine 2.1.3, 2.2.3
  formation 19.2
  gender 2.1
  infinitive used as 2.1.5b
  masculine 2.1.2, 2.2.2, 2.3.2
  neuter 2.1.4, 2.2.4
  plural, *see* plural of nouns
  prefix 19.2.3

suffix 19.2.2
weak, *see* weak masculine noun
numbers
    cardinal 20.1.1
    fractions and decimals 20.1.3
    ordinal 20.1.2
nur 7.2.14

ob 17.3.3b
ob ... oder ... 18.2.4a
object
    accusative 1.1.2a, 1.1.2d, 1.1.2e
    dative 1.1.5a
    direct or indirect object TIP p. 8
    genitive 1.1.3c
    prepositional 13.1
    word order of objects 18.3.2
    see also verbs + cases
obschon 18.2.2
obwohl 18.2.2
oder 18.2.1a
ohne 9.1.6
ohne dass 14.1.1d, 17.4.6d
ohne ...zu 14.1.1d
one of ... 4.5.4c
ordinal numbers 20.1.2
Ostern 2.2.11c

parenthetical clauses 18.2.4b
participle
    as noun 19.2.1b
    see also past participle, present participle
particle (modal) 7
passive voice **15**
    agent *by* 15.1.2
    alternatives to 15.2
    dative objects 15.1.3
    formation 15.1.1
    impersonal/subjectless 15.1.4, 16.3g
    impossible with certain verbs 15.1.6
    infinitive constructions 15.1.7
    sein passive 15.1.5
    subject of 15.1.3
    werden passive 15.1
past participle 14.2
    see also passive voice, perfect tense, pluperfect
        tense
perfect tense, *see* tense
personal pronouns 4.1
    how to remember 3rd person pronouns TIP
        p. 46
    replaced by definite article 4.1.2c
    translation of *it* 4.1.2a
    with prepositions 4.1.4
pluperfect subjunctive, *see* subjunctive
pluperfect tense, *see* tense
plural of nouns 2.2
    double plurals 2.2.7

feminine nouns 2.2.3
masculine nouns 2.2.2
neuter nouns 2.2.4
of weights and measures 2.2.11b
plural in English, singular in German 2.2.9,
    2.2.11a
plural in German, singular in English 2.2.8,
    2.2.10
-s plural 2.2.5
summary of forms 2.2.1, TIP p. 19
words of foreign origin 2.2.6
possession
    dative preferred 1.1.5e
    genitive 1.1.3a
possessive (*my, your*)
    determiner 3.4
    pronouns 4.4
predicative adjective, position 18.3.1
prefix
    in adjective formation 19.3.3
    in noun formation 19.2.3
    noun gender 2.1.5a
    on verb – inseparable 19.5.2
    on verb – separable 19.5.1
    on verb – variable 19.5.3
    separable – word order 18.1.1, 18.1.4
preposition **9**
    + accusative 9.1
        accusative: how to remember TIP p. 94
    + accusative/dative 9.3
    contraction 9.6
    + dative 9.2
        dative: how to remember TIP p. 97
    followed by infinitive clause 14.1.1d
    + genitive 9.4
    to: how to translate 9.5
    with adjective 5.4
    with verbs, *see* verbs +prepositions
prepositional adverbs (**darauf**, etc.) 13.2
    instead of pronoun 4.1.4
    + infinitive clause 13.2.1
    + subordinate clause 13.2.1
prepositional object 13.1
present participle 14.3
    present participle or gerund (verbal noun) TIP
        p. 167
    as adjective 14.3.2a, 14.4.1, 19.3.1
    as adverb 14.3.2c
    as noun 14.3.2b
    present subjunctive, *see* Subjunctive 1
present tense, *see* tense
pronouns **4**
    pronouns and determiners – summary 3.7
    demonstrative 4.3
    indefinite 4.5
    interrogative 4.6
    personal 4.1
    possessive 4.4

pronouns (cont.)
  reciprocal 4.2.3
  reflexive 4.2, 12.7, 14.2.2b, 14.3.2a, 16.2b
  relative 4.7, 14.4.3c
punctuation 20.5

quantities 20.1.4
question
  in reported speech 17.3.3
  interrogative adverbs 6.7
  interrogatives determiners 3.5
  interrogative pronouns 4.6
  wer? 4.6.4
  wo(r)- ? 4.6.1
  word order 18.1.3a, 18.2.2f
quotation marks 20.5.2

reflexive pronoun, *see* pronouns
reflexive verb 12.7, 15.2c
relative clause 4.7
relative pronoun 4.7, 14.4.3c
  after **derjenige** 3.3.3
reported speech 17.1.4, 17.3.1–4
requests (polite) 17.4.4
root word 19.1.1

same 3.3.4
sämtliche 3.6.12, 3.6.15b
schneiden 12.4, **21**
schon 7.2.15
sehen 14.1.2d
sein
  as auxiliary 10.3.3
  conjugation 12.4, **21**
  copular verb 1.1.1b
  impersonal constructions 12.6.1
  + infinitive 15.2d
  in passive 15.1.5
sein + **zu** + infinitive 15.2d, 16.3e
seit 9.2.7, 18.2.2
seitdem 18.2.2
selber, selbst 4.2.2
selbst wenn 17.4.2c
sentence 18.1
separable verb 10.3.1, 19.5.1
  one word or two? 20.3.1
sich 4.2.3, 12.7
Sie or **du/ihr?** TIP p. 47
simple past tense, *see* tense
sitzen 12.4, **21**
so dass 18.2.2
so ein 3.3.2c
so...wie 8.3c
sobald 18.2.2
sogar wenn 17.4.2c
solange 18.2.2
solcher 3.3.2, 3.6.15b, 4.3.3
sollen 12.2, 12.3.5, 16.3c

some TIP p. 31
  see also **ein paar, einige, etwas, manche,**
    irgendeiner, welcher
sondern 18.2.1
sonst 18.2.5
sowie 18.2.2
speech marks 20.5.2
spelling
  capital or small? 20.2.1
  one word or two? 20.3
  ss or ß? 20.4
spüren 14.1.2d
ss or ß? 20.4
statt 9.4.1a
statt dass 14.1.1d
statt ... zu 14.1.1d
stehen 12.4, **21**
strong adjective declension 5.1.3
subject (word order) 18.1.1, 18.1.4a
subjunctive **17**
  conditional + **würde** 17.2.3b, 17.3.1b,
    17.4.1
Subjunctive 1
  avoidance of in indirect speech 17.3.4
  formation 17.1, **22**
  use 17.3
Subjunctive 2
  after **als ob** 17.4.6
  formation 17.2, **22**
  use 17.4
subjunctive mood **17**
  conditional 17.2.3b, **22**
  conditional in the past 17.2.4, 17.5, **22**
  for unlikely conditions 17.4
  in 'future in the past' 17.4.5
  in indirect speech 17.3
  in polite requests 17.4.4
  in wishes and commands 17.3.5, 17.4.3
  pluperfect subjunctive 17.2.4, 17.5
subordinate clause 18.1.4, 18.2.2, 18.2.4
subordinating conjunction 18.2.2
such 3.3.2
suffix
  adjective 19.3.2
  adverb 6.3.3, 19.4
  noun 19.2.2
  noun and gender 2.1.2b, 2.1.3b, 2.1.4b, 2.1.5,
    19.2.2
superlative **8**
tense
  formation **10**
  use **11**
  guide **22**
  continuous (progressive) tenses (English) TIP
    p. 125
  future
    formation 10.5, **22**
    use 11.4

future perfect
 formation 10.6, **22**
 use 11.5
 in passive voice 15.1.1
perfect
 auxiliary (**haben, sein**) 10.3.3
 formation 10.3, **22**
 use 11.2
pluperfect
 formation 10.4, **22**
 use 11.3
present
 formation 10.1, 12.1, 12.2, **22**
 use 11.1
simple past
 formation 10.2, 12.2, **22**
 use 11.2

Time–Manner–Place rule 18.3.3, 18.3.4c
to – how to translate 9.5
transitive verb TIP p. 114, 12.5
trotz 9.4.1b
trotzdem 18.2.5
tun 12.4, **21**

über 9.3.6, 13.1.9
überhaupt 7.2.16
übrigens 18.2.5
um 9.1.7, 13.1.10
um ... zu 14.1.1d
umlaut
 comparative of adjectives 8.1.1–2
 comparative of adverbs 8.1.1–2
 formation of adjectives 19.3.2b–g
 formation of nouns 19.2.2b–c, 19.2.2i, 19.5.4
 in subjunctive 17.2.3a
und 18.2.1
unter 9.3.7

verb
 auxiliary, *see* auxiliary verb
 conjugation **10**, **12**, **22**
 copular 1.1.1b
 formation 19.5
 impersonal 12.6
 infinitive 14.1
 inseparable 10.3.2b, TIP p. 219, 19.5.2
 irregular 12.4, **21**
 mixed 12.1, **22**
 modal 12.2, 12.3, 14.1.2a, **21**
 of motion 10.3.3, 14.1.2e
 of perception 14.1.2d
 past participle 14.2
 prefix (inseparable) 19.5.2, 19.5.3
 prefix (separable) 19.5.1, 19.5.3
 present participle 14.3
 reflexive 12.7, 15.2c
 separable verb 10.3.1, 19.5.1

strong 10.1.2, 10.2.2, 10.3, **21**
tenses, *see* tense
transitive/intransitive TIP p. 114, 10.3.3, 12.5
weak 10.1.1, 10.2.1, 10.3
verbs + cases 1.1.1a, 1.1.2a, 1.1.5a, 13.3
 + dative 12.6.1a, 13.3.1
 + dative and accusative 13.3.2
 + genitive and accusative 13.3.4b
 + genitive object 13.3.4
 + prepositional object 13.1
 + two accusative objects 13.3.3
viel, viele 3.6.13, 3.6.15, 4.5.14
vielleicht 7.2.17
von 6.3.3, 9.2.8, 9.6.1, 13.1.11, 15.1.2
vor 9.3.8, 13.1.12
Vorfeld (first position in main clause) 18.1.2

während 9.4.1c, 14.4.3a, 18.2.2
wann 6.7, 18.2.2f
warum 6.7, 18.2.2f
was 4.6.1, 4.7.2, 4.7.3, 18.2.2f
was ... auch 18.2.4a
was für 3.5.2, 4.6.2
weak adjective declension 5.1.1
weak masculine noun 2.3.2
 feminine forms 2.3.2b
 how to recognise TIP p. 28
 neuter form (**das Herz**) 2.3.2e
weak verb, *see* verb
weder ... noch ... 18.2.3c
wegen 9.4.1d, 13.1.13
weights and measures 2.2.11b, 20.1.4
Weihnachten 2.2.11c
weil 18.2.2
weiter 14.4.4c
welcher 3.5.1, 4.6.2, 4.7.1f
welcher ... auch ... 18.2.4a
wenig, wenige 3.6.13, 3.6.15a, 4.5.14
wenn 17.4.2, 17.5, 18.2.2e
 omission of 17.4.2d
wenn ... auch 17.4.2c
wer 4.6.3, 4.7.3, 18.2.2f
werden
 as auxiliary 10.5–6 15.1, 17.2, 17,4.1
 as copular verb 1.1.1b
 conjugation 12.4, **21**
 impersonal constructions 12.6.1
weshalb 18.2.2f
wessen 18.2.2f
weswegen 18.2.2f
when 18.2.2e
wider 9.1.8
wie 6.7, 14.4.3b, 18.2.2
wie viel(e) 6.7a, 18.2.2f
wieso 6.7
wishes (unlikely) 17.4.3
 accusative case 1.1.2f
wissen 12.4, **21**

wo 6.7
    as conjunction 18.2.2f
    as relative pronoun 4.7.4
wobei 14.4.3a
woher 6.7, 18.2.2f
wohin 6.7, 18.2.2f
wohl 7.2.18
wollen 12.2, 12.3.6
+ preposition **wo(r)**- 4.6.1, 4.7.2d, 6.7
word formation **19**
word order **18**
    adverbs 18.3.3, 18.3.4
    in commands 18.1.3b
    in infinitive clauses 18.5
    in main clauses 18.1.1, 18.1.5, 18.2.1, 18.2.4, 18.2.5
    in questions 18.1.3a
    in subordinate clauses 18.1.4, 18.2.2, 18.2.4

objects 18.3.2, 18.3.4
of **nicht** 18.4
predicative adjective 18.3.1
prepositional phrases 18.3.2e
pronouns and nouns 18.3.2
relative clauses 4.7.1e
separable verb prefix 18.1.1, 18.1.4
Time-Manner-Place 18.3.3
verb complement 18.3.3d
würde conditional 17.2.3b, **22**

ziehen 12.4, **21**
zu 9.2.9, 9.5.1b, 9.6.1, 13.1.14
zufolge 9.2.10d
zuliebe 9.2.10e
zwar 7.2.19, 18.2.5
zwischen 9.3.9

Lightning Source UK Ltd.
Milton Keynes UK
UKOW05f0629050616

275587UK00006B/180/P